D1050748

# The 8 PILLARS
### of
## Financial Greatness

**8 PILLARS**

TM

**Also by Brian Nelson Ford**

Marshmallows AND Bikes
*Teaching Children (and Adults) Personal Finance*

Financial Wisdom
*Timeless As Nature*

332.024
FORD

505810

$17.95

c.1

Bowen and Taylor

3-24-14

# The **8 PILLARS**
## of
## Financial
## Greatness

# Brian Nelson Ford

**Outskirts Press, Inc.**
**Denver, Colorado**

PROPERTY OF
EGF CAMPBELL LIBRARY

DISCARDED

The opinions expressed in this manuscript are solely the opinions of the author and do not represent the opinions or thoughts of the publisher. The author has represented and warranted full ownership and/or legal right to publish all the materials in this book.

This publication is designed to provide accurate and authoritative information in regard to the subject matter covered. This book is strictly educational in nature and is sold with the understanding that neither the publisher nor the author are engaged in rendering accounting, investment, tax, legal, or other professional services by publishing this book. If legal or other professional advice, including financial, is required, the services of a competent professional person should be sought. The publisher and author specifically disclaim any liability, loss, or risk which is incurred as a consequence, directly or indirectly, of the use and application of any of the contents of this book.

The stories described in this book are based on true experiences but in many cases the names and situations have been slightly altered to protect each individual's privacy.

The term Realtor® is a collective membership mark owned by the National Association of Realtors® and refers to a real estate agent who is a member thereof.

Certified Financial Planner® or CFP® is a federally registered mark owned by the Certified Financial Planner Board of Standards, Inc.
</br>

The 8 PILLARS of Financial Greatness
All Rights Reserved.
Copyright © 2009 Mainstay, LLC
Soft cover - V1.0  R1.1

Cover Photo © 2009 Mainstay, LLC
Book design by Stephanie Winzeler

**8 PILLARS**

*8 Pillars, The Greatness Gap, The Financial Momentum Circle, Financial Confidence Account, Marshmallows AND Bikes, The Greatness Continuum, 8 Pillars University, The Financially Fatal Rule, Self Projection Reinforcement Model, The Five Mousetraps of Investing, The Value Creation Matrix,* and *The Five Levels of Financial Merit* are trademarks of Mainstay, LLC.

This book may not be reproduced, transmitted, or stored in whole or in part by any means, including graphic, electronic, or mechanical without the express written consent of the publisher except in the case of brief quotations embodied in critical articles and reviews.

Outskirts Press, Inc.
http://www.outskirtspress.com

ISBN: 978-1-4327-3748-1
Library of Congress Control Number: 2008939545

Outskirts Press and the "OP" logo are trademarks belonging to Outskirts Press, Inc.

PRINTED IN THE UNITED STATES OF AMERICA

PROPERTY OF
EGE CAMPBELL LIBRARY

*This book is dedicated to my father, Edward L. Ford.
Without his love, mentoring, and support this book would not exist.*

*Thank you.*

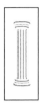

# CONTENTS

# ACKNOWLEDGMENTS

This book is the product of many positive influences in my life. First and foremost, I would like to give thanks and praise to my Heavenly Father. Second, I am grateful for the wonderful family that raised me. My parents, Ed and Jeanie Ford, brought me up with so much love and kindness that negativity still seems foreign to me.

Throughout my childhood, my siblings repeatedly whispered the message in my ear that *you are amazing*—and I believed them! Thank you Peyton, Paige, Troy and Scott for giving me the confidence to do things I never would have thought possible otherwise.

I want to say thank you to my church leaders for helping me become the person I am today. As a young man, spiritual teachers and advisors shaped and molded me in ways that will forever bless my life. Among these many leaders, I would like to personally thank James and Bonnie Parkin for their guidance during my missionary service in England.

I love my best friend and spouse, MeKette. I would like to express appreciation for her love and support. I feel very blessed to be married to such a glorious individual.

My children bring me unspeakable joy! The deep happiness that springs from my relationships with my children allows me to be creative and enjoy life on an elevated level. Thank you, love Daddy.

I have always loved the subject of personal finance. I pride myself on original thought, but I would be remiss if I did not acknowledge that the writings of many great authors have shaped the way I think and view the world. Thank you to every writer who truly cares about financial education—please, keep teaching and inspiring us.

More specific to this book, I would like to thank my able body of editors: Jason Palmer, Christy Stevenson, Kelsey Ann Hannon, Robin

Olson Peterson, Marilyn Stevenson, Mieke Ann Nielson and Kendra White. I appreciate and respect your writing prowess.

I appreciate my graphics designer, Stephanie Winzeler. Her creativity has breathed life into my words and allowed my thoughts to be displayed visually throughout the book. Stephanie is truly multi-talented. She is responsible not only for the graphics but also the cover art, design and layout of the book—thanks Stephanie!

Finally, I would like to acknowledge my good friend and chief editor Jason Palmer. I can certainly say with no hesitation that without Jason's intelligence, creativity, writing ability, editing skills, and overall desire to produce wonderful content, *The 8 Pillars of Financial Greatness* would not have become the book I envisioned. Jason, I appreciate all of the late nights, Saturdays, and phone time you spent helping me fulfill one of my greatest dreams. You deserve a massive "Thank You!" Even beyond our partnership on this project, I am most grateful for your friendship and example of greatness.

As you can see, I can hardly take credit for the book you are now reading. I will be forever grateful for all of the wonderful people that surround me. I am truly blessed by their friendship, support, and collaboration.

Brian Nelson Ford

# INTRODUCTION

## THIS BOOK WAS WRITTEN FOR YOU

I am optimistic about your financial future. The fact that you picked up a book with "Financial Greatness" in the title tells me something about you: you already understand that financial health plays a key role in your overall happiness and well-being.

I believe the word *greatness* means something to you. You sense that no matter what your current income or net worth, your financial situation impacts the quality of your life in pivotal ways. You want to improve your life, and you know improving your financial health plays a powerful role in doing so. This book provides you with the enduring principles to unlocking true Financial Greatness.

## HOW THIS BOOK IS UNIQUE

This book is unique among current personal finance literature. Many financial books and systems today teach about the importance of being entrepreneurial, owning your own business, becoming a real estate investor or other money-making options. I agree with the methods that many of these books present and subscribe to their wisdom. I am an entrepreneur. I own my own business, and I actively invest in real estate. I believe the majority of these books are good tools (with a few exceptions). However, most of these books fail to teach the bedrock principles of true financial success. In an effort to sell more books, they skip over fundamental principles of Financial Greatness and focus on exciting and flashy ideas that don't apply to everyone.

Further, many of today's financial systems fail to connect money to areas in our lives of deeper importance (our values). This book is different—once you master *The 8 Pillars*™ you will have the foundation necessary to reach your dreams using any sound money-making methods you choose (including the traditional professions, corporate careers, or higher education-based vocations that seem so out of favor in today's financial literature).

## THE END OF THE BEGINNING

I value your time. I am honored that you are reading *The 8 Pillars of Financial Greatness*. This book blueprints the way to a fantastic financial future. As a result of building your financial house with *The 8 Pillars*™, many unexpected but wonderful things will come into your life. These principles become the bridge to a lifetime of financial discovery and freedom. Equally important, these principles help put your financial health in harmony with your deepest values. Beyond the methods presented, this <u>fundamental approach</u> to Financial Greatness is what makes this book most unique among its peers.

I am excited about your future. I believe that you have an amazing life before you. No matter what your particular dreams are, following *The 8 Pillars of Financial Greatness* will help you reach them more quickly while ensuring that your success is sustainable. This book and its financial principles are sure and true. I am honored to be a part of this journey with you and am optimistic that your time with this book will be well spent.

Brian Nelson Ford
brian@8pillars.com
www.8pillars.com

## CHAPTER 1

# WHAT IS FINANCIAL GREATNESS AND HOW CAN YOU ACHIEVE IT?

What is Financial Greatness? Most people talk about financial success in terms of income ("he makes six figures") or in terms of net worth ("she's a millionaire," or "that family is loaded"). True Financial Greatness is more than outward prosperity and has less to do with dollar signs and zeroes than it does with how money affects your life and your relationships. Society lacks objective methods to evaluate and measure real Financial Greatness, so we tend to fall back on familiar numbers to gauge success in the area of personal finance.

The problem with viewing our financial health through the objective lens of cold, hard numbers is that *life does not occur to us objectively.* We may compare two individuals based on income and net worth, but all we learn about them by doing so is that one makes more money or has more assets than the other. We don't know whether they have satisfaction, balance, and peace of mind about their financial situations. If the numbers told us that, we could easily determine the income level or net worth at which a person or family achieves Financial Greatness. If life were an objective experience, we could teach that everyone who had a certain net worth was financially secure. Since each of us experiences life differently, YOUR measures of Financial Greatness depend on the goals, needs, and aspirations that YOU bring to the table.

Now, I know what some of you are thinking: "I don't need to read a book about being happy with what I already have—I want more from my financial life! Also, I'm tired of big promises that fail to deliver, and I'm not interested in another get-rich-quick idea—but I *do* want to be *rich!*"

Rest assured, what you will learn from this book has everything to do with being rich. Keep reading.

Consider briefly the many meanings of the word "rich." A rich harvest refers to a yield that has great value and worth; rich land refers to abundant resources; a rich cake brings to mind something exceptionally heavy and sweet. You might refer to a full and melodious voice, a vivid color, a good joke, or a meaningful interaction all as "rich." What we usually mean when we talk about being rich is being wealthy, moneyed, affluent, loaded—what we might call *filthy rich*. I say this in good humor, not intending to say that people with money are somehow filthy. Rather, my point is that becoming rich does not always equate to Financial Greatness. *The 8 Pillars*™ demonstrate how to build real riches by applying enduring financial principles to your entire life.

Whether you make $50,000 or $500,000 a year, you can achieve Financial Greatness. That does not mean Financial Greatness is a short-term goal, but it does mean you don't have to wait until you have a high income before you get started. By implementing the proven financial principles in this book, you will learn to systematically focus on achieving what you value most. I am writing this book to give you the blueprints you will need to get from where you are now to true Financial Greatness.

In architecture, pillars function as both supportive structures and decoration; they not only hold up the building, they increase its aesthetic value. I chose this metaphor purposefully. After applying the concepts you will learn in *The 8 Pillars*™, you will experience the riches of greater happiness, health, peace, and family relationships in your life. Financial Greatness comes from creating harmony between your finances and your values, akin to the harmony of form and function that architects achieve using pillars in their designs.

Financial Greatness comes down to taking care of what you can control. Of all the challenges you face in life, money issues should be among the easiest to handle. Why? Because money is an object; money is subject to our management. Ultimately, you have the real power over your financial future because *financial challenges are manageable.* No matter how powerless you may feel now, the cornerstone of this book is the principle that you can control your personal finances.

# THE WAY TO GREATNESS

Why then do so few people seem to achieve Financial Greatness? In reality, tens of thousands of "rich" people practice what I will teach you in *The 8 Pillars*™ and reach Financial Greatness. In this book I will share some of their examples and stories with you. Although many people already enjoy the fruits of Financial Greatness, the vast majority of people don't have a plan that will get them from where they are to where those "fortunate few" now stand. Imagine the divide between financial meagerness and Financial Greatness to be like the Grand Canyon. The less control you have of your personal finances, the wider the gap becomes. I call this chasm *The Greatness Gap*™, and to cross it you need a solid understanding of the principles taught in *The 8 Pillars*™.

The Greatness Gap™

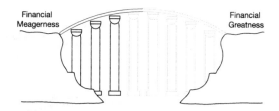

I write this book primarily to combat what I see as the two leading contributors to *The Greatness Gap*™:

**First**, we are flooded with information today regarding personal finance, and not all of it is sound. Contradictory advice and confusing excesses of information seem to only make the canyon deeper and more daunting. People struggle with where to begin and what to believe. *The 8 Pillars*™ brings simplicity and sound principles to bear on your financial life.

**Second**, most people get their information from financial professionals such as insurance agents, so-called "financial planners," or mortgage lenders. While many of these individuals are well-intentioned and knowledgeable, they often make their living through commissions on the products they sell. I believe that the inherent conflict of interest created by this arrangement most often results in poor advice and poorer client education.

This book provides pure and simple advice—advice that I follow and share with my clients, closest friends, and family members. *The 8 Pillars™* will help you sift through the complex universe of financial information and implement a simple yet successful personal plan. Yet no matter how good my advice is, you won't bridge *The Greatness Gap™* without having the right mindset.

People who have what I call a *Financial Greatness Mindset* take responsibility for their own results. They are willing to change their attitudes, behaviors, and habits to bring them into alignment with the principles of Financial Greatness. I urge you to adopt a *Financial Greatness Mindset* as you read this book. Seize control of your money by taking full accountability for your financial outcomes.

Financial Greatness is about practicing proven and timeless principles so money is no longer a significant driving force in your life. Being in control of your money allows you to focus on what you value most. The principles in this book are tested and true, and I am committed to teaching and writing about only the best and most successful financial principles. If you know of other universal financial truths that will lead people to greater happiness and overall well-being, please visit www.8pillars.com and share them with me.

**Thoughts, Feelings, and Ideas** – What are some of the thoughts or feelings you had while reading Chapter One? What insights occurred to you while reading? Did any particular action ideas pop into your mind as you read?

_____

_____

_____

_____

_____

_____

_____

_____

_____

_____

_____

_____

_____

_____

## CHAPTER 2

# THE BEDROCK PRINCIPLES OF FINANCIAL GREATNESS

In this chapter, I will lay the foundations or bedrock concepts that *The 8 Pillars*™ stand on. The focus of future chapters will be on how to integrate the individual pillars into your life. You will benefit more from the pillars themselves if you take a moment to understand the following principles completely:

**To Know and To Do**
**Logic or Emotions**
**Clarify Your Values**
**The Financial Momentum Circle**™
**Fighting Friction**
**Changing for the Better**

These precepts will help illuminate the "why" of *The 8 Pillars*™, creating a solid and working foundation for the "how to" presented later.

## TO KNOW AND TO DO

Understanding *The 8 Pillars*™ is crucial to your success, but it is important to remember that *to know how to do something* and <u>*to do it*</u> are two very different things. If everyone did what they knew was good for them, we would all be exercising regularly, saving money, choosing healthy diets, and avoiding needless debts. While countless people do engage in these kinds of simple yet vital activities, far too many do not. Some try to act on their basic knowledge then give up because it seems too difficult and perhaps not *unusual* enough. *The 8 Pillars*™ are not complex—in fact, they are very simple to learn. Do not let their simplicity fool you. In the search for a secret solution—the "magic bullet" that will solve all their money problems—many people look beyond time-tested financial wisdom.

Knowing how to read is extremely important as well as incredibly empowering for an individual. Yet if a literate person never read anything, they would have no more power to learn than someone who could not read at all. Our financial understanding works the same way. If you learn a true financial principle that will lead to a better life but do not follow through and act on that knowledge, you are no better off than the person who never learned the principle at all. This book is designed to take you beyond just knowing; everything I teach is meant to be put into action systematically. A wise man once said that we need to be doers and not hearers only. To help facilitate your becoming a "doer," I have provided a **"Doer Checklist"** at the end of each chapter that calls for immediate action. These to-do lists can be your launching points to crossing *The Greatness Gap*™ and arriving at enduring Financial Greatness.

As you read, you are likely to have a few ideas sparked that apply directly to your personal situation. Take advantage of such thoughts and ideas—these intuitions can make all the difference in your eventual success. In addition to the 'Doer Checklist' at the end of each chapter, I have included a section for you to note important thoughts as soon as they occur to you. Do not be afraid to write in this book. This book is only valuable when you take action, make the principles your own, and experience change for the better.

## LOGIC OR EMOTIONS

How can we bridge the gap between just comprehending true principles and actually *living* them? The problem lies with merely understanding finances logically—using only our minds. Logic does not always lead to action. Why? For the same reason that life is not an objective experience—*we are emotional beings.*

I remember when I was in college and did not understand this principle. I took great pride in always making sound, logical decisions.

In fact, I believed that when it was time to settle down and get married, finding a wife should be a fairly straightforward process. It would be a relatively simple matter to meet and identify the woman that fulfilled all of my logical specifications for compatibility. As you may have guessed, that was not quite the way it worked out!

One night, concerned that my rational plans were not leading me any closer to a marriage partner, I called home to speak with my father. After some small talk regarding the subject, my voice became more serious. "Dad, how will I know when I have found the girl I am supposed to marry?" My father realized that I was earnestly searching for advice. With experience and conviction guiding his words he calmly responded, "Brian, you will just know."

After our conversation ended and I hung up the phone, his words bothered me as they echoed in my mind: "…you will just know." This made no sense to me. I expected him to speak about compatibility, red flags, how long we should date before getting serious, or the importance of getting along with her family. I was hoping that making such a major commitment could be a purely objective, logical choice. My father has been faithfully married to my mother for more than 43 years, and he certainly understands the seriousness and importance of marriage. Yet his advice was, "You will just know."

At the time, I did not buy it. I resolved not to "fall in love" unless everything made complete logical sense. Six months later I met my wife MeKette. We were compatible; there were no red flags; and yes, I even got along with her family. But these facts had little bearing on my decision to marry her. Knowing we were logically compatible was not enough to elicit a marriage proposal from a young college kid like myself. Perhaps there were many other "compatible" women on that very campus. What made the difference? I fell in love and experienced one of the happiest times of my life. I "just knew" that she was the woman I wanted to make a permanent commitment with. My father wisely understood that our emotions play a vital, motivating role in the decisions we make.

I now admit that most of our decisions are based on emotion. If a particular activity makes us feel better at the moment, we are more likely to engage in it. Likewise, we avoid certain activities because of the sadness, confusion, insecurity, or pain we associate with that behavior. To succeed financially we need to understand how our emotions affect our financial lives. We need to emotionally bond ourselves to positive financial behavior that will lead to Financial Greatness. Conventional wisdom says that financial decisions should never be emotional decisions, but that concept only holds true when the decision is a negative one. We need to avoid making hasty, uninformed, panicked, and spiteful financial decisions whenever we can, and understand that those kinds of decisions only come from fearful, negative emotions. The positive and good feelings we have can be powerful tools for moving us to positive action.

For you to take action on the principles I teach, it is important for you to become emotionally involved with *The 8 Pillars* ™. You need to speak and act as though your health, happiness, and closest family relationships depend on your mastering *The 8 Pillars*™—because they do! This book will provide a sound understanding of how finances work. Yet knowledge without action will do little to help you achieve your dreams and live your values. We learn best with our hearts—not with our heads. Recognizing this is crucial to adopting a *Financial Greatness Mindset*. You will improve most when you are emotionally committed to a better financial future. The next section will explain where to find that kind of commitment.

## CLARIFY YOUR VALUES

This section on values may be the most important in the entire book. It certainly is the most important "bedrock principle" to achieving Financial Greatness. Your values can help you form powerful emotional connections to the actions you want to take.

What do you value? What is most important in your life? Money without meaning will not bring lasting happiness, nor will wealth alone motivate you to bridge *The Greatness Gap*™. When you understand *The 8 Pillars*™ in terms of what you personally value most, your odds of reaching Financial Greatness skyrocket.

Some of the things I value most are family, health, spirituality, deep happiness, security, safety, freedom, and balance. These values are my motivation for Financial Greatness. Notice that I list neither money nor financial status among my values. Why? Because money is an object to manage; without the meaning and purpose I give it (what it means to my family, health, and so on), it cannot bring lasting joy. Money is only a means to a much deeper end—and it is not the only means in most cases. I value money as far as it can serve what really matters in my life and empower the people and causes I care about. This principle is one of the fundamental keys to reaching Financial Greatness.

A lack of healthy financial responsibility can seriously affect your values. When your financial life is out of balance, the rest of your life (and the people in it) will suffer. I have seen too many brilliant and talented people crushed by their own poor financial habits. When you evaluate your money behavior in terms of your values, you begin to take control of your money. Knowing what values you want your money to serve will help you break poor habits and stick with great ones.

The purpose of this book is to help you reach *greatness*—not just *financial* greatness. This is an awkward way of reiterating that money is not your end goal. The happiness of your family, the contributions you make in life, and the dreams you pursue are your end goals. Obtaining Financial Greatness enables you to put your money worries behind you so that you can focus on living a fantastic life. I want you to worry about your finances *now* so that you don't have to worry about your finances *for the rest of your life*. When you connect your values and emotions with your financial life while implementing sound financial habits, you make a direct investment in your future Financial Greatness. Over time, such investments will yield the true riches of more time for your family, for serving others, and for pursuing your dreams.

As you implement *The 8 Pillars™*, you will be able to enjoy the freedom to live without money being a significant driver in your life. By placing money in its proper perspective, you gain financial control of your life. This process will be liberating! When money no longer controls any part of you, something deep within you will be freed to make a profound difference in this world. I commend to you the words of Marianne Williamson from her book, *A Return to Love* and later quoted by Nelson Mandela during his Inauguration Speech in 1994:

Our deepest fear is not that we are inadequate. Our deepest
fear is that we are powerful beyond measure. It is our light, not
our darkness that most frightens us. We ask ourselves, '*who
am I to be brilliant, gorgeous, talented, fabulous?*' Actually,
who are you not to be? You are a child of God. Your playing
small does not serve the world. There is nothing enlightened
about shrinking so that other people won't feel insecure
around you. We are all meant to shine, as children do. We were
born to make manifest the glory of God that is within us. It is
not just in some of us; it is in everyone.

I believe that every person is unique and amazing. I believe that
you have wonderful gifts that you are meant to develop and share. Your
gifts may be meant for the whole world or they may be reserved for the
people who live within the walls of your own home, who reside in your
neighborhood, or who support the same causes that you do. This book
aims to be less about finances in general and more about what finances
mean to you.

I want you to reach your full potential, no matter how frightening it
may feel to gaze across *The Greatness Gap*™ at first. Connecting with
your values counters the fear of change. This book will help you put your
financial life in harmony with your values so that you are free to fully live
them and accomplish your dreams. At the end of this chapter, I would like
you to write down your values. Clarifying and committing your values
to writing will be very important to your success. Please take the time to
complete this exercise—it will be critical to the remainder of the book.


## THE FINANCIAL MOMENTUM CIRCLE ™

The process I teach in this book is circular in nature and designed to
create momentum in your life. Your values are the fuel and motivation
for implementing *The 8 Pillars*™. When you begin to implement *The
8 Pillars*™ and emotionally tie them to your deepest values, Financial
Greatness begins to occur systematically. Although you may not reach
Financial Greatness suddenly or quickly, it *will* begin to take effect in your
life *while* you focus on your values.

Almost anything worthwhile comes incrementally, as part of a process; Financial Greatness is no exception. Every small success on the way to complete Financial Greatness narrows *The Greatness Gap*™. Each financial victory gives you more control over money, more freedom from financial bondage, and a clearer perspective on your own values. Seeing your financial life in harmony with your values will in turn strengthen your resolve to keep going. You will begin to understand *The 8 Pillars*™ better and can better connect to them emotionally. As you cycle through this process you will build tremendous momentum—your life will change forever. I call this circular process *The Financial Momentum Circle*™.

THE FINANCIAL MOMENTUM CIRCLE ™

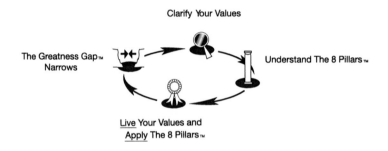

FIGHTING FRICTION

Perhaps the most important principle to understand about the process of achieving Financial Greatness is that it is *a process.* For financial success to endure and become Financial Greatness requires more than one trip around *The Financial Momentum Circle*™. Although I have designed the process you will follow in this book to naturally generate momentum, you need to watch out for the forces of financial friction that can grind your momentum to a halt. The primary detractors to financial momentum come in the form of negative feelings, thoughts, and words.

Are you optimistic about your financial future? I believe that wonderful blessings are in store for you. In large measure, your ability to achieve Financial Greatness depends on how you feel, think, and speak about your financial life. Positive and proactive feelings, thoughts, and words have a tremendous amplifying effect on your momentum—especially in your financial life. They are also an essential component of a *Financial Greatness Mindset.*

Before I began writing *The 8 Pillars of Financial Greatness* I made a very deliberate decision not to focus on the negative aspects of our financial lives. If you have read other financial books, you will recognize that this approach is rather unique. The majority of today's financial literature speaks in great detail regarding negative subjects, such as how ill-prepared we are for retirement, what our average credit card debt is, how the number of bankruptcies and foreclosures are rising, and how low our savings rate has become. Outside of that last sentence, you will not find much of this kind of information in *The 8 Pillars of Financial Greatness*. This book is not about meagerness and mediocrity—it is about greatness. I am convinced that learning about and dwelling on poor financial behavior does not effectively motivate people to live better financial lives.

You and I are more likely to take action when we feel good about the future—when we believe in our chances for success. We often give too much attention to what is wrong or even what *might* go wrong. I would like you to focus on doing the right things so that you can expect things to go right. I want you to speak about the future optimistically and talk about what you can and will accomplish. I want you to follow the examples of Financial Greatness that I will share with you in this book, and determine to keep your outlook and thoughts positive regarding your financial situation. Here are some samples of the kind of positive ideas you need to be feeling, thinking, and expressing about your financial future:

*Good things are in store for me.*
*I feel that my financial life will improve.*
*I am grateful for my job.*
*I have complete control over my money.*
*I am optimistic that I can improve my financial life.*
*My life is rich with blessings.*
*I value money as far as it can help me obtain what really matters in my life.*
*One day, I will own my dream home.*
*By continuing to live correct principles, I will be financially free.*
*I am fortunate to have so many things to be grateful for.*
*Saving and investing feel good because I look forward to living my dreams.*
*My financial life is on track.*

Remember: in large measure your ability to achieve Financial Greatness depends on how you feel, think, and speak about your financial life. The primary detractors to financial momentum come in the form of negative feelings, thoughts, and words; positive feelings, thoughts, and words amplify your momentum and the results you will experience in your financial life.

## CHANGING FOR THE BETTER

My experience has proven that most people, when they truly understand correct principles, will take the actions necessary to change their lives for the better.

*We can change if*:

1. We understand correct financial principles. (*Logical Understanding*)

2. We know that the principles will change our lives for the better. (*Emotional Connection*)

3. We take action. (*Becoming a Doer*)

4. We use our feelings, thoughts, and words to reinforce our momentum. (*Fighting Friction*)

5.We learn from someone who has lived the principles. (*Having a Mentor*)

The 8 Pillars™ will teach you correct financial principles, helping you understand them logically and connect to them emotionally. This book also stresses the importance of being a <u>Doer</u> and helps you to take immediate action on the principles taught in each chapter. Further, *The 8 Pillars™* gives you real-life stories and concrete statements to help you think, feel, and speak about your financial life in positive, momentum-building ways.

But the final factor in the process of enduring change involves finding a successful mentor to provide perspective, practical knowledge, and objective feedback along your journey to Financial Greatness. A living resource like this can never be contained between the covers of a book. If you do not have a person like this in your life, my company, **8 Pillars, LLC** offers personalized financial coaching with no strings attached.

The importance of real, live help cannot be overstated. Even with a good map (this book) and good survival tools (the concepts I've covered in this introduction), wise explorers will enlist the help of a guide who knows the terrain whenever they undertake a serious expedition. Your personal financial life is more like a jungle path than a freeway, and having a trusted, experienced personal guide can make all the difference. Visit us at www.8pillars.com to learn more about our 8 Pillars™ Coaching Programs and tools.

**Thoughts, Feelings, and Ideas** – What are some of the thoughts or feelings you had while reading Chapter Two? What insights occurred to you while reading? Did any particular action ideas pop into your mind as you read?

_____

_____

_____

_____

_____

_____

_____

## DOER CHECKLIST – CHAPTER 2

☐     I understand my values (what is most important to me), and I have committed them to paper.

### My Values:

1. _____

2. _____

3. _____

4. _____

5. _____

6. _____

7. _____

8. _____

## CHAPTER 3

# OVERVIEW OF THE 8 PILLARS

Throughout the remainder of this book, I devote one section to each of *The 8 Pillars™*. Before you set out to fully explore each principle, orient yourself by reviewing this brief explanation of *The 8 Pillars™* and the fundamental questions they answer:

### PILLAR ONE – Establish a Financial Confidence Account™

How can you protect yourself and your family from the unexpected? Start by establishing what I like to call a *Financial Confidence Account™*. Many of my clients call it a "save-your-marriage account." The bottom line: you need a "no-touch" account specifically set aside for life's little surprises. How much money do you need and where do you save it? Pillar One will educate you and help you achieve empowering peace of mind.

### PILLAR TWO – Organize and Systematize for Success

Do you have a financial plan? Will you be able to stick to it? How can you make your financial plan as simple and sure-fire as possible? Systematic financial organization plays a key role in your answers to these questions. Pillar Two will help you effectively organize, automate, and simplify your financial life. This book teaches you how to put effective systems together so that saving money, budgeting, keeping track of tax deductions, and paying your bills will not keep you from enjoying life.

**PILLAR THREE – Break Your Financial Bonds and Barriers**

What forms of economic bondage can keep you from achieving Financial Greatness? What forms of debt are acceptable? How do you control your debt? Do you know what your credit score is and how to improve it? Debt and credit can become financial tools rather than shackles when you learn to manage them wisely. Pillar Three will help you master both.

**PILLAR FOUR – Take Care of "What if?"**

What if a major life event occurs unexpectedly—will your finances hold together? Insurance acts like a safety net, protecting your financial plan from otherwise fatal falls. Pillar Four first educates you on which types of insurance are essential and which are optional. This chapter will guard you against being under or over-insured so you won't be let down by inappropriate insurance products and pushy insurance salespeople.

Further, Pillar Four will teach you how to approach estate planning and help you get started. Very few people have their estate plan up to date or complete. Why? Because they're confused about what they need to do and worried about how much it will cost. For most households, it will be a reasonably simple and inexpensive process once they eliminate the white noise. This chapter will help you begin before it's too late.

**PILLAR FIVE – Invest for Happiness Now and in the Future**

You understand the importance of saving and investing with your head (logically), but what about with your heart (emotionally)? Do you associate investing with your happiness, your dreams, your health, and better family relationships? If not, chances are you are not saving and investing enough. Pillar Five will help you simplify your options and educate you on where to put your funds for retirement, major purchases, and your children's college needs.

## PILLAR SIX – Make Your Home the Heart of Money Matters

Should you rent or buy? How much home can you afford? What type of mortgage should you use? Should you make extra payments on your home? How does your home affect the rest of your financial decisions? Your home can either be an area of great enjoyment and financial reward or a source of ongoing headaches and grief. Pillar Six will help you make your home a wonderful and enriching aspect of your life.

## PILLAR SEVEN – Maximize Your Money-Making Machine

Are you confident that your income won't be interrupted? Do you rely on only one source of income, or are you working towards multiple income sources? I believe that the size of your paycheck matters less than the proper management of that paycheck. However, I also recognize that your ability to increase and safeguard your income is the engine that drives your financial plan. Pillar Seven addresses ways to tune up your economic engine and maximize your fundamental income-earning asset—you!

## PILLAR EIGHT– Get Perspective by Giving Back

Donating your time and money to worthy causes feels good! An immense amount of satisfaction can be found by giving back to society. Not only is it the right thing to do, but it will yield tremendous benefits in your financial life. When you give back, you feel more in control of your money and learn to manage your remaining assets better. Through giving, you also gain the perspective on money that leads to the true abundance and riches at the heart of Financial Greatness. Pillar Eight will educate you on how to effectively give back.

**Thoughts, Feelings, and Ideas** – What are some of the thoughts or feelings you had while reading Chapter Three? What insights occurred to you while reading? Did any particular action ideas pop into your mind as you read?

_____

_____

_____

_____

_____

_____

_____

_____

_____

Can you see how your ability to reach Financial Greatness will improve your life?

How will your life specifically improve by implementing _The 8 Pillars_™?

_____

_____

_____

_____

_____

_____

## DOER CHECKLIST – CHAPTER 3

☐    I am committed to reaching Financial Greatness by completing each of _The 8 Pillars_™!

# PILLAR ONE

**Establish a Financial Confidence Account**

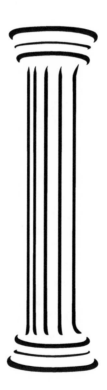

## CHAPTER 4

# WHAT IS A FINANCIAL CONFIDENCE ACCOUNT?

What is a *Financial Confidence Account™*? When I ask this question during my seminars, the audience usually falls silent. No matter how long it takes, I wait for a response. Because the answer seems obvious, most people suspect a trick question, so no one dares to speak up first. Many of the seminar participants are thinking: "It's an emergency account, we get it—let's move on." Sometimes the continuing silence in the room begins to feel uncomfortable. At this point, someone usually blurts out, "It's an emergency account!" almost always without raising his hand. But occasionally a seminar participant answers my question very differently. After raising her hand, a more reserved individual will give a thoughtful response. As she begins to speak, I can tell that experience, not conventional wisdom, is about to impart a financial pearl to everyone present. The answer comes in the form of a personal story—much like the one I am about to share with you.

When my wife was only a little girl, about the age of three, she was thrown from a car in a terrible accident. She landed face first on the pavement, knocking out her four front teeth. She eventually recovered from the accident without any noticeable scarring. The doctors were hopeful that her adult teeth would be completely normal. Unfortunately, the damage was more extensive than originally thought. As her permanent teeth came in, it became apparent that they would not be so permanent. She was fitted with caps and veneers to give her a gorgeous smile.

Fast forward to today. During the time I began to write this book, something unexpected happened to my wife. One evening she called me on the telephone, obviously distressed and shaken. Immediately a wave of worry swept over me as I sensed her distress and prepared myself for the worst. With a tremulous voice she explained that while at dinner, she had bitten into some food and broken one front tooth off completely, cracking the other one in half. I must admit that after hearing the explanation, I was somewhat relieved that she was safe and that nothing life-threatening had transpired. However, she was clearly very upset by the experience—having her teeth fall out in a social situation had been understandably quite embarrassing.

The next day we visited with her dentist. We expected to have the missing tooth replaced and the cracked tooth repaired as soon as possible, but the dentist had other unexpected news. He said that the root was so damaged due to the early car accident that my wife needed a dental implant. We soon learned that "dental implant" really meant a titanium screw placed into her jawbone. Her root needed to be extracted and the screw put in its place. The bone then needed to heal around the screw for at least six months before a crown or veneer could be built on top of the implant. The prognosis was unpleasant enough, but on top of that we were informed that the entire procedure would cost around $6,000! We are self-employed and pay for our own medical and dental insurance. Because the condition of my wife's teeth was "pre-existing," the cost would be completely out-of-pocket for us.

Back to our original question: what is a *Financial Confidence Account™*? It is a completely liquid and safe account that brings peace and security during times of difficulty and financial stress. Let me be even more specific: this must be a no-touch, separate account that is set aside specifically for financial emergencies. Remember, Financial Greatness comes down to taking care of what you can control. Can you control every possible situation that comes up in your life? Of course not. Unexpected and trying challenges will come to all of us. I believe that our response to difficult situations truly shapes our character. Having a *Financial Confidence Account™* in place before financial hardships occur gives you more control over your *response* to challenges when they happen.

If we did not have a *Financial Confidence Account™*, our responses to my wife's dental needs would have been very limited. Most likely we would have taken on expensive debt or had to burden a family member by asking for their help or charity. These alternatives would have further complicated an already unpleasant situation. Fortunately, because we do have a *Financial Confidence Account™*, this dental emergency did not turn into a financial or marital emergency. We were financially prepared. The situation was discouraging, but knowing that we had money specifically set aside for unforeseen life events made a tough situation much more manageable. My wife did not have to add financial worries to the burden of her long treatment process. I could focus on her comfort and recovery rather than on trying to come up with the money to pay for it. Further, because we could pay up front with cash, we received a 15% discount that saved us $900! A *Financial Confidence Account*™ can bring an immense amount of reassurance to a relationship or family during stressful times. You can probably understand why many of my clients call this a "save your marriage account."

Anticipating life's little surprises and expecting that they *will* occasionally occur does not mean being pessimistic—it means being responsible. Reliable cars sometimes break down, accidents can happen even to careful families, and capable individuals may lose their jobs by no fault of their own. Preparing realistically for the future is not pessimism but rather a sign of financial intelligence and responsibility. Expanding your "response-ability" (and therefore the number of financial factors you control in your life) plays a crucial role in achieving Financial Greatness.

## THE PRESENT VALUE OF A FINANCIAL CONFIDENCE ACCOUNT™

Having a *Financial Confidence Account*™ in place can pay huge peace dividends when financial difficulty arises. However, many people put off preparing for future emergencies because the anticipated benefits seem so far removed from their everyday lives. Yet the future calm you can experience when disaster does strike is only half of the reason for establishing a *Financial Confidence Account*™.

In reality, you will gain the assurance created by having money set aside whether an emergency actually happens or not. When you have liquid assets at your disposal, something occurs deep inside you—something difficult to describe. Your subconscious need for security is met, appeasing psychological worries and fears about your ability to survive, cope, and overcome financial challenges. This feeling can be more important than the money itself—it instills a *Financial Confidence Account*™ with *present and immediate* value.

When we are internally at ease and secure we are more open to being our best selves, tapping into our creative vision, and making personal changes to improve our lives. Feeling at peace results in greater confidence in yourself and your relationships. Sometimes this feeling results in the assurance to take an important relationship to the next level and consequently experience greater joy. At other times it begets the courage to take the necessary risk to start a business, change careers, or make a significant investment. The term *Financial Confidence* refers to the immediatley empowering effect of knowing you have financial reserves available.

## WHY FIRST?

I often get the question, "Brian, why is this pillar first?" It's a fair question, especially since traditional financial planning says to pay off debt before you begin to save. I did not create the sequence of *The 8 Pillars*™ academically in a classroom—I developed it for use with real people in the living room. I agree that debt elimination should come before saving and investing *considerable amounts* of money, but Pillar One is specifically designed to create immediate, sustainable action.

Having a reserve of money and confidence operates like a reservoir of warm water filling *The Greatness Gap*™. When you have a *Financial Confidence Account*™ in place at the start of your journey to Financial Greatness, you no longer face hundreds of feet between you and jagged rocks below. As you begin to take your first steps across the bridge towards Financial Greatness, you can look down and see calm water not far beneath your feet. The safety of this reservoir provides you with great peace of mind and confidence. Because of this added confidence you can begin to think of better, faster ways to build your bridge. In this way a *Financial Confidence Account*™ gives you the ability to build momentum and endure fewer setbacks as you pursue Financial Greatness.

## The Greatness Gap™

Financial Meagerness · Financial Greatness · Financial Confidence Account

With Pillar One, I intend for you to tackle a very specific goal right from the start so that you can begin to build momentum. Paying off debt only to fall into it again due to an unexpected emergency can kill momentum very quickly. Further, setting real money aside without touching it requires tracking your expenses, living below your means, and sticking to a plan. All of these important behaviors happen to be the same actions you will need to take to successfully pay off debt. We will discuss each of these areas in more detail in the chapters for the next two pillars.

When I meet with new clients and we begin working on *The 8 Pillars*™, one spouse sometimes says, "Well, we don't have an actual account for emergencies but we know we could pull a little here and a little there from all of our other accounts (like our checking and savings)." Don't settle for financial mediocrity by cutting corners on your *Financial Confidence Account*™. This is the first pillar in the bridge to Financial Greatness, and if you aren't willing to implement Pillar One correctly you will struggle even more with subsequent pillars. I will be very clear about this again: you need a separate, liquid, no-touch account specifically set aside for emergency use only.

**Thoughts, Feelings, and Ideas** – What thoughts, feelings or insights occurred to you while reading Chapter Four? What particular action ideas popped into your mind as you read?

_____

_____

_____

_____

_____

_____

_____

_____

_____

_____

Can you see how taking the steps to _Establish a Financial Confidence Account_™ will improve your life?

How will your life specifically improve once you _Establish a Financial Confidence Account_?™

_____

_____

_____

_____

_____

_____

_____

_____

_____

_____

_____

## CHAPTER 5

# HOW MUCH AND WHERE?

## Part I: START "GRAND"

You accomplish Pillar One in two parts. Your initial goal is to save $1,000 in a *Financial Confidence Account™*. This is the <u>first part</u> to Pillar One—one grand in the account. You need to understand that $1,000 is the <u>minimum</u> you need to have set aside in order to complete <u>part one</u> of this pillar. Once you have *started* by saving $1,000 in the proper place, move on to Pillar Two. After completing pillars two through four, revisit Pillar One and begin to work on <u>part two.</u> Keep reading and you will understand why I want you to proceed this way.

## Part II: ACCOUNT FOR CONFIDENCE

To complete <u>part two</u> of Pillar One you need to have three months of living expenses in your *Financial Confidence Account™*. Living expenses are not necessarily the same as your monthly income. "Living expenses" means the amount you need to pay all of your bills and take care of your basic necessities. If you do not know how much your living expenses cost you, it will be worth your time to start tracking them for three months or more to understand how much of your money goes to pay for basic needs. The average American household earns $42,000 per year ($3,500 per month). Typically, a family with this level of income would require 80% or $2,800 a month to just get by. In this example, our "average" family would need $8,400 in their *Financial Confidence Account™* ($2,800 monthly living expenses times three).

If this seems like a lot of money, take a deep breath and realize that it takes some time for most people to accomplish this part of Pillar One. You can only cross *The Greatness Gap*™ one step at a time, and your focus right now should be to complete <u>part one</u> of Pillar One—begin immediately to save $1,000 and move on to Pillar Two.

Ambiguity does not lead to reaching specific goals. For this reason, I have provided a chart that illustrates differing levels of income and living expenses with the corresponding amounts needed to fully fund a *Financial Confidence Account*™. Choose the row that is closest to your personal situation and make minor adjustments as needed to make sure that you are saving for the appropriate target amount.

| Annual Income | Monthly Income | Average Monthly Living Expenses | Amount needed in your Financial Confidence Account |
|---|---|---|---|
| $15,000 | $1,250 | $1,000 | $3,000 |
| $25,000 | $2,083 | $1,667 | $5,001 |
| $50,000 | $4,167 | $3,334 | $10,002 |
| $75,000 | $6,250 | $5,000 | $15,000 |
| $100,000 | $8,333 | $6,600 | $19,800 |
| $125,000 | $10,417 | $8,334 | $25,002 |
| $150,000 | $12,500 | $10,000 | $30,000 |
| $200,000 | $16,667 | $12,500 | $37,500 |
| $250,000 | $20,833 | $15,625 | $46,875 |

## WHERE SHOULD I KEEP IT?

The purpose of your *Financial Confidence Account*™ is to provide a financial cushion during unexpected stressful periods of your life. When you need this money the most, you should be able to access it without any hassle. In addition, this account needs to be liquid—a fancy way of saying it can be converted to cash quickly and easily without penalties or risk of loss. For this reason, I do not recommend *investing* any portion of your *Financial Confidence Account*™. It may help you to think of our example of the reservoir of water again—your *Financial Confidence Account*™ should be as liquid and accessible as that water. A dry reservoir would be the last thing you would want to see below you in a financial emergency.

## 85% In the Bank

I recommend keeping 85% of your *Financial Confidence Account*™ in a simple <u>online savings account</u>. An online savings account provides liquidity and a modest rate of return with little-to-no risk. At the same time, it avoids becoming *too* accessible like a checking account would be. You typically won't have a debit card, ATM access, or branch offices to allow you to make withdrawals any time you are tempted. Instead, you request an electronic transfer of funds or a check to be mailed out when you need to access the account. This slight delay in receiving funds can be an excellent deterrent to casually spending your emergency money or borrowing from it unnecessarily.

To set up an online savings account you will need to bank online. If you are not yet comfortable opening an account over the Internet, you can use a regular savings account *at a separate bank* from the one where you have your checking account. Don't make it too easy to cheat on your *Financial Confidence Account*™ by keeping it in virtually the same place as your operating cash. A regular savings account at a bank you don't normally visit will provide the same benefits as an online savings account but at a lower interest rate—usually 2-3% lower than an online savings account. (I will discuss online banking further during the next chapter on Pillar Two.)

## 15% Cash On Hand

I recommend that 15% of your *Financial Confidence Account*™ be held in cash in a locked home safe. For the majority of financial emergencies, your separate savings account will provide adequate accessibility. However, if a major local or national disaster occurs, it may become more difficult to get your money out of a traditional or online savings account. If the power is out, you may not be able to access your money online, and traditional bank ATMs and systems may stop working. In addition, during an urgent type of emergency there may be very little time to act, and having cash on hand could make all the difference.

Possibly you already have your first $1,000 of *Financial Confidence Account*™ money and just need to allocate it to a separate savings account and cash safe. The ratio of 85% savings account and 15% cash on hand is important to maintain. You should not have more than 15% of your *Financial Confidence Account*™ in cash. Because of inflation, your cash will be losing 3-5% of its purchasing power every year while earning no interest whatsoever. Further, having too much cash around the house can increase the risk of loss by theft or accident. I recommend you obtain a good fire/water-proof safe and keep it in a low-visibility, low-traffic area of the house. Never mention to anyone that you keep cash in your home or disclose the location of the safe to anyone but your immediate family and the executor of your estate.

## TAKE ACTION IMMEDIATELY!

If you already have what you need to fund a *Financial Confidnce Account™*, congratulations—all you may need to do in order to implement the 85/15 rule is move the money to the right places. If not, you need to start setting money aside each month until you reach your target amount. How much can you currently save every month in your *Financial Confidence Account™*? No matter what amount you start with, start *this month*. As mentioned earlier, saving money takes tracking your expenses, living below your means, and sticking to a plan. I will cover these areas in greater detail in Pillar Two. For now, commit to saving a certain amount every month, whether $25, $250 or more. Write this amount down.

Remember that no matter what particular financial goals you establish, living *The 8 Pillars of Financial Greatness* will help you reach them more quickly while ensuring that your success is sustainable. An important part of sustainability is allowing *The 8 Pillars™* to work for you without constant worry. You should be able to set a goal, map out a plan to reach it, take the first steps to put the plan in motion, and then leave the plan on autopilot. For Pillar One, that means setting up an automatic transfer or payment from your checking account to your *Financial Confidence Account™* to be taken out every month. If you have to think about making a deposit or transfer every month, your sustainability will go down—not only might you simply forget to make a monthly deposit to savings, but you might also be tempted during financially difficult months to intentionally forego the monthly transfer. If you put your *Financial Confidence Account™* funding on autopilot, you will experience faster and more enduring success.

It is important to realize that after completing Pillars Two and Three, you will have tremendous momentum and you will be able to double or triple the amount you save. For now, I just want you to begin saving a small but fixed amount of money <u>each month,</u> <u>automatically,</u> <u>no matter</u> <u>what</u> else is going on in your financial life. Once you have committed and begun to save this way in your *Financial Confidence Account™*, move on to Pillar Two: *Organize and Systematize for Success™*.

## WHAT IF I HAVE AN EMERGENCY?

Whether you have fully funded your *Financial Confidence Account™* or only just begun to move money into it each month, *use the account* when you have a real financial emergency. Sometimes people forget the purpose of their *Financial Confidence Account™* and begin to treat it with too much reverence. They don't want to touch the funds or dip into the account for anything, and as a result make poor decisions because of their unwillingness to access their own money. Keep in mind the reasons why this pillar comes first: to help you make more confident financial decisions, to protect the rest of your financial plans from the unexpected, and to give you momentum with an immediate and actionable goal. When you handle a financial hardship well because you prepared for it in advance, you reinforce all of these benefits—your confidence grows, your other goals remain unfazed, and financial friction does not slow your momentum.

However, I don't intend for you to drain dollars from your *Financial Confidence Account™* every time you experience a small financial hiccup. If an "emergency" will only cost you a small amount of money to deal with, it may not require emergency money to cover it. Before you tap into your emergency fund, ask yourself the following questions:

I    "Do I have other funds available that would be more appropriate to use for this expense?"

I    "Can this expense wait until I have saved money specifically for paying it?"

I    "Does this expense represent a financial inconvenience rather than a true hardship for me?"

If you answered any of these questions in the affirmative, you should avoid dipping into your *Financial Confidence Account™*.

## MAINTAINING A FINANCIAL CONFIDENCE ACCOUNT™

Once you have completed <u>part two</u> of *Establish a Financial Confidence Account™*, you will have three months' living expenses set aside (85% in a savings account and 15% in a home safe). Keeping too much money in low-paying accounts can add drag to your entire plan, therefore turn your automatic savings transfer off when you have hit your target balance. After utilizing your *Financial Confidence Account™* in an emergency, turn your automatic transfer back on until you replenish the account. Real emergencies don't usually happen on a regular schedule or back-to-back, so don't panic when you have to use your *Financial Confidence Account™*. Just go back to <u>part one</u> and <u>two</u> of Pillar One and start saving monthly again. Get the first $1,000 back into the account as soon as you can, then leave the funding on autopilot until you reach your mark of three months' living expenses.

One final note on Pillar One: always go to your savings account first in an emergency, reserving the cash you keep in your home safe as a last resort. Your cash on hand should be used in only the most urgent circumstances, then immediately replaced from the savings account portion of your *Financial Confidence Account™* whenever possible. Unless the emergency prevents you from utilizing your savings account, you would be well served to forget you even have cash on hand until you absolutely have to use it.

**Thoughts, Feelings, and Ideas** – What thoughts, feelings or insights occurred to you while reading Chapter Five? What particular action ideas popped into your mind as you read?

_____

_____

_____

_____

_____

_____

_____

_____

_____

_____

_____

# DOER CHECKLIST – CHAPTER 5

**Part I:**

☐ I have at least $850 saved in a separate, no-touch online or regular savings account.

☐ I have $150 cash in a fire/water-proof safe that I can access immediately.

It is important to remember that you do not need to have these items checked off before moving on to Pillar Two. However, you do need to take immediate action before moving on: start saving a fixed amount of money every month in your _Financial Confidence Account™_ and put this savings process on autopilot. Once you have begun to save, you can keep your momentum going by moving on to Pillar Two: _Organize and Systematize for Success™._

**Part II:**

☐ I have 85% of 3 months of my living expenses saved in a separate, no-touch online or regular savings account.

☐ I have 15% of 3 months of my living expenses saved as cash in a fire/water-proof safe that I can access immediately in my home.

After checking off these two items, you should be very proud of yourself—you have successfully completed Pillar One! If you have been following the program closely, this means that Pillars Two through Four are likely also complete or under way. You are now ready to Invest for Happiness by understanding Pillar Five.

# PILLAR TWO

## *Organize and Systematize for Success*

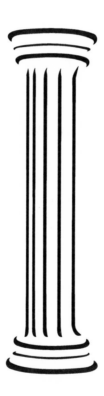

## CHAPTER 6

# CREATE YOUR
# FINANCIAL GREATNESS BLUEPRINT

## MY FAVORITE PILLAR

Occasionally people ask me, "Brian, what is your favorite pillar?" or "Which pillar is most important?" These questions can be dangerous. *The 8 Pillars*™ are each important and interrelated, and achieving Financial Greatness requires the successful implementation of every one of them. However, if I had to select one favorite pillar it would be Pillar Two: *Organize and Systematize for Success*™. Why? Because the principles of this pillar can help you accomplish so much for so little cost. With no additional income required, systematically organizing your financial life can make a dramatic difference in how you feel about your money and the financial goals you will accomplish with it.

Have you ever walked through a fully furnished model home? I love touring model homes. They often have such a great feeling to them. I like how they are so simple, clean, and organized. I want you to have the same great feeling when you "walk through" your financial house. An organized, uncluttered financial house with systems in place to keep it that way will bring a new level of confidence into your life.

Pillar Two teaches you how to gain control over your finances without having to first earn more money. I stated in Chapter One that no matter how powerless you may feel now, the cornerstone of this book is the principle that you can control your personal finances. Remember that the less control you have over your money, the wider *The Greatness Gap*™

(between you and Financial Greatness) becomes.

I emphatically believe that your ability to control your personal finances will be the cornerstone to your Financial Greatness. In a masonry foundation, the builders place every stone in reference to the initial cornerstone. The way the cornerstone is set literally determines the position and orientation of the entire structure. Pillar One gave you a specific and immediate goal designed to increase your financial control and confidence with your very first step towards Financial Greatness. Pillar Two will give you the tools you need for creating, implementing, and sustaining a successful financial plan—setting your financial cornerstone in place. A solid financial plan anchors the other seven pillars to the firm bedrock of your own values and guides the placement of each successive pillar toward the achievement of your unique goals.

## YOUR FINANCIAL GREATNESS BLUEPRINT

Imagine you are building your dream home. Your general contractor vaguely asks you a couple of questions before beginning construction. He asks how large you want the house to be and what your overall budget is. He then tells you he will locate a suitable site, draw up a plan, and build your home without any further input from you. That's it! You will have very little control over the specifics of your home and end up with the floor plan and location the builder chooses for you.

This may not sound like the best arrangement for building the home of your dreams, yet many people approach the construction of their financial plans in exactly this way. Rather than planning for the outcomes that they value, they let professional advisors, the media, or their friends and neighbors dictate what they plan for.

Let me give you a real life example. Very few people would place owning a fancy car ahead of spending time with family on their list of priorities. Yet too often many people make this choice, almost always unconsciously, by working long hours to pay for their cars and spending less time with their spouse and children. The same can be said for designer clothes and extravagant homes.

Instead of living life "unconsciously," we need to act rather than be acted upon. In other words, *The 8 Pillars*™ must be founded on your values and the other bedrock principles discussed in Chapter Two, or they will not lead to true Financial Greatness. Remember, money is merely a means to a much deeper end—and it is not the only means possible in most cases. We only value money as far as it can serve what really matters in our lives.

Before we move on to creating your *Financial Greatness Blueprint*, I want to stress the importance of identifying your deepest values—such as your relationships, spirituality, security, and health. You will frame every financial goal you set in the context of how it will affect your most important values. Do this just as deliberately and thoughtfully as you would if you were designing the layout and features of your dream home. Every room in a home has unique purposes and provides specific benefits that set it apart from the other rooms, just as each pillar does for your financial life. Every great home includes the same basic types of rooms, just as every great financial plan incorporates *The 8 Pillars*™. But from these fundamental elements of design, an infinite variety of needs can be met and dreams realized. The 'Doer Checklist' for Chapter Two asked you to write down your values; I recommend completing or reviewing that assignment before you move on. The clearer your values become to you, the better your ability will be to set meaningful financial goals.

Once you have clear values identified, the importance of setting specific, written financial goals cannot be overstated. Having a master plan in your head may be great if you never want to actually build anything, but to create your financial house you will need to sketch out blueprints on paper first. Your *Financial Greatness Blueprint* will consist of:

I     A current financial inventory

I     Values-based written goals with specific action steps and
      timeframes attached to them

**TIP:** See ***The 8 Pillars Workbook*** for a comprehensive outline to help
you design your own *Financial Greatness Blueprint.*

Let's look at creating your financial inventory and values-based goals in more detail.


## TAKE FINANCIAL INVENTORY:
### "YOU ARE HERE"

Have you ever found yourself wandering through an amusement park or a shopping center unable to find the ride or store you are looking for? When I have been lost in such places, no sight is more welcome than one of those large anchored maps with a big dot on it marked "**YOU ARE HERE**." I value the relief of knowing exactly where I am in the maze of attractions, and I appreciate the time that map will save me by showing me where my goal is in relation to my current position. After I know where I am on the map, I can quickly find where I need to go.

The same principle applies to your *Financial Greatness Blueprint*. In addition to determining where you want to end up financially, you need to find out where you are right now. Taking inventory of your finances places a dot on the map that will make a huge difference in deciding what you will do next. Facing the reality of your financial situation can be scary, but it is absolutely critical in creating an accurate and effective *Financial Greatness Blueprint*. A full inventory includes three major components:

**Part I:** You need to understand your personal <u>net worth</u> by creating your own simple balance sheet.

**Part II:** You need to fully understand your <u>expenses</u>. This involves tracking your spending habits and bills for two months or more to determine the fixed and variable costs of running your household.

**Part III:** You need to know where your money is coming from and whether you are currently living within your means. To do this, you will put together an <u>income statement</u> and a household <u>budget</u>.

Most people have never really completed a personal financial inventory. I often speak with couples who tell me they can't believe the incredible increase in awareness and motivation they experience just by doing these three simple exercises. The process of looking hard at your own money habits and taking stock of your financial reality can and does inspire people to action. People with a *Financial Greatness Mindset* immediately recognize the potential benefits involved. Thus your financial inventory becomes a crucial part of the *Organize* portion of Pillar Two: *Organize and Systematize for Success* ™.


## FINANCIAL INVENTORY PART I:
## YOUR NET WORTH

Determining your Net Worth does not have to be difficult or complicated. You simply:

1. List the name and dollar value of each of your assets (what you own). Add them together to find your total assets.
2. List the name and dollar value of each of your liabilities (what you owe, or your debts). Add them together to find your total liabilities.
3. Subtract your liabilities from your assets to arrive at your total net worth.

Example:

| | |
|---|---|
| Assets | $136,000 |
| - Liabilities | - $129,000 |
| = NET WORTH | = $7,000 |

On my website **8Pillars.com** you will find a tool called, *Financial Quick Look*. This *Financial Quick Look* has all of the categories listed for your assets and liabilities and will calculate your net worth and graphically display it as a pie chart.

## FINANCIAL QUICK LOOK

### ASSETS

**Cash & Cash Equivalents**

| | | |
|---|---|---|
| Cash on hand | $ | 3,500 |
| Checking Account | $ | 2,200 |
| Bank Savings | $ | 1,700 |
| Money Market | $ | 3,500 |
| Children's Savings | $ | 1,400 |
| Other | $ | 2,000 |
| Sub-total | $ | 14,300 |

**Securities**

| | | |
|---|---|---|
| CD's | $ | 1,000 |
| Bonds | $ | 3,000 |
| Mutual Funds | $ | 5,000 |
| Exchange Traded Funds | $ | 3,000 |
| Individual Stocks | $ | - |
| Cash Value of Insurance | $ | - |
| College 529 Plans | $ | - |
| Other | $ | - |
| Sub-total | $ | 12,000 |

**Retirement Accounts**

| | | |
|---|---|---|
| 401k | $ | 76,000 |
| 401k (2) | $ | 123,000 |
| Roth IRA | $ | 16,400 |
| Roth IRA (2) | $ | 4,200 |
| Other | $ | 4,000 |
| Other | $ | - |
| Sub-total | $ | 223,600 |

**Real Estate**

| | | |
|---|---|---|
| Personal Residence | $ | 562,000 |
| Personal Residence (2) | $ | - |
| Rentals & Investment Property | $ | - |
| Other | $ | - |
| Sub-total | $ | 562,000 |

**Use Assets**

| | | |
|---|---|---|
| Automobile (1) | $ | 22,500 |
| Automobile (2) | $ | 14,300 |
| Recreational | $ | - |
| Other | $ | - |
| Other | $ | - |
| Sub-total | $ | 36,800 |
| **Total** | **$** | **848,700** |

### LIABILITIES & NET WORTH

**Liabilities**

| | | |
|---|---|---|
| Mortgage(s) | $ | 376,000 |
| Automobile (1) | $ | 5,600 |
| Automobile (2) | $ | - |
| Credit Card (1) | $ | - |
| Credit Card (2) | $ | - |
| Line of Credit | $ | - |
| Rental Property | $ | - |
| Other | $ | - |
| Other | $ | - |
| **Total** | **$** | **381,600** |
| **NET WORTH** | **$** | **467,100** |
| Life Insurance Death Benefit(s) | $ | 550,000 |
| Total Estate Net Worth | $ | 1,017,100 |

**Insurance**

| | Provider | | |
|---|---|---|---|
| Life | xx | $ | 50,000 |
| Auto | xx | $ | 5,000 |
| Health | xx | $ | 1,000,000 |
| Jewelry | xx | $ | 5,000 |
| | xx | $ | 500,000 |

**Credit Scores**

| | Score | Date checked |
|---|---|---|
| You | 723 | |
| Spouse | 765 | |

**Goals & Notes** — **By (Date)** — **Completed (Date)**

1 Health Savings Acc.
2 Pay off Car
3 Pay off house
4 Donate $1,500 to Shelter
5 Start College 529 Plan
6 Other
7 Other

Your net worth can be a powerful measuring stick for overall financial progress.

Seeing your net worth increase gives you quantifiable evidence that you are going in the right direction. You can only do two things to raise your net worth—either increase your assets or decrease your liabilities. While it is important to do both, the typical American household stands to gain the most initial benefit by paying off liabilities. People who constantly borrow money usually fail to save and invest and end up wallowing in financial meagerness. The less consumer debt you carry, the faster your net worth can grow. Increasing assets becomes easier when you are not overburdened by debt, especially credit card payments (we will discuss debt in more detail in Pillar Three: *Break Your Financial Bonds and Barriers™*).

Keep in mind that there are two very different types of assets. Some of your assets (what I call *performing assets*) have the potential to increase or appreciate in value over time. These assets represent your money at work for you earning interest, dividends, and equity. The more performing assets (securities, real estate, savings, and so on) you invest in, the higher your net worth can grow.

Other assets will decrease or depreciate in value over time. Assets that depreciate (such as cars, furniture, electronics, some jewelry, and recreational vehicles) are usually called *use assets*. Rather than working for you, these assets lose their value the longer you use them.

Think about the principle that net worth can teach us: when you invest more money in performing assets than you spend on use assets, your net worth will increase. On the other hand, if you own very few appreciating assets and spend the majority of your money on use assets, your net worth will decrease. You need to understand this distinction clearly. Many people who own expensive cars, nice boats, designer clothes, luxury homes, and opulent jewelry (*use assets*) may appear to be wealthy when in reality they are not. In fact, some of the wealthiest-looking people in your area may actually have a negative net worth!

## FINANCIAL INVENTORY PART II:
## YOUR EXPENSES

Every household has three types of expenses or costs to manage: fixed costs, variable costs, and unplanned expenses. Implementing Pillar One*: Establish a Financial Confidence Account™* prepares you for the variety of unplanned or emergency costs that hit all of us at one time or another. Since unexpected costs cannot be <u>planned for</u> or counted on, we exclude them from our expense analysis and instead <u>prepare for</u> them with a *Financial Confidence Account™*. Implementing the principles in Pillar Two will help you manage and control the more typical expenses of bills and discretionary spending—costs that you <u>can</u> plan for and anticipate.

**The process for analyzing your expenses has four steps:**

**First**, list the expenses that come directly out of your paycheck. The idea is to be aware of what you may be spending on taxes, health insurance, and retirement plans that you do not think about on a regular basis. What is the average monthly dollar amount you are expending on these items? This number is called your <u>total payroll deductions</u>. You may also want to calculate the percentage of your gross income represented by these deductions.

**Second**, list the dollar amounts of your regular monthly bills (fixed costs). For regular bills you pay that are the same amount every month, as well as bills that fluctuate slightly from month to month, simply list the average monthly cost of each bill. Add them up to determine your total average <u>fixed costs.</u>

**Third**, list the average amount of money you spend on discretionary items each month (variable costs). Include necessities like gas, groceries, clothing, medical costs, and household supplies, as well as your typical spending on entertainment, travel, gifts, eating out, and consumer goods (electronics, appliances, toys, home improvement projects, etc.). Add these up to determine your total average <u>variable costs.</u>

**Fourth**, add the totals from each of these categories of expenses to find your baseline monthly average expenses. At this point you will have your *estimated* expense analysis.

## Example

| | | |
|---|---|---|
| Total Taxes Withheld | $878 per month average | 16.2% |
| Health Insurance/Benefits | $313 per month average | 5.8% |
| 401(k) Contributions | $325 per month average | 6% |
| **Total Payroll Deductions:** | **$1,516 monthly average** | **28%** |
| Mortgage Payment | $755 per month average | |
| Charitable/Tithes | $650 per month average | |
| Utilities | $210 per month average | |
| Car Payments/Insurance | $340 per month average | |
| Credit Card Payments | $100 per month average | |
| Phone (inc. cell phones) | $95 per month average | |
| Internet Service | $35 per month average | |
| Cable | $45 per month average | |
| **Total Fixed Costs:** | **$2,230 monthly average** | |
| Groceries/Household | $450 per month average | |
| Gas, parking | $230 per month average | |
| Clothing | $100 per month average | |
| Consumer Goods | $150 per month average | |
| Entertainment/Restaurants | $130 per month average | |
| Medical | $90 per month average | |
| Gifts | $60 per month average | |
| Travel and Misc. | $100 per month average | |
| **Total Variable Costs:** | **$1,310 monthly average** | |
| **Total Average Expenses:** | **$5,056 per month** | |

I strongly recommend that you track every dollar you spend for a minimum of two months to see how accurate your estimates really are. Most families are shocked to find out how much they spend on entertainment, restaurants, medical care, and so forth in the course of a year. By keeping careful track of what you are actually spending money on, you will discover a feeling of financial control and awareness that may surprise you. You can do this in a notebook, a spreadsheet program, or any way you like. Whichever method you use, I strongly urge you to complete this exercise so that you can better understand where your money goes each month.

## FINANCIAL INVENTORY PART III: INCOME STATEMENT (NET CASH FLOW) & BUDGET

The final component of your "YOU ARE HERE" financial inventory involves determining whether you are living within your means or not. Having calculated your net worth and totaled up your monthly expenses, you now need to examine how your income fits into the picture.

We will delve more deeply into the subject of income in Pillar Seven: *Maximize Your Money-Making Machine™*, so for now we only need to look at one simple formula:

> Gross Monthly Income
> - Total Monthly Expenses
> = Net Cash Flow

Staying with the same expense numbers as our previous example would give us the following results:

$5,417 Gross Monthly Income ($65,000 annual salary)
- $5,056 Average Monthly Expenses
= $361 Net Cash Flow per month

In this example, our hypothetical family has $361 per month available to fund their financial goals. In other words, they live within their means and can direct that "left over" money towards the priorities in their *Financial Greatness Blueprint*. A positive net cash flow enables a family to put their money to work for them, increasing their net worth and giving them choices with their budget.

## The "B" Word

Is the word "BUDGET" a bad word for you? Many people feel budgets are too restrictive and time consuming. Such an attitude towards budgets is a good indicator of someone who has never properly used one. When implemented well, budgets become liberating for anyone with a *Financial Greatness Mindset*.

My wife and I occasionally go out to eat at nice restaurants without any financial guilt or concern. Why? This is because we budget for the expense ahead of time. We are not spending money on our date nights that we have not already planned for. In fact, we have an entire "Fun/ eating out/babysitter" category to our budget. We rely on our budget to keep us from spending money on things that do not add value to our lives. Many people without budgets spend money aimlessly, and at the end of the month they wonder where it all went. The typical household spends nearly all of its income regardless of how much it earns and yet has very little to show for it in the long run.

If you are serious about achieving Financial Greatness, you must create and adhere to a workable household budget. Creating a budget requires that you first understand where you are in terms of income and expenses (part of your Financial Greatness Inventory) and then actively decide what expenses you will continue or discontinue, increase or decrease.

One of the most critical success factors will be reaching a consensus among everyone in the household about the spending allocations in the budget. Without having each person who contributes to income or spending on board, the budget may fail. If you are married, please be patient with your spouse. Ideally, I would have both of you read this book together. If that is not possible, it is important to realize that in many relationships, one spouse may be more financially inclined than the other. If that describes you and your marriage, be encouraging towards your spouse. Kindly invite him or her to be a part of the budgeting process, but don't force participation or give ultimatums. Further, if you have children at appropriate ages, you can slowly begin to include them in simple budgeting conversations.

Sticking to a budget requires restraint, discipline, and continuous tracking of what you spend. Having a budget does not mean you can never make allowances for special circumstances, needs, or opportunities; however, it does require you to commit to living within your means.

Budgeting formats and systems come in many varieties. Some people keep receipts and bills in a file and others track everything online. Some people create computer spreadsheets for their records and others use spiral-bound notebooks. One family might write out checks for almost everything, listing their budget categories in the check memo field. Another family might put bills on automatic payment and run all of their purchases through a credit card to get rewards points. I have even seen people divide their net pay into envelopes of cash, one for each budget category. When an envelope's allotment of cash runs out, they can't spend more on that category until next month. <u>Do what works for you!</u> The important thing is to decide together on a system and on amounts that everyone involved can agree on and commit to. Utilize whatever methods and systems will make following your budget easiest for you. Trying to follow someone else's best approach usually makes discipline harder than it needs to be.

On my website **8Pillars.com** you will find a tool called *Super Budget Calculator*. *Super Budget* will calculate your net cash flow and graphically display where your money goes. Use the tool to see where you can make changes to your spending habits and improve your net cash available for saving and investing.

# S U P E R  B U D G E T  Calculator

| MONTHLY EXPENSES | $ | 7,033 |
|---|---|---|

**Monthly House Expense**

| | | |
|---|---|---|
| House Payment | $ | 2,100 |
| Home Maintenance | $ | 200 |
| Misc | $ | 100 |
| Other | $ | - |
| Sub-total | $ | 2,400 |

**Monthly Loan Payments**

| | | |
|---|---|---|
| Auto Payment | $ | 387 |
| Auto Payment 2 | $ | - |
| Credit Card Payments | $ | 100 |
| Bank Service Charge | $ | - |
| Other | $ | - |
| Misc. | $ | - |
| Sub-total | $ | 487 |

**Monthly Insurance Expense**

| | | |
|---|---|---|
| Auto Insurance | $ | 120 |
| Health | $ | 350 |
| Life | $ | 56 |
| Home | $ | 112 |
| Other | $ | - |
| Misc. | $ | 100 |
| Sub-total | $ | 738 |

**Monthly Utilities**

| | | |
|---|---|---|
| Electric | $ | 92 |
| Gas | $ | 75 |
| TV/Cable | $ | 65 |
| Telephone (land line) | $ | 30 |
| Cell Phone | $ | 120 |
| Internet | $ | 36 |
| Other | $ | 100 |
| Misc. | $ | 10 |
| Sub-total | $ | 528 |

**Other Monthly Expenses**

| | | |
|---|---|---|
| Food | $ | 650 |
| Auto Gas and Maintenance | $ | 550 |
| General Merchandise | $ | 175 |
| Travel and Entertainment | $ | 155 |
| Child Care Expense | $ | 100 |
| Donations | $ | 1,000 |
| Gift Expense | $ | - |
| Medical | $ | 100 |
| Other | $ | 150 |
| Other | $ | - |
| Other | $ | - |
| Misc. | $ | - |
| Sub-total | $ | 2,880 |

| MONTHLY INCOME (combined) | | | $ | 7,800 |
|---|---|---|---|---|

| Income | | YOU | | SPOUSE |
|---|---|---|---|---|
| Gross Pay (Monthly) | $ | 7,000 | $ | 3,000 |
| Taxes withheld (optional) | $ | 1,300 | $ | 300 |
| Insurance and benefits | $ | 300 | $ | - |
| Company retirement savings plan | $ | 300 | $ | - |
| Other | $ | - | $ | - |
| Other | $ | - | $ | - |
| Monthly Net Pay (take home) | $ | 5,100 | $ | 2,700 |
| Sub-total | $ | 5,100 | $ | 2,700 |

| AVAILABLE FOR SAVINGS | $ | 767 |
|---|---|---|

| Goals & Notes | Date Completed |
|---|---|
| 1. Increase Savings | |
| 2. Open 529 Plan | |
| 3. Automate Savings | |
| 4. Open Roth IRA | |
| 5. Increase Deductible | |
| 6. Pay off Car | |
| 7. | |
| 8. | |
| 9. | |
| 10. | |

**Thoughts, Feelings, and Ideas** – What are some of the thoughts or feelings you had while reading Chapter Six? What insights occurred to you while reading? Did any particular action ideas pop into your mind as you read?

_____

_____

_____

_____

_____

_____

_____

_____

_____

Can you see how creating your *Financial Greatness Blueprint* will improve your life?

How will your life specifically improve after you create your *Financial Greatness Blueprint*?

_____

_____

_____

_____

_____

_____

_____

_____

_____

## DOER CHECKLIST – CHAPTER 6

☐    I have clarified my core values / dreams and committed them to
paper.

☐    I have calculated my net worth, and I am committed to growing
it in a balanced way.

☐    I have tracked my expenses and taken inventory of my fixed and
variable costs.

☐    I have analyzed my income and determined my net cash flow.

☐    I have a working budget that the entire household is committed
to supporting.

## CHAPTER 7

# WHERE ARE YOU GOING?

Once you have clarified your values and taken a thorough inventory to determine where you are financially, you are ready to work on the rest of your *Financial Greatness Blueprint*. After finding the "YOU ARE HERE" dot on the map, you have to identify the attractions in the park you want to visit. You need a plan for getting from where you are currently to the destination you want to arrive at in the future. This is where written goals come into play.

## THE IMPORTANCE OF GOALS
## IN YOUR FINANCIAL GREATNESS BLUEPRINT

Thinking about your goals in terms of results—what you ultimately want to have happen for you financially—creates the vision you will need in order to stick to your plan (including your budget). Many people fail to reach their goals because they never think about the real results they want to achieve. You need to have meaningful, values-based long-term goals in place (parallel to which attractions in an amusement park you want to visit).

## LONG-TERM GOALS

**Long-term goals** are very different from short-term goals. You may set a few long-term goals where the path ahead is unclear; this is perfectly fine. Do not be afraid to set long-term goals just because you are unsure how you will achieve them. My father often tells me, "You set the goal first and then you see; you never see first." Where long-term goals are concerned, that's a profound statement.

Too many people wrestle with the problem of exactly how they will achieve a potential dream before they even set the goal to reach it. None of us can anticipate everything that will happen to us 7-10 years down the road; every one of us has uncertainty and uncontrollable circumstances in our future. This should not stop us from setting challenging goals. By setting long-term *written* goals, you clarify the destinations you want to reach and give yourself purpose and motivation for working towards them.

When I was in college, I set a goal to create a world-class financial education company. The thought almost overwhelmed me at the time. How would I get started? Where would I come up with the capital? Who would listen to me and become my customers? At the time, the road ahead was unclear. Ten years later my goal has become a reality. Without the long-term goal and dream to inspire me, I would not have been able to see through the fog of setbacks or move past the obstacles in my path.

## SHORT-TERM MILESTONES

Once you know where you are now and where you want to end up, you need to set short-term goals that map out specific steps required to get from point A to point B. When I was young, my father used to say, "If you tell me where you are and your specific plans to move forward, I will tell you where you will end up." I thought he sounded a bit corny at the time, but I now realize the wisdom in my father's statement.

Short-term goals act like milestones on the way to a desired future result, marking your progress in manageable and measurable intervals. Short-term milestones call for immediate action and have a direct impact on your financial decisions and situation. When you have a specific plan to move forward from where you are, your likelihood of success increases dramatically. These milestones should be concrete actions that you can implement right away and accomplish in the next two years. As you work towards your long-term objectives, you may need to update or modify your short-term milestone goals along the way.

I gave you two specific milestones to reach for in Pillar One, and spent a significant amount of space explaining the importance of those results. If you complete the Doer Checklists at the end of each chapter of this book, you will find that they continue to give you clear milestones to mark as you sketch out your *Financial Greatness Blueprint*. Financial Greatness is the ultimate result I want for everyone who reads *The 8 Pillars*™. As such, the milestones I assign to you in the Doer Checklists are core elements of Financial Greatness that apply to everyone. However, keep in mind that major aspects of Financial Greatness will depend on your particular values. Financial Greatness in its fullest sense can mean different outcomes for different people. The concepts and principles in *The 8 Pillars*™ will provide the fundamentals of your plan, but you also need to connect your plan to what *you* value. Otherwise you will be following *my* plan and not yours, which may not correspond with your long-term goals.

At the risk of sounding like a broken record, I want to reiterate the importance of connecting your goals to your core values. Further, for your goals to be effective they need to be written, specific, and measurable. Your goals will give direction to every other facet of your *Financial Greatness Blueprint*. When you find yourself off course once in a while, your long-term goals will give you something concrete to come back to. When you feel like your efforts are getting you nowhere, your short-term milestone goals give you something to measure your overall success against.

## EXAMPLE OF A BLUEPRINT GOAL

Now that we have examined "goal theory," we need to put it into practice. I would like to take you through an example of the kind of goals that will make up your *Financial Greatness Blueprint*.

**Long-Term Goal:** *"I will be prepared for financial opportunities and emergencies before they present themselves. I never want to lose sleep over money issues nor do I want to lose control over my financial plan."*

## Action Plan:
These are the steps (short-term goals) I need to take in order to reach my long-term goal:

**Milestone #1:** *"I will track all of my expenses for the next two months and have a working budget in place within three months." (List the date)*

**Milestone #2:** *"I will set aside $150 per month for the next ten months for a week-long family vacation next summer (list the vacation year)."*

**Milestone #3:** *"One year from now (list the date), I will have saved $5,000 in my Financial Confidence Account™. I currently have $1,200 in a Financial Confidence Account™ – This requires saving $300 per month starting now."*

## <u>Values that Relate to My Goal:</u>
**Balance** - having peace of mind and gaining financial discipline
**Family** - avoiding excessive stress on my relationships
**Safety / Security** - building momentum, being prepared for emergency or disaster, and gaining financial freedom and control

If you are struggling to put specific goals into words, you may want to look to the Doer Checklist at the end of each chapter. Each "to-do" item can be a short-term milestone on your path to Financial Greatness. Make the goals more personal by rewording the ones you would like to focus on. Try not to overwhelm yourself by tackling all of them at once. Choose a few (2-3) that relate to your particular situation and specify when you will accomplish each goal.

Also, take the time to understand why you want to accomplish each specific goal. The questions that precede each checklist are intended to help you connect your values to your short-term goals. By pondering how your life will specifically improve by accomplishing each goal, you will discover the "why" behind the specific to-do items. Whether you create your own financial goals or use the Doer Checklist as your milestones, it is important to take immediate action.

**Thoughts, Feelings, and Ideas** – What are some of the thoughts or feelings you had while reading Chapter Seven? What insights occurred to you while reading? Did any particular action ideas pop into your mind as you read?

_____

_____

_____

_____

_____

_____

Can you see how setting long-term goals and short-term milestones will improve your life?

How will your life specifically improve once you have set long-term goals and short-term milestones?

_____

_____

_____

_____

_____

_____

## DOER CHECKLIST – CHAPTER 7

☐   I have written down specific long-term financial goals that connect with my values.

☐   I have developed a plan to achieve my long-term financial goals by identifying and writing out short-term milestone goals.

## CHAPTER 8

# FOUR WORDS:
## BALANCE, AUTOPILOT, SIMPLIFY, ORGANIZE

### IMPLEMENTING YOUR
### FINANCIAL GREATNESS BLUEPRINT

Successfully implementing Pillar Two does require some discipline, and I make no attempt to gloss over that fact. Organizing your financial house demands thoughtful evaluation of your values and goals, as well as your time and effort in taking a thorough financial inventory. After creating a *Financial Greatness Blueprint*, you may identify luxuries and indulgences you currently enjoy that need to be sacrificed for now in order to achieve your long-term goals. To me, the word sacrifice has positive connotations—it means giving up something valuable now for something even better in the future. Those who reach Financial Greatness understand the importance of a long-term outlook and are willing to make sacrifices for their deepest long-term values. It takes discipline to avoid negative distractions from the media or other outside influences.

With that said, I want to be clear that Financial Greatness does not require putting your life on hold for several years while you devote every penny to its pursuit. Your lifestyle may need some temporary changes to put you on the path to success, but this does not mean you have to sacrifice every comfort you currently enjoy or live in poverty-like conditions in order to reach your goals. Experiences with thousands of families and individuals have taught me that people quickly lose momentum and perspective when financial goals feel too demanding. If sticking to your

*Financial Greatness Blueprint* requires constant willpower, eventually the mental and emotional effort can overwhelm you to the point of giving up on it.

Two important principles should guide you as you implement your blueprint day by day. First, you must exercise good judgment to maintain **balance** between your financial life and the things you live for. Second, whenever possible, you need to put the plans you make on **autopilot**. Let me explain how applying these two principles will keep you on track without causing you to burn out.

## PRINCIPLE ONE:
### FINDING FINANCIAL BALANCE

Remember, obtaining Financial Greatness enables you to put your money worries behind you so that you can focus on living a fantastic life. I do want you to worry about your finances *now* so that you don't have to worry about your finances *for the rest of your life*. However, this does not entail growing your net worth at all costs or spending all of your time and energy scrimping and budgeting. I do not expect you to eat only rice, shop only with coupons, and cut all entertainment and long-distance calls out of your budget just so you can retire wealthy. Most of us can think of someone who lives like this. They are so consumed with pinching pennies that they forget to live life here and now.

On the opposite end of the spectrum, we all know people who spend money like crazy—money that they don't have. They sacrifice their freedom and the security of their families by "living it up" now without regard to the future. I want you to find the right balance between the present and the future. It is important to enjoy life along the way to Financial Greatness and this means spending some money. At the same time, your net worth should be steadily rising over time; a declining net worth tells you that you are spending more than you make. Finding *Financial Balance* depends on your unique values and circumstances, but you can get a good idea of the extremes to avoid by reviewing this graphic.

| Spends, Spends, Spends | Saves, Saves, Saves |
|---|---|
| No ability to delay gratification | Consumed with delaying gratification |
| Happiest when spending | Happiest when saving |
| Always keeping up with the Joneses | Never buys anything unessential |
| Foolish with money | Miserly with money |
| Lives for the moment | Lives in the future |

**Ignore Net Worth Completely**                    **Grow Net Worth at all Costs**

**Financial Balance**

## PRINCIPLE TWO:
### AUTOMATE YOUR PLAN

Perhaps the most important part of financial discipline is <u>not asking too much of your own willpower</u>. Any financial plan that requires your constant supervision, restraint, and vigilance will sap your energy and lead to its own collapse. This is why the second half of Pillar Two tells you to *Systematize* your way to Financial Greatness. I define a system this way: *any organized and coordinated way of doing things*. Systems are the methods and procedures you follow to accomplish a task or produce a result. No matter how well you organize your *Financial Greatness Blueprint*, it will not amount to much if the plans exceed your ability to carry them out. Your steps from point A to point B need to be coordinated and methodical if they are to work effectively. The idea behind systematizing your plan is simple: put as many of your financial goals as possible on autopilot.

In other words, you need to remove the *need* for endless discipline by putting automated systems in place that do not rely entirely on your integrity and willpower for their maintenance. You need to make <u>the way you implement</u> your blueprint as automatic as possible. Let me refer to the Long-Term Goal example we have already used to give you an idea of how you might put your plan on autopilot.

This Long-Term Goal involved being prepared with a fully-funded *Financial Confidence Account*™ and some monthly savings for next year's vacation. The milestones specified saving a total of $450 per month after the initial effort of tracking expenses and budgeting appropriately. How could you automate this goal?

First, utilize a "set it and forget it" automatic transfer from checking to savings each month. Most banks and credit unions now offer convenience services such as this, and many will even offer you better account packages for setting up automatic transfers. The idea is to choose the best day of the month for each transfer (such as the 15th or the 25th) depending on when your other bills are due, then the bank will make the transfer for you every month on that date. Once you turn it on, the feature will keep making the transfers for you without any effort on your part. Your only job is to leave the savings account alone until you have reached your savings target.

Second, use a separate savings account for each goal—one for the vacation and one for the *Financial Confidence Account™*. This way you don't have to think about how much money you have saved for each goal—the accounts are clearly segregated. This encourages you to leave them alone by tying them more closely to their respective results. Most banks and credit unions allow you to "nickname" your separate accounts for further organization and convenience. Any time you have a new goal that requires setting money aside, open a separate account to save money in and turn on the automatic transfers.

Many tools are available to you for automating your financial systems, including:

I     Direct deposits
I     Automatic transfers
I     Online bill pay
I     Purpose-specific segregated accounts
I     Automatic payment plans

I will discuss systematic investment and protection plans, as well as other aspects of your finances that can be put on autopilot as we come to them in future chapters. For now, take to heart the principle of automated, systematic action, and you will find your road to Financial Greatness much easier to travel.

## SIMPLIFY:
## THROW OUT THE CLUTTER

Often when people reach this point in Pillar Two, they start imagining all of the ways they could better organize and automate their financial lives. If the principles I am teaching have not fully sunk in, one of two things happens: either the very thought exhausts them and they do nothing, or they open a whole slew of savings accounts in their overabundant enthusiasm and get bogged down in keeping track of all the transfers and resultant overdrafts they cause.

Remember the analogy of model homes? One of the keys to their appeal is simplicity. Part of Financial Balance is keeping things simple enough that you don't make your situation worse when you take action. If you sketch out your *Financial Greatness Blueprint* only to discover that your goals call for nine separate savings accounts, you have taken on too much at once. Pare down those goals to make them manageable. Unless you stay in control of your goals and systems, they will only become clutter in your financial house. Here are a few ways to further eliminate typical financial clutter from your life:

1.  Give your personal information only to reputable businesses where you are a current customer (this will reduce unwanted junk mail).

2.  Follow my <u>*One or Two Rule*</u>: Work with one or two primary banks or credit unions, one or two major insurance carriers, and one or two financial professionals. The principle of diversification applies to specific types of investments, not to the number of institutions where you keep your money! Limit the number of credit cards you use to one or two; avoid store charge cards and store financing like you would a disease.

3.  Put yourself on the National Do Not Call Registry at www.donotcall.gov and remove yourself from as many mailing lists as possible. Opt-out of credit and insurance offers at www.optoutprescreen.com. Tell the companies you do business with not to send solicitations to you.

4.      Never give out financial information via email; delete unsolicited email without reading it. Any emails regarding foreign sweepstakes, lotteries, and inheritances are known fraudulent scams.

5.      Call your bank and tell them you want to "Opt-out" of all phone, mail, and email solicitations. Companies who can claim you as a customer are exempt from Do Not Call/Do Not Mail rules unless you specifically opt-out.

6.      Keep all of your financial records and important documents in one place (your fire/water-proof home safe or a safe deposit box). Make sure that your emergency contacts, estate executors, and attorney all know where your records are kept (I will discuss what financial records to keep on file below).

7.      Use Online Banking and go with paperless statements whenever possible. This reduces your risk of identity theft while saving you time and hassle. Keep a list of your usernames for any online accounts, but do not write your passwords down (more about Online Banking below).

8.      Avoid changing service providers too frequently. Loyalty is often rewarded by financial institutions, and switching over accounts costs you time and energy that is often not worth it.

## PUT YOUR FINANCIAL RECORDS IN ORDER

I put the topic of organizing your financial records towards the end of this chapter for one simple reason: you can get by initially without a rigorous filing system. I would rather have you start abiding by a budget and leave your records a total mess than put off budgeting until you feel completely organized. My emphasis will always be on taking action by doing the most important things first.

It also becomes easier to decide what your filing system will be after you already have a couple months of budgeting under your belt. The possibilities for keeping your records organized are staggering, so don't get overwhelmed. Many people do just fine with one catch-all financial file drawer and a box for receipts and check registers. Others prefer clearly labeled folders in large filing cabinets holding several years' worth of sorted information. Whatever method you decide on, keep it simple and functional so that you can stick to it. Take the time to file records as they come so that you never find large piles of momentum-killing paper staring at you. Immediately shred any paper files you don't need to reduce space, clutter, and risk of theft.

## THE FINANCIAL GREATNESS FILING SYSTEM

Keeping your financial records organized will increase your level of financial control, but only when the method you implement works for your lifestyle. You need to ask yourself this important question: When I need to find a financial document (a bill, a warranty, an account statement, etc.) how long does it take me to find it? If you cannot answer "one minute or less," you need to work on your filing system. Setting up a filing system and keeping it current will allow you to spend time on more important activities and will give you a greater sense of control over your money.

What financial records are essential to file and where should you keep them? Whether you use an electronic or hard copy filing system (or both), the following categories provide a high-level summary of the records you should create and keep. Within each category you would place individual files. Remember that you do not need to keep paper copies of statements that are stored electronically.

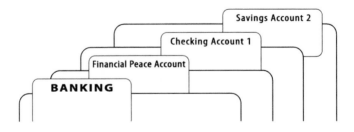

**Banking (3 years)**
>  Checking account statements
>  Savings account statements

**Investing (7 years)**
>  Brokerage account statements
>  Retirement accounts (401(k) / IRA)
>  Rental properties
>  Other accounts and investments

**Insurance (Keep policies forever, statements 5 years)**
>  Life
>  Health
>  Auto
>  Homeowners
>  Disability
>  Long-Term Care

**Taxes (7 years)**
>  Tax returns (by year)
>  Receipts (for tax deductible items – by year)
>  Income documentation (W2s, pay stubs, etc.)

**Household Accounts (3 years)**
>  Electric company
>  Gas company
>  Cable company
>  Phone and cell phone providers
>  Medical providers
>  Other accounts

**Credit Scores (5 years)**
>  My credit score and reports (by month and year)
>  My spouse's credit score and reports (by month and year)

**Mortgages (5 years)**
>  Account statements
>  Other important documents

**Debt (3 years)**
>   Credit card account statements
>   Loan account agreements and statements
>   Lines of credit (HELOC, etc.)

**Receipts (As long as you own the item)**
>   Receipts of major purchases
>   Warranty information

**Financial Greatness File**
>   Your *Financial Greatness Blueprint*
>       -   Net worth
>       -   Expenses
>       -   Budget
>       -   Value-based goals
>   Your Financial Greatness Doer Checklists
>   Financial coach / planner information

**Other Files**
>   Employment history
>   Educational history
>   Residential history
>   Letters of recommendation and reference
>   Important articles

**What to Keep in Your Locked Fire/Water-Proof Home Safe (Or Safe Deposit Box):**

I   The cash portion of your *Financial Confidence Account*™ (home safe only).

I   Important personal documents such as passports, birth certificates, marriage certificates, social security cards, and so on.

I   Legal documents such as your wills, trusts, powers of attorney, legal contracts, settlement papers, and other estate documents.

I   Titles to property such as homes, vehicles, condos, and any other tangible physical goods.

I   Physical certificates for stocks, bonds, and other securities and investments.

I    A current list of your online financial accounts along with
     instructions for accessing them if you are dead or incapacitated.
     Include a list of any passwords you use.
I    An "EXTREMELY CONFIDENTIAL" file for the keys to your
     safe deposit box and spare keys for any other safes, properties, or
     vehicles you own (home safe only).
I    Credit cards that you do not carry with you and debit/ATM cards
     you would only use in an emergency.
I    An inventory (on paper, on video, or both) of your possessions
     for insurance claims in case of flood, fire, or other disaster.
I    The names and contact information for the people who need
     to be notified if you die or are incapacitated (the executor of
     your estate or a very trusted family member should have the
     combination or a key to your safe).

Having a well-organized filing system will greatly facilitate your
ability to reach Financial Greatness. Whether you adopt an outline like the
one above or create your own, make sure that your personal information
stays secure and that you don't spend more time filing than you do working
on your *Financial Greatness Blueprint*!

## A WORD ABOUT ONLINE BANKING

If you do not currently bank online, you should! Online banking offers tools
that can benefit every facet of Pillar Two. Online account access enables
you to better track your spending, manage your bills, stay on budget, and
automate your savings plans. The best online banking sites store your
account statements and tax records, allow transfers and payments between
accounts, let you sort and download account activity by type of purchase,
and give you year-end account activity summaries.

The only serious objections I hear about online banking have to do
with security. Let me be clear: customers who bank online are much better
protected than those who don't. Financial Institutions already store your
information electronically, and accessing it yourself does not expose that
information to anyone but you. As long as you safeguard your passwords,
no one else will ever see your information. Most banks are very aggressive
in dealing with online security, fraud issues, and customer privacy.

I highly recommend online bill pay to all of my clients. In addition to saving you time and money, it will simplify your financial life and help keep you organized. Beyond these benefits, it will help protect your financial information. Every time you write a personal check, you are giving potential thieves your name, address, account number, routing number, and the institution you bank with. Personal checks are the least secure way to pay for goods and services and the most difficult to settle disputes over. Debit cards offer fraud protection guarantees, but if your card is stolen and money leaves your account fraudulently, you may not get your money back right away while you file claims and settle disputed charges. Credit cards offer more protection against fraud because you are not out any money while disputed charges are researched and reversed. Online bill pay offers the maximum in security because all payments are guaranteed by the bank, preauthorized by you, and made either electronically over a secure connection or via official bank check (which leaves your account number out of the picture).

The benefits of banking and paying bills online far outweigh any concerns you may still harbor about the Internet. If you are not part of the Internet age yet, get one of your children, grandchildren, nieces or nephews to teach you how to use it. You can avoid almost all online scams and dangers by following two simple rules: First, remember that no legitimate financial institution will ever ask for your financial information in an email or a pop-up message. Second, never get involved with anyone who claims you won a foreign lottery, wants you to wire funds on a cashier's check they will send you, or offers to give you a share of the estate of a wealthy person that supposedly has no living heirs. These are all common scams and are never legitimate.

## REVIEWING YOUR
## FINANCIAL GREATNESS BLUEPRINT

Once you have organized your finances, you need to implement one additional important procedure: an ongoing feedback system. At regular intervals you need to systematically review your *Financial Greatness Blueprint* and measure your progress on each goal. Think of this as financial housekeeping. All of the systems you put in place need regular maintenance to ensure they are performing at optimal levels for you. So balance your checkbook, review your account statements, monitor your credit, check your balances, verify your interest rates, and update your goals on a regular basis. Again, most of these activities can be done online in a matter of minutes. Keeping up on the financial housework helps you maintain your momentum.

At a minimum, you need to review your budget and your investment portfolio annually (ideally twice per year). You can also shred all outdated statements and records at that time so that your filing cabinet does not take over your house. I recommend taking a brief financial inventory and balancing your checkbook once per month (hopefully online). That way you can note any milestones you have reached and make sure you are not letting anything important slip through the cracks. Whatever schedule of review you decide on, make it systematic. Put it on your calendar or in your PDA as a set of appointments you will keep.

## THE IMPORTANCE OF ENLISTING HELP

For most of my students, the closer they come to Financial Greatness, the more complex and specialized their financial needs will become. When you have gained control of your money and want to see it work harder for you, professional advice can make all the difference.

Over time, you will probably assemble a "team" of professionals who act as resources and consultants to help you reach your financial goals. This team may include:

- Accountant or tax professional (preferably a CPA – Certified Public Accountant)
- Estate planning attorney
- Reputable insurance specialist (from a large, highly-rated insurance company)
- Financial Planner or investment advisor (preferably a CFP® – Certified Financial Planner®)
- Banker (from a strong, reputable bank)
- Financial Coach (certified in *The 8 Pillars*™)

A good financial advisor will help you review your plan, recommend solutions, refer you to other competent professionals, and facilitate your continuing financial education. Be wary of paying high commissions to sales people or paying asset managers a percentage fee on investments that already carry sales charges or high internal fees.

As discussed in Chapter Two, an important factor in the process of enduring change involves finding a successful mentor to provide perspective, practical knowledge, and objective feedback along your journey to Financial Greatness. A living resource like this can never be contained between the covers of a book. If you do not have a person like this in your life, **8 Pillars, LLC** (my financial education company) offers personalized financial coaching with no strings attached. The importance of real, live help cannot be overstated. Even with a good map (this book), and good survival tools (the concepts we cover in this book), wise explorers will enlist the help of a guide who knows the terrain whenever they undertake a serious expedition. Your personal financial life is more like a jungle path than a freeway, and having a trusted, experienced personal guide can make all the difference.

## PILLAR TWO IN A NUTSHELL

Implementing Pillar Two takes a lot of work. There is a reason why not everyone reaches Financial Greatness. Most people would rather float through life and be acted upon instead of taking action. Take a deep breath and pause for a moment to review in your mind's eye everything we have covered in Pillar Two (Chapters 6, 7 and 8):

1.  Creating a *Financial Greatness Blueprint* including:
    a.  A financial inventory examining your net worth, expenses, income, and net cash flow
    b.  An effective budget that everyone in the household agrees on
    c.  Values-based long-term written goals
    d.  An action plan made up of short-term milestone goals
2.  Maintaining balance and simplicity in your financial life
3.  Automating your action plan by putting systems and procedures on autopilot
4.  Creating your *Financial Greatness Filing System*
5.  Systematically reviewing your plans with the appropriate professionals on your team

Imagine for a moment how good it will feel to have these five aspects of Pillar Two under control. Implementing Pillar Two frees you from worry and uncertainty while positioning you to take effective action on the other seven pillars. That is why if I had to pick a favorite pillar, it would be this one. Few decisions can bring more satisfaction than putting your financial house in order and taking control of your money.

**Thoughts, Feelings, and Ideas –** What are some of the thoughts or feelings you had while reading Chapter Eight? What insights occurred to you while reading? Did any particular action ideas pop into your mind as you read?

_____

_____

_____

_____

_____

_____

_____

_____

_____

_____

_____

Can you see how organizing, simplifying, and automating your plans will bring a new level of peace into your life?

How will your life specifically improve after you have organized, put systems in place, and thrown out financial clutter?

_____

_____

_____

_____

_____

_____

_____

_____

## DOER CHECKLIST – CHAPTER 8

☐    I have eliminated as much financial clutter from my life as possible and will continue to keep my finances as simple as I can.

☐    I have my savings plans and financial goals on autopilot.

☐    I have a fire/water-proof home safe with my vital documents and cash portion of my *Financial Confidence Account*™ in it.

☐    I have an organized financial filing system.

☐    I have scheduled systematic and regular reviews of my *Financial Greatness Blueprint* and my automatic plans.

# PILLAR THREE

## *Break Your Financial Bonds and Barriers*

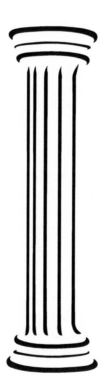

EAST GRAND FORKS CAMPBELL LIBRARY

## CHAPTER 9

# THE CHAINS OF CONSUMER DEBT

## A DIFFERENT PILLAR

Pillar Three is different from the other pillars. Throughout Pillar Three, we discuss what may hold you back from Financial Greatness as opposed to learning about the proactive steps that move you toward it. Without understanding certain economic bonds and barriers, you may never bridge *The Greatness Gap™*.

Now that you have established a *Financial Confidence Account™* (Pillar One) and your financial house is in order (Pillar Two), it is time to break through any bonds or barriers that may be limiting you or standing in your way. The most common form of financial bondage comes disguised as the freedom to buy whatever you want: the chains of consumer debt. This chapter will teach you how to break those chains and keep them off forever. The following two chapters will address two common obstacles to Financial Greatness: poor credit and lack of knowledge. These barriers act like roadblocks to anyone trying to bridge *The Greatness Gap™*, walling off their progress and limiting their opportunities. Learning to manage your credit and educating yourself financially will help you to break through these barriers to Financial Greatness.

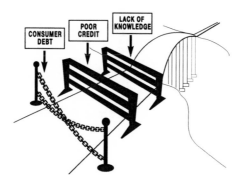

Even if you are debt-free with an outstanding credit score, I encourage you to read these three chapters. Remember, *The 8 Pillars*™ not only help you achieve success, they help you maintain it. Understanding Pillar Three will encourage you to re-connect emotionally with your own values and how they are impacted by your consumer debt, credit score, and financial knowledge. One of the most important sections of this entire book is the chapter on "Lack of Knowledge." I am constantly reading additional financial literature to gain new insights in an effort to continually re-commit myself to maintaining Financial Greatness.

## HEAVY CHAINS

I often have the opportunity to speak at high schools and universities across the country. During my presentations, I always ask for a volunteer. On the stage I have a large, 20-foot metal chain spread across the floor. I ask the volunteer to pick up one end of the chain and I ask, "Is that heavy?" The volunteer normally says, "Not really." I quickly respond by saying, "You're right, that's not too heavy—that's just a flat screen TV purchased with no money down and no payments for a year—not that big of a deal."

I then ask the volunteer to put down the end of the chain and pick up the middle section of the chain. "Is that heavy?" I inquire. In response, the participant usually says something like, "The middle is a little heavier than the end but not that heavy." I nod my head with a bit of a smirk on my face and respond, "Yes, that section of the chain is a little heavier but still not too bad—that's just a new SUV with a payment of $380 a month."

Finally, I ask them to pick up the other end of the chain, and I inform them that this end of the chain is a new credit card with a balance of $1,500 and a minimum payment of $25 a month—not a big deal right?

I then take the entire 30-pound chain and wrap the volunteer with it. At this point, the crowd is laughing. I then ask, "How does that feel?" With a smile on his face, the chain-wrapped victim almost always says, "Not good!" I usually laugh a little and quickly respond, "Not good— hmm. Well, it can't be that bad—you're still smiling. I mean, you have a new flat screen TV, a good looking car to cruise in, and a bunch of cool clothes and fun things you just charged on your credit card." With not-so-subtle sarcasm in my voice, I conclude, "That sounds fun to me."

After this exchange, my tone alters and I get a little more serious as I ask the volunteer, "What about wearing those chains for the rest of the day—what about sleeping in them?" The volunteer and the crowd begin to realize that individually, each of the debts did not seem like a big deal, but collectively, and over time they can become very heavy.

I pause for a few seconds, and the auditorium falls silent. In a quiet voice, almost a whisper, I say, "Now picture me in these chains. As I come home from work, I can barely get the front door open because of the weight around my neck. My two little girls come running, and they shout, 'Daddy, Daddy, we have been waiting all day to play hide-and-go-seek with you.' With a depressed look on my face, I respond, 'Girls, I've had a rough day, and Daddy needs to do some work—I'm sorry.' My wife also expresses that she needs to speak with me about something important. Instead, I go downstairs to my office to be alone. Not only am I worried about the money I owe, I am saddened because I realize that the chains are affecting my most important values—including my family."

Now, am I saying you cannot be an effective parent or spouse when you have consumer debt? Absolutely not. What I am saying is that you will not be as effective as you could be, in any area of your life, when you are burdened with the chains of consumer debt. We have been subtly sold the idea that consumer debt is a normal way of life and that it is not a big deal. IT IS A BIG DEAL!

Credit card debt is simply not acceptable. My clients that have reached Financial Greatness understand the destructive subtleties of credit cards and often stay away from them altogether. Later in this chapter, we are going to speak about the importance of a good credit score. We will discuss the role credit cards play in establishing good credit. For now, it is important to understand that credit card usage can become a slippery slope to disaster. I have seen people with an understanding of interest and the importance of staying away from debt get into financial trouble using credit cards irresponsibly. To reach Financial Greatness, I have a simple rule for credit cards:

> **Pay your credit card(s) off, in full, every month.**
>
> **If you cannot do this - you need to cut them up and get rid of them**

It's that simple! No excuses. Later in this chapter we will go through a debt reduction plan to completely eliminate consumer debt.

I feel very fortunate to have been taught at an early age the dangers of credit card debt. I have always prided myself on using my credit cards and then paying them off in full every month, but recently I have taken my understanding of credit cards to the next level. I realized that even though I paid my credit cards off in full every month, I was missing something. I began to notice that my use of credit cards was prohibiting me from reaching some of my financial goals. Even though I was following my simple rule of paying my cards off every month, I admitted to myself that I was not investing as much as I should have been.

Now, I rarely use my credit cards at all. I choose to use my debit cards instead. I realized that a psychological shift took place for me when I knew that the money was coming directly out of my checking account. I was more prudent about what I purchased, and I budgeted with greater care.

Sometimes I feel my spending gets a bit off-track while using only my debit cards (even with my credit cards stashed away in a safe). When this occurs, I go to a completely cash system for a time. I now use my credit cards very sparingly and with a high degree of consciousness (when renting a car, for example). I encourage even my high-net-worth clients to think about their use of credit cards and how these little pieces of plastic may be keeping them from greater financial success. Several studies have concluded that people spend more money when they use plastic to pay. The first step is to make sure you can pay your credit cards off, in full, every month while developing your credit history. Once you have developed a fantastic credit score and no longer need your credit cards, I would suggest you consider using your credit cards very sparingly and move to a debit card / cash system.

## INTEREST – YOU EITHER UNDERSTAND IT
## OR YOU PAY IT

The reason that consumer debt is crushing our nation's families goes much deeper than my simple story about chains. Most people would agree that overwhelming consumer debt, over time, produces negative outcomes in our personal and professional lives. This is only half of the story. Remember, our goal is Financial Greatness.

What is your debt <u>keeping you from</u>? Even if you have the ability to sleep at night and your relationships do not suffer because of consumer debt, the bigger questions are: does your debt prevent you from achieving Financial Greatness? Do the chains of interest sap your ability to reach your most important goals and dreams? I have not met a client yet with significant consumer debt that has achieved Financial Greatness. This kind of debt has too great an impact on our deepest values to coexist with them long term. That is why consumer debt and Financial Greatness are negatively correlated. Like water and oil, they simply do not mix.

At the heart of this principle lies a correct understanding of interest, especially <u>compound</u> interest. Albert Einstein once said that one of "the most powerful forces in the universe is compound interest." Why do people want to loan you money in the first place? It is because they understand the power of compound interest. Why do people who have achieved Financial Greatness invest? They, too, understand the power of compound interest. The point is very simple: you either understand interest or you pay it.

Let me ask you a question: do you want one of the most powerful forces in the universe (compound interest) working for you or against you? When I ask this question in my seminars, almost 100% of the participants emphatically respond that they want that force on their side. But when

I meet individually with seminar participants, only about half of them really get it. Remember that *to know* something and *to do* it are two very different things. Compound interest is one of those financial principles that is easy to understand with our heads but not with our hearts. How can we bridge the gap between just comprehending interest as numbers and actually realizing its impact on the things we value most? The problem lies with merely understanding the principle of interest logically—using only our minds. Remember from Chapter Two that because we are emotional beings, logic does not always lead to action.

From a very young age, we have been solicited through a multitude of advertisements to accumulate *things*. We have been relentlessly sold the idea that we should buy things, even if we cannot afford them. Advertising does work. I am acutely aware of the subtleties of advertising, and I will admit that I am affected by their messages. Advertisers know that you do not want to pay interest, but they also know that emotions are more important than reason in your decision-making process. Advertisers are amazingly effective at getting us emotionally involved with a product through the use of humor, sex appeal, good feelings, or fear.

I ask you to be more aware of your feelings about money and why you buy things. Are you more concerned about impressing others than you are about your long-term financial success? We need to ask ourselves before a purchase: "Will this add value to my life? Will purchasing this item get me closer to reaching Financial Greatness?" I can tell a lot about a person's values by looking at how they spend their money. The more aware you are of your feelings and the clearer you understand your values, the better financial decisions you will make.

## What Forms of Debt are Acceptable?

Let's get specific. What forms of debt are acceptable? Here is my list:

I    Education (Student Loan)
I    Car (Auto Loan)
I    Mortgage (Home Loan)
I    Business (Investment Loan)

Why are these forms of debt acceptable? They all have something in common—they either appreciate or add value to your life. Each one of these forms of debt has the potential to help in your ability to reach Financial Greatness.

**Education Loans:** There is a direct statistical correlation between the amount of education people have and the amount of money they earn. Your ability to make money by creating value in others' lives depends mostly on what you know. Studies have consistently shown that as your level of education goes up, so does your level of income. I am very pro-education. I encourage young people to go as far as they desire with their education, and I teach adults that education is a lifelong process.

**Automobile Financing:** It is very important to understand how your car relates to Financial Greatness. You may be saying, "Brian, a car depreciates very quickly—how does an automobile fit this criteria?" You are right—on paper. A car is a depreciating asset, but it also gets you to work and allows you to earn an income. Your ability to earn money is one of your greatest assets. Your earning ability is your economic engine that will power you towards Financial Greatness (we will discuss your income in greater detail during Pillar Seven: *Maximize Your Money-Making Machine*™). You must keep in perspective how your car relates to your financial goals. Additionally, many of your deepest values (time with family, community and religious service, hobbies and activities, and so on) may depend on reliable transportation.

I will not ask you to drive a car so cheap that it continually breaks down and is not safe. On the other hand, because your car *will* depreciate very quickly, it does not make financial sense to have a new, expensive car all the time. Having a car that is safe and that you feel good about is important. I recommend buying a car that is a couple of years old with 20,000-50,000 miles on it. Further, you should keep your car for at least 3-4 years. Whenever possible, avoid financing your vehicles at all. Saving for your next car ahead of time will give you more power to negotiate, encourage you to shop more carefully, and keep you from buying more car than you can really afford. By following these simple guidelines, you will save yourself a large sum of money while still driving a safe car that you enjoy. People who view their vehicles from this perspective help put themselves on the road to Financial Greatness.

**Home Mortgages:** Your home not only provides a nurturing environment to raise a family in, it also appreciates in value over time. Home ownership and Financial Greatness are closely correlated. Almost all of my clients that have reached Financial Greatness own their homes (we will discuss home ownership in more detail during Pillar Six: *Make Your Home the Heart of Money Matters™*).

**Business Debt:** Business ownership can be a great way to increase your income and put you on the fast track towards Financial Greatness. I wholeheartedly encourage entrepreneurialism. Is starting your own business essential to reaching Financial Greatness? No. If it were, I would have identified a specific pillar for the subject. I believe that a school teacher has the same opportunity to reach Financial Greatness as a successful business owner. Remember, Financial Greatness has less to do with your salary and more to do with your values and taking care of what you can control. I simply want to point out that a reasonable business loan is acceptable as a form of leverage (debt that you invest for greater long-term returns than the cost of interest).

Even though these forms of debt are on my allowed list, we still need to be careful with "acceptable" forms of debt. Many people will justify luxury cars, extravagant homes, unnecessary student loans, and risky business investments as acceptable forms of debt. These excesses are NOT ACCEPTABLE!

My wife and I both have four-year degrees, and I have a Master's degree. We chose not to get student loans to pay for our educations. Instead, we both held two jobs and worked our way through school. We drive reasonable cars that are paid off in full. Further, we waited to purchase our first house until we had saved a 20% down payment. We used a conservative 30-year fixed mortgage and made sure that we could afford the monthly payments. I am also very careful with business debt. I would rather grow my company slowly and steadily (with minimal debt) than rapidly and aggressively (with risky levels of debt). I only borrow for specific projects that will increase my company's revenue. Further, I only borrow what I am confident I can pay back.

My clients who reach Financial Greatness understand the need to be very careful, even with acceptable forms of debt. On the other hand, they understand that consumer debt is completely out of the question and not an option for them. If you have debt that falls outside of this list of acceptable forms of debt, it's time to get rid of it—it is keeping you from reaching Financial Greatness.

We know that certain items depreciate or go down in value. Let me ask you a question: does it make sense to buy something that goes down in value while the amount you owe on the item goes up? Even though this makes no sense at all, people frequently buy depreciating items on credit.

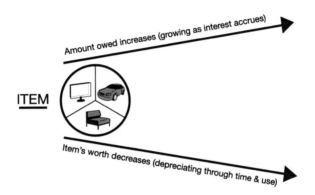

As the gap widens between what an individual owes and what the item is worth, so too does the gap widen between them and Financial Greatness.

Some examples of inappropriate consumer debt include:

**Carrying Credit Card Balances or Purchasing on Payment Plans**

- Vacations you couldn't afford at the time
- Hobbies you financed before you had money to invest in them
- Impulsive purchases of items you didn't really need
- Spending money you don't have on entertainment, restaurants, and so forth
- Appliances, Electronics, Furniture, and other big-ticket items

**Recreational Vehicles ("Toys")**

- Boats, ATV's, Snowmobiles, Motorcycles, Motor Homes, and so on

You can finance just about anything these days; this list is by no means all-inclusive. These are only some of the things that we should not go into debt for. Please don't misunderstand what I am saying: there is nothing wrong with wanting to purchase some of these items. Many of the things on this list are a lot of fun and can add to our standard of living. Further, some of these items can create lasting memories and provide valuable experiences to our families. But we cannot rationalize going into debt for these consumable (depreciating) items.

If we want to spend money on "toys" or other big-ticket items that will depreciate over time but do allow us to improve our quality of life, we can do one of two things:

**1. We can set a goal, save, and pay in cash.** This does not mean you bring a suitcase of money to buy a boat. I am talking about paying for the toy in full at the time of purchase. I recommend this option if you particularly enjoy a specific toy and know you will use it often. Not only does this save you from paying for the item more than once (when you count the interest), it can also save you on the purchase price. Businesses are often willing to give significant discounts to customers who pay up front. I know I would much rather get a 10% discount up front than pay 10% interest over the life of a loan, especially on items that depreciate.

**2. We can rent instead of buying.** Renting is definitely the way to go for my family. By renting (not with your credit card but with cash), you get the opportunity of playing with some expensive toys without paying interest. In addition,

I    You skip the maintenance and storage issues
I    You get to play with the latest and greatest toys
I    You lose the guilt associated with not using your expensive toys often enough
I    You give your family more flexibility to choose activities rather than "needing" to use that specific toy every time
I    You can save for much less expensive goals with clearly defined costs

The most important thing is that we are not going into debt for items that depreciate. At the heart of this issue is a principle called "delayed gratification." This is a vital characteristic for achieving Financial Greatness and a key element of a *Financial Greatness Mindset*. Your ability to delay gratification and pay with cash will largely determine your financial happiness. In fact, I will take that statement a step further. Your ability to delay gratification *in general* will largely determine your overall, long-term happiness in life.

The principle of delayed gratification is so important that I have written a children's book on the subject. It is entitled **Marshmallows AND Bikes** – *Teaching Children (and Adults) Personal Finance*. I believe that learning the lesson of delayed gratification at a young age gives children a much better chance to apply it as adults.

If you have young children, please do them a favor: go to my website www.8pillars.com, purchase the book, read it to your children, and begin to teach them about the importance of this principle at an early age.

## The Million Dollar Question

For you to reach Financial Greatness, it is absolutely essential that you understand the principle of interest. The difference between understanding interest (earning it) and not understanding interest (paying it) may be larger than you realize. Let me illustrate my point by asking you a "Million Dollar Question." Have you ever heard someone preface a question by saying, "Here is the million dollar question..."? The question may be important but usually will not help you actually obtain a million dollars. Well, my question literally is a million dollar question—one that can mean millions of dollars more over your lifetime:

## What does paying 14% interest really mean to you?

When I ask this question in my workshops, I give the example of a credit card interest rate of 14% on a $15,000 balance. So what does that 14% credit card actually cost? Many people say 14%, or $2,100 per year in interest. Both of these answers are good but are not completely correct. If you understand the principle of compound interest, the real answer is **a million dollars**.

You see, if you do not understand how interest works and you end up paying interest your entire life, you are not just spending 14% every year on finance charges. You are failing to <u>earn</u> the interest you *could* have by investing that $15,000. Let's say your average investments earn you 12% per year. The difference between paying 14% on that balance and earning 12% by investing it is more than one million dollars! I'll explain why. If you invest $15,000 (instead of spending it) then add $2,100 (the interest you would have been paying) every year, after 30 years averaging a 12% return, your money would compound to $1,017,103. Now you can see why I call this a "Million Dollar Question" and why I insist consumer debt is a big deal. It can be a million dollar big deal.

I learned early on in my life that small things over time can make a big difference. I want you to see that two small principles can get you a lot closer to Financial Greatness:

I    First, consumer debt is not an option for you.

I    Second, if you are serious about reaching Financial Greatness, you want to *earn interest* rather than pay it!


## CONSUMER DEBT COMMITMENT

The challenge for most people is not merely getting out of debt—for most of us, it is <u>*staying out*</u> of consumer debt. I will show you a simple plan to eliminate your debt, but before you begin any debt elimination process I want you to make a fundamental decision. In order to reach Financial Greatness, you need to commit to stop borrowing money for consumer items. That commitment becomes an emotional investment in *The 8 Pillars*™ because you now understand that your values are on the line.

Take a moment to realize that your life will be forever changed for the better without consumer debt. Make a decision now to reach Financial Greatness by putting consumer debt behind you FOR-EVER. Resolve now to not only get out of debt, but to stay out of debt by not borrowing money for things that lose value. You must be able to say, " I am finished borrowing money! I want to earn interest rather than pay it!" Once you have made this decision, take the steps necessary to keep your promise to yourself:

1. Set a specific goal to not borrow money for consumer items. Let your close friends and family members know of your decision and ask them to keep you accountable. If you need a mentor, please enlist the help of an *8 Pillars Certified Coach*™ who will help keep you on track (www.8pillars.com).

2. Take your credit cards out of your wallet or purse immediately and put them in your safe for emergencies. Move to a cash or debit card system. If you have serious credit card debt ($5,000-$10,000+) because of poor spending habits, I would encourage you to get rid of your credit cards altogether—cut them up and throw them away. Once your credit cards are destroyed, you won't be tempted to use them anymore.

3. Commit to staying within your budget. Remember that a budget should be simple; it needs to be a system that works for you long term. This may take some time to develop, but don't procrastinate doing it. Even my very wealthy clients use a budget. Your budget should be a living tool that changes over time but that also holds you accountable to spending within your means.

4. Once you have eliminated any consumer debt you owe, you will free up a significant amount of monthly cash flow. Decide now, before you even get out of debt, where that cash will be directed. To remain debt-free, you will need to save for larger consumer items and pay for them up front. Decide now to put an automatic savings plan in place with the extra monthly cash flow. Once you are free from consumer debt, open a

second savings account at the institution where your *Financial Confidence Account*™ is set up, and nickname the account "Major Purchases." Then put the funding on autopilot by setting the specific amount to be taken out of your checking account and moved directly into your "Major Purchases" account on the same day every month.

## CONSUMER DEBT ELIMINATION PLAN

The debt elimination method I teach is not complicated or difficult to understand, but it does take discipline and a decided heart to see it through. Let's look at how a typical couple I will call Sarah and Jacob tackled their debt using *The 8 Pillars*™ debt elimination plan. Sarah and Jacob began by listing <u>ALL</u> of their debts in order from the smallest balance to the largest. They even included their "acceptable" forms of debt. Please see the spreadsheet provided.

Next, Sarah and Jacob put stars next to their "acceptable" forms of debt. They understood that they needed to get rid of their consumer debt first in order to reach Financial Greatness. The acceptable debts (their mortgage, student loan, and two auto loans) were moved to the bottom of the list, even though one had a lower balance than one of the consumer debts.

Conventional financial planning typically says pay off your highest interest rate balance first. I agree with this advice in instances when you are dealing with amounts over $1,000 or with only one or two balances. Because Sarah and Jacob have a store credit card and a furniture balance *under* $1,000, I recommended paying off these smallest balances first, regardless of their monthly payment or interest rate. Remember, I did not create *The 8 Pillars*™ academically in a classroom—I developed it for use with real people in the living room. I knew that when Sarah and Jacob paid off those small amounts of debt first, it would give them a tremendous amount of financial momentum and a feeling of accomplishment. It also freed up cash flow more quickly than any other method we might have followed, which helped them increase their momentum.

In this example, Sarah and Jacob have two forms of consumer debt that are above the $1,000 mark (Credit Card 1 and Credit Card 2). Because Credit Card 1 has a higher interest rate than Credit Card 2, they attacked this debt next, even though Credit Card 2 was a smaller balance. After modifying the order of their debts and rounding them off for simplification, the list looked like this:

| Description | Remaining Balance | Monthly Payment | Interest Rate |
|---|---|---|---|
| Store Credit Card | $450 | $25 | 11% |
| Furniture | $800 | $25 | 15% |
| Credit Card 1 | $3,800 | $100 | 18% |
| Credit Card 2 | $1,400 | $60 | 11% |
| *Jacob's Car | $3,200 | $230 | 8.5% |
| *Sarah's Student Loan | $14,000 | $150 | 7% |
| *Sarah's Car | $17,500 | $280 | 6% |
| *House | $180,000 | $1,200 | 7.25% |
| | | $2,070 Total | |

* acceptable form of debt

Sarah and Jacob realized that they did not want to make a bad situation worse. To maintain their credit score, they understood the importance of making every minimum payment on time, every month. All of their minimum payments added up to $2,070 per month. They factored this $2,070 into their budget along with their basic needs. After making sure their minimum payments and basic living expenses were covered, they were determined to aggressively pay down their consumer debts.

Paying the minimum payments did not satisfy Sarah and Jacob. They were completely focused on paying off each debt as quickly as possible. By using a budget for the first time, they realized that they had more money available than they originally thought. Further, after accomplishing part one of Pillar One ($1,000 *Financial Confidence Account*™), they took some of the money they were using to establish this account and shifted it to their debt elimination-plan.

The plan was simple: begin at the top of the list and eliminate each debt in order. They would put whatever extra monthly cash flow they could into the first debt on the list. When the store credit card was paid off, they shifted their extra payments (along with the $25 they had budgeted for the minimum payment) to the second item on the list. When the furniture account was paid off, another $50 per month was freed up to apply towards Credit Card 1. As each debt was eliminated, they freed up more and more cash flow to apply toward the next item on the list. Many people call this process a "debt snowball" because it works like a snowball rolling down a hill. The bigger the snowball grows, the faster it picks up snow—growing in size exponentially. The more minimum payments you eliminate, the more cash flow you have for paying off the remaining debts—accelerating your debt payoff rapidly over time.

Sarah and Jacob put every extra dollar they earned toward the particular debt at the top of the list. In addition to their normal jobs, they picked up extra cash by taking on side jobs. Rather than spend this extra cash, they put it right into the debt at the top of the list. They visualized what it would feel like to be free of consumer debt. With these extra payments, they paid off their store credit card ($450) in just three weeks. They felt a tremendous and well-earned sense of accomplishment.

They immediately took the money they had been using to pay the store card and plunged it into the furniture bill. They calculated that at the rate they were going, it would take 2 ½ months to pay off the furniture. This gave them confidence and greater momentum. They set goals with time horizons for each debt on the list and had fun trying to beat their goals. They also had confidence that with their $1,000 *Financial Confidence Account™*, even if something unexpected came up, they were prepared to handle it without altering their debt-elimination plan. By sticking to their plan, Sarah and Jacob were completely out of consumer debt and had also paid off Jacob's car loan in 15 months. They then had an extra $440 a month to fund other financial goals.

## COMPLETELY DEBT-FREE?

Should Sarah and Jacob continue down the list and eliminate all of their debt? Let us go back to our standard of Financial Greatness. In order to reach Financial Greatness, do Sarah and Jacob need to be completely debt-free? No, the prerequisite to Financial Greatness is the absence of consumer debt and not using "acceptable" forms of debt in excess to buy cars and homes beyond our incomes. Because their "acceptable" forms of debt (one car, one student loan, and a mortgage) were not disproportionate with their incomes, I encouraged them to take their extra $440 and do three things:

**First**, I encouraged them to take $150 and turn back on the automatic savings plan for their *Financial Confidence Account™*. With $1,000 already in the account and adding $150 a month at 3.5% interest, they will have about $4,740 in two years. It is important for Sarah and Jacob to accomplish <u>part two</u> of Pillar One.

**Second**, I recommended taking $200 per month and setting up an automatic savings plan into their "Major Purchases" account. This account will allow them to stay out of debt by paying cash for consumer items and will eventually help them to eliminate their need for auto loans. As time goes on, their incomes will increase. I encouraged Sarah and Jacob to increase their savings plans in proportion with their increased income.

**Third**, Sarah and Jacob were quick to point out that they still had $90 remaining. They were surprised when I said that this could be used for a new column in their budget—"Date Night." You see, in the beginning of this process, they had expressed to me that they greatly value their marriage. In fact, their marriage was one of their most significant motivations for getting out of debt.

I reminded them that as they cycle through the *The Financial Momentum Circle™*, they need to continue to "<u>live</u> their values" as they "<u>apply</u> *The 8 Pillars™*."

THE FINANCIAL MOMENTUM CIRCLE ™

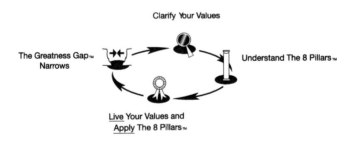

Clarify Your Values

The Greatness Gap™ Narrows

Understand The 8 Pillars™

<u>Live</u> Your Values and
<u>Apply</u> The 8 Pillars™

Budgeting for a weekly "Date Night" was a simple reminder of why they were working so hard at achieving Financial Greatness. Not only did this put smiles on their faces, it gave them greater confidence in their financial plan because they could see and appreciate the fruits of their labor.

**Thoughts, Feelings, and Ideas** – What are some of the thoughts or feelings you had while reading Chapter Nine? What insights occurred to you while reading? Did any particular action ideas pop into your mind as you read? _____

_____

_____

_____

_____

_____

_____

Can you see how eliminating the chains of consumer debt will bring a new level of peace into your life?

How will your life specifically improve after you have overcome the bonds of consumer debt?

_____

_____

_____

_____

_____

## DOER CHECKLIST – CHAPTER 9

☐    I understand the principle of interest and the idea of depreciating assets. I am committed to elimating and completely avoiding consumer debt.

☐    If I have consumer debt, I have a plan to eliminate it.

☐    I understand what "acceptable" forms of debt are. I will be very careful to only use "acceptable" forms of debt to help me reach Financial Greatness.

## CHAPTER 10

# YOUR ADULT REPORT CARD:
# YOUR CREDIT SCORE

Credit is a concept surrounded by misconceptions and false information. In this chapter, I will cut through all of the white noise and provide you with the simple facts about credit scores. My objective is to arm you with the most important concepts and strategies for earning a fantastic credit score.

## WHY DO YOU WANT A HIGH CREDIT SCORE?

Your credit score quantifies the risk you pose to potential lenders. In other words, your credit score gives lenders an idea of how likely you are to pay back borrowed money. The higher your score, the more likely you are to pay back the loan and the less risk you represent to the lender. What this translates into is having more, and often better, options when you need to borrow money for "acceptable" items. An attractive credit score allows you to shop and negotiate for the best interest rates and loan terms. Remember, Financial Greatness comes down to taking care of what you can control. Ultimately, you have complete control over your credit score.

In high school, some of my friends earned good grades and some did not. When it came time to select a college, my friends with good grades had the most options to choose from. Some of my friends with exceptional grades received scholarships that covered their tuition and books. Although this money was not "free" (they paid their dues in hours of homework and study), my more studious friends did not have to pay as much *money* for college. Their grades made them more attractive to potential colleges.

A credit score functions a lot like school grades, and lenders behave similarly to universities in the above example. When you have a good credit score and you need to borrow money, you will have multiple lenders to choose from. Having several options will allow you to get the best interest rates and terms on the loan you need. Some lenders will even give you additional incentives if your credit is attractive enough. It is very important that when you do need to borrow money for "acceptable" forms of debt, you maintain as much financial control as you can. When you do have to pay interest, you need to get the best rate and terms possible.

In addition to affecting meaningful purchases, such as a home or car, your credit score can impact the rates you pay on several types of insurance. Some auto insurers now rely almost exclusively on credit scores to rate their policies. Employers also frequently check credit scores when evaluating potential job candidates. A low credit score could therefore impact your attractiveness to employers and affect your money-making potential over time. What is your credit score saying about you?

## <u>YOUR</u> SCORE

Before reading any further, I want you to consciously take ownership of and responsibility for YOUR credit score. The credit ranking system is what it is, and the sooner you learn the rules of the game, the better the whole credit score picture will look for you. Begin to think of your credit score as your grown-up report card. When a student gets bad grades, he can blame the teacher, his unfavorable circumstances, or even inaccurate information (like a transcription error). The fact still remains: that student has a bad grade attached to his name! A credit score is no different. No matter what excuses you might make for it, the number does exist, and it has your name on it.

When I was in college, my friends frequently scratched their heads in puzzlement at my knack for getting good grades without seeming to overwork myself. They knew me too well to believe it was due to raw intelligence! What helped me was my ability to quickly assess the teacher and the rules and requirements for success in each class. I never wasted extra energy on areas that were not important to that specific teacher or on things that would not directly affect my grade. I approach my credit score the same way.

After you read this section and apply what you learn, you will be headed for a fantastic credit score because:

1. You will take responsibility for your credit score.
2. You will understand the rules of the game that affect your credit score.
3. You will be prepared to consistently play by the credit score rules.

## THE RULES OF THE GAME

In its simplest form, your credit score comes from your credit history, your payment records, and your debt ratios. I have friends who do not understand any more than the previous sentence who have very high credit scores. Many times we try to complicate issues when we would be better off keeping things simple. To have a good credit score you need to:

I   Have a long credit history
I   Always pay your bills on time
I   Not carry excessive consumer debt

If you follow these simple rules, over time your credit score will rise automatically.

## TECHNICAL ANALYSIS

Simplicity may be best at times, but in the case of your credit score, it helps to be armed with additional knowledge. I will break down the mechanics of how your credit score is determined to assist you in raising it more aggressively. The following graph gives you a visual idea of what areas make up your credit score. I will outline tips and helpful information in order for you to receive high marks in each specific category.

| Payment History | Amounts Owed | Length of Credit History | New Credit | Types of Credit Used |
|---|---|---|---|---|
| 35% | 30% | 15% | 10% | 10% |

**35% of your credit score is derived from your <u>Payment History</u>**

I    You need credit in the form of a loan or a credit card to show
     a history of payments. If you have never borrowed money,
     you have no payment history. For your first loan or credit card,
     you may need to secure the loan with collateral (money in the
     bank) or have a co-signer (someone with good credit already
     established).
I    Always pay your loan payments on time and as agreed with the
     lender. Consistently paying your bills and loan payments on time
     is the simplest action you can take to have a good credit score.
     Having a bill sent to a collection agency can quickly drop your
     score.

**30% of your credit score is calculated from your <u>Amounts Owed</u>**

I    Do not max out credit limits or carry high balances on any
     accounts.  More specifically, do not borrow more than 50% of
     your credit limit. (Example: if your credit card limit is $1,500, do
     not ever exceed a $750 balance on that card.) Your credit score
     will factor in your highest recent balance on each account.
I    Pay more than the minimum amount required by the lender.
     (Example: If your minimum payment on your credit card is $25,
     pay at least $50-$100. Better yet, pay off your card in full every
     month.)
I    When you have multiple lines of credit, do not carry balances on
     all of them at the same time. (Example: if you have 6-7 lines of
     credit, never owe money on more than 3-4 at any one given time.
     Having a balance on all of your lines of credit at the same time
     may negatively affect your score.)

**15% of your credit score is determined by your <u>Length of Credit
History</u>**

I    The longer you can show responsible use of credit, the better
     your score will be. (Example: a person who has responsibly
     managed his/her credit for 7 years will have a higher credit score
     than an individual who has responsibly managed his/her credit
     for 2 years.)

I    It is important to use your credit accounts and show a history of paying on time. (Example: just having a credit card or access to a loan but never using the lines of credit will not build a history. You need to actually borrow the money and responsibly pay it back in order to establish good history.)

## 10% of your credit score is derived from a category called <u>New Credit</u>

I    Do not open multiple lines of credit in a short amount of time. (Example: opening up 3-4 lines of credit within a two-month period may lower your score.) When starting out, it is best to open lines of credit slowly, over time, as needed. (Example: you may begin by opening up a cash-secured credit card. Six months to a year later, you may need to get a reasonable student loan. A year later, you may get a small and manageable auto loan, etc.)

I    Avoid having multiple lenders check your credit score in a short period of time. (Example: if you are applying for multiple loans with many different lenders and your credit score has been checked 7 or 8 times in one month, this may lower your score.) Checking your own score every 6-12 months will NOT negatively affect your score. You should be checking your own credit score at least once a year.

## 10% of your credit score is determined by the <u>Types of Credit Used</u>

I    Do not have too many credit lines in any one category. (Example: remember the *One or Two Rule* discussed in Pillar Two? Avoid having more than one or two credit cards, one or two auto loans, one or two of any kind of loan, and stay away from store charge cards completely.)

## BEAT THE SYSTEM

The financial system is perfectly aligned to create consumers who are dependent on borrowed money. I find it interesting that to build a good credit score, we need to show a history of repaying debt. It takes responsibly using debt, which eventually we want to get rid of, in order to establish credit history. It is true that responsibly using one or two credit cards can help build your credit score. Because of this fact, if individuals are not financially intelligent, over time the system will create the need to operate on debt. Those who reach Financial Greatness learn to beat the system.

Many people on the road to Financial Greatness have the goal of buying a home in the future. (We will discuss more about real estate in Pillar Six: *Make Your Home the Heart of Money Matters*™). They understand that having a good credit score will greatly help to secure a mortgage at a competitive interest rate and decide early in their financial journey to beat the system.

People who reach Financial Greatness build their credit score by responsibly using multiple lines of credit (including credit cards) in a strategic way. In other words, they *utilize* credit lines but never become *dependent* on borrowed money. You should only use borrowed money to pay for necessities (not wants) that you already have the money to pay for. Once your credit score is established, use low levels of "acceptable" forms of debt to maintain a good score. With a fantastic credit score, no consumer debt, low levels of "acceptable" forms of debt, and a good source of income, you will be in a position of power. You will be able to act rather than be acted upon. You will remove the roadblock that a poor credit score presents on the way to Financial Greatness.

## WHAT'S THE SCORE?

To win the game you need to know the score. What is your credit score right now? I recommend getting your score from all three credit bureaus—Equifax, Experian, and TransUnion. Take the average of these three scores to find your grade.

| Grown-Up Report Card Grading Scale | | | |
|---|---|---|---|
| Credit Score | 600 or less | 600-650 | 650-730 | 731 or higher |
| Grade | D or F | C | B | A |

Most people will want to build a credit score of at least 720 in order to reach Financial Greatness.

The first thing you should do once you receive your credit score (along with your credit report) is look for mistakes. If you find any errors, it is important to report these mistakes to the appropriate credit bureau right away. Continue to follow up with the credit bureaus until the errors are corrected or removed.

One of the most frustrating aspects of credit scores is the businesses that provide them—they can be sneaky. There are no free rides in the credit industry. You will pay in one way or another (in money, frustration, a monthly fee, or being heavily advertised to) in order to view your credit score.

Recently, because of new laws, you are entitled to one free credit _report_ each year. Your credit report is different from your credit _score_. The report contains the information used to generate your score, but the score itself is not part of the actual report. Most companies that provide your "free" credit report will attach a service to the report that, if not canceled in the first 30 days, will begin costing you money on a monthly basis.

Once you order your "free" credit report, they might still charge you to view your credit score. My point is to be wise when ordering your credit score. If you are only going to check your report (for errors and so on), you can avoid most of the gimmicks by going to www.annualcreditreport. com. However, in order to get your credit score, you will likely have to pay a small fee. Remember, when selecting a source for your score, it is important to know your scores compiled from all three major credit bureaus.

### TIP – Where to get your credit score:

I get my credit score at least once a year at MyFICO.com. I pay about $50, but I know what I am getting and I do not have to play games. I do not usually mention specific companies in my written literature, but I know how frustrating it can be to simply get your credit score with no strings attached. I am in no way endorsing MyFICO.com. In addition to offering credit scores, they sell many products that I do not agree with. You will find advertisements for all kinds of other products that you do not need, so be careful.

No matter what your score is right now, commit to playing by the rules and your score will improve over time. If your score is lower than you would like, own up to it. Taking responsibility for a poor credit score can be liberating. When you acknowledge that you are the cause of your bad credit score, you also begin to clearly see that you have the power to improve it! By knowing the score and playing by the rules, you will be in a position to beat the system.

For more details regarding credit scores, or if you have special circumstances that need more specific recommendations, please see *The 8 Pillars Workbook* or visit www.8pillars.com.

**Thoughts, Feelings, and Ideas** – What are some of the thoughts or feelings you had while reading Chapter Ten? What insights occurred to you while reading? Did any particular action ideas pop into your mind as you read?

_____

_____

_____

_____

_____

_____

_____

_____

Can you see how improving your credit score to 720 or higher will help you reach Financial Greatness?

How will your life specifically improve by having a credit score of 720 or higher?

_____

_____

_____

_____

_____

_____

## DOER CHECKLIST – CHAPTER 10

☐   I know my credit score.

☐   I am committed to playing by the rules and achieving/ maintaining a credit score of 720 or higher.

## CHAPTER 11

# LACK OF KNOWLEDGE

Lack of knowledge is no ordinary financial barrier. While consumer debt can drag you down and credit woes can trip you up, lack of knowledge can keep you from ever making progress at all. Financial education and the proper application of knowledge form the keystone that secures Financial Greatness.

## THE KEYSTONE

One of the strongest, most stable structural elements is the arch. In ancient times, masons used stone archways to create doorways that could bear tremendous weight without sacrificing beautiful design. In a stone arch the most important piece is the keystone.

The Keystone

KNOWLEDGE

The keystone locks all of the other stones in place, and without it the arch would ultimately collapse. Just as the keystone is essential for the strength and longevity of a stone arch, *knowledge* will be your indispensable key to reaching and sustaining Financial Greatness. Every person I know who has reached Financial Greatness was and is a diligent seeker of financial education.

I have a friend who has made a hobby of studying influential people from history. He enjoys reading the biographies of individuals who have shaped our world in a positive way. Whether they were scientists, statesmen, artists, spiritual leaders, military commanders, athletes, philosophers, or just ordinary people who made a profound difference in the world, he loves reading about them. As he studies their lives, he tracks the essential characteristics and attributes that made these people great.

My friend once told me something very interesting that I will never forget. He said that there were many characteristics that showed up repeatedly among those who impacted the world for the better. However, he found only one trait that ALL of them had in common—every one. The single attribute that they all shared was their love of reading. These amazing individuals were voracious seekers of knowledge and wisdom!

## THE SPECIALIZATION TRAP

Because we live in a complex world, specialization has become a necessity. We have endless information available to learn in myriad fields of study. In an effort to save time, we rely on so-called "experts" to tell us what we need to know. Some of these specialized experts include doctors, auto mechanics, spiritual leaders, builders, physical trainers, and financial advisors. Many highly-trained professionals possess true expert knowledge and skill requiring years of concentrated study and practice to master. These individuals provide critical services and become invaluable resources to society.

Unfortunately, some "professionals" tend to overcomplicate basic subjects in order to protect their professions and justify higher charges for their services. The more complex and incomprehensible a subject seems, the more people develop feelings of dependence on experts for information and direction. Such "experts" often have little formal training or education in their field and so feel obligated to inflate their own importance by claiming exclusive knowledge. These are the so-called experts to avoid.

Stay away from any professional who claims to have privileged information or a secret solution, as well as any who are not willing to educate you about their profession. Some of these individuals will stir up your emotions in order to sell you poor advice and products that may hinder your progression. Two of the most common emotions that they will try to exploit are greed and fear, usually by taking advantage of what you don't know.

Specialization is important, and I certainly agree with getting quality counsel from competent and qualified professionals. Yet some people use specialization as an excuse to never branch out, to stop seeking knowledge outside their own field or occupation. When we limit or curtail our own education, we run the risk of becoming too dependent on outside advice. We become easier targets for those who would take advantage of uninformed customers. Conversely, the broader and deeper our own reserves of knowledge become, the better equipped we are to find the answers and advice that are best suited to our personal circumstances. Any true professional will spend almost as much time educating you as they will spend treating, advising, or serving you.

If you ever find yourself being pressured to make a purchase out of fear or a desire to get rich quickly (greed), you need to be very careful. If these negative emotions are accompanied by a lack of understanding about the product or service, then you need to be extremely cautious. Never purchase anything based on a negative emotion. Likewise, don't follow advice that you do not understand. The key to avoiding major financial mistakes is financial education. The more you learn, the less you will have to fear. In addition, as you apply your understanding, you will guard yourself against greed and see money as a means to a much deeper end.

I believe that lack of knowledge keeps more people from wealth than any other single factor. The most common element I have observed among those who reach Financial Greatness is their wealth of knowledge. Consequently, I am a passionate advocate of paying for quality financial education and wise, unbiased advice. Even with my education and financial background, I still utilize a trusted team of financial professionals that I pay for and take counsel from.

## YOUR ADVISORS GET SMARTER AS YOU DO

The best financial professionals advise time-tested solutions, educate us about the principles behind them, and motivate us to implement the ones that we feel best suit our goals. The more intelligent and knowledgeable you are, the less likely you are to choose poor advisors. An individual who is financially intelligent will never settle for a mediocre financial professional. The better we understand fundamental principles in any area of our lives, the more prepared we are to choose competent advisors in that field.

Interestingly, the more you know personally, the more valuable your trusted advisors become—especially in the area of personal finance. A great storyteller by the name of Andy Andrews often says, " The quality of your answers depends on the quality of your questions." In other words, qualified money advisors (attorneys, insurance agents, CPAs, financial planners, etc.) become more effective and valuable as you become more financially intelligent.

Let me use two of my friends to illustrate this principle. One friend, whom I will call Bill, is constantly complaining about how much money he pays in taxes. Every year when the month of April rolls around, Bill vows to find a new CPA that can show him the way to better tax savings. Another friend, whom I will call Steve, is always bragging about how amazing his CPA is. Steve is confident that he is doing everything within his power to minimize his tax obligation.

I found this very interesting. With their permission, I looked at their tax returns. I found that they were both telling the truth. Bill was indeed paying more than his fair share of taxes and was not utilizing every tax break available. On the other hand, Steve's tax return looked great. I could not find even one area that could be improved on.

The most fascinating part of this story is that Bill and Steve use the same CPA! And this situation is more common than you might think. What makes the difference? Steve takes responsibility for learning as much as he can and comes to meetings with his CPA prepared with specific and well-researched questions and possible solutions. I am confident that your financial professionals will get smarter as you do.

## THE GREATNESS CONTINUUM ™

Chances are, you agree with me and already understand the importance of education. After all, you are reading a book about personal finance in order to improve your life. You should be commended! In order to reach Financial Greatness, you will need to continue seeking knowledge beyond this book. I am very passionate about the principle of gaining knowledge; passionate enough to have founded a quality financial education company, write multiple books, and work hard promoting financial literacy.

Sound education and the wise implementation of knowledge is the key to not only *obtaining* Financial Greatness but *becoming* something great. As I have persistently reiterated, this book aims higher than helping you *obtain* material possessions. *The 8 Pillars™* aspires to help you to *become* something better by living your values. The key to becoming a person of greatness is continually learning and consistently applying what you learn. If you are committed to learning and applying sound wisdom, over time I have no doubt that you will become a person of greatness. I call this process *The Greatness Continuum™*.

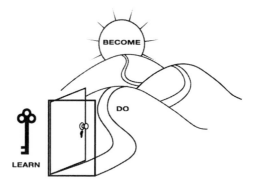

In an effort to facilitate this process of attaining greatness, I have created a financial education curriculum called *8 Pillars University™. 8 Pillars University™* is a complete learning system that provides real-world financial education for an affordable price. Participants gain a mastery of *The 8 Pillars of Financial Greatness* by completing the program at their own pace. But *8 Pillars University*™ includes much more than just an educational system. Students and graduates gain membership to a community of people committed to living their values and achieving Financial Greatness. It becomes an ongoing financial resource for continuous learning, development, and principle-based personal finance management.

Without going into great detail, enrollment in *8 Pillars University*™ includes:

+ A printed workbook
+ The 8 Pillars of Financial Greatness – Audio Book
+ An interactive CD ROM with important Financial Worksheets including the Financial Quick Look™ and the Super Budget™
+ A DVD orienting you to the curriculum and explaining how to use the system
+ Financial Wisdom – Timeless as Nature (full color hardback inspirational quote book)
+ Access to The 8 Pillars™ monthly newsletter
+ Discounts on workshops, seminars, coaching, and our annual 8 Pillars summit
+ Access to a members-only online portal with:
    • *Dozens of financial articles indexed by subject*
    • *High-quality financial calculators*
    • *A fully-indexed financial glossary*
    • *The 8 Pillars™ Wizard (a proprietary piece of technology that helps you reach Financial Greatness)*
    • *A special question-and-answer forum to address current financial issues*
    • *Hours of video and flash-animated online learning modules*

My goal for *8 Pillars University*™ is simple: I want to give people access to high-quality, no-strings-attached education in some of the most important subjects they never had the chance to take. *8 Pillars University*™ has been carefully designed to be simple and useful. It is not merely a class to sit through—it is a living resource designed to save you time and money through practical education and interactive tools. Every aspect of the system is indexed so that you can continue to reference *8 Pillars University*™ materials as a trusted source of knowledge. Unlike other financial education systems and websites, you will not find a single advertisement or a host of unnecessary services proffered.

I am well aware that different people learn in different ways. *8 Pillars University*™ delivers education through a variety of formats (watching, reading, listening, and doing) to help each individual learn the material in the way most effective for him or her. Do you have a spouse or an adult child that is not as interested in reading about personal finance as you are? I designed *8 Pillars University*™ to be interesting, engaging, and easy to navigate. Each online learning module is 10-15 minutes in length in order to keep things simple and focused.

If you are committed to learning and seeking financial wisdom, please visit 8pillars.com and click on the *8 Pillars University*™ link to learn more.

**"If a man empties his purse into his head, no man can take it away from him. An investment in knowledge always pays the best interest."**

*- Benjamin Franklin*

**Thoughts, Feelings, and Ideas** – What are some of the thoughts or feelings you had while reading Chapter Eleven? What insights occurred to you while reading? Did any particular action ideas pop into your mind as you read?

_____

_____

_____

_____

_____

_____

Can you see how having greater financial knowledge will improve your life?

How will your life specifically improve as you learn more and increase your financial knowledge?

_____

_____

_____

_____

_____

_____

## DOER CHECKLIST – CHAPTER 11

☐      I understand that knowledge is the keystone to Financial Greatness.

☐      I commit to becoming a person of greatness by continually furthering my financial education. I have visited www.8pillars. com to learn more about *8 Pillars University*™.

# PILLAR FOUR

*Take Care of "What if?"*

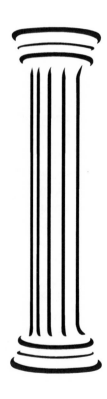

## CHAPTER 12

# INSURANCE: YOUR SAFETY NET

## "WHAT IF" WHAT?

What if you were involved in a serious car accident? What if one of your children needed emergency surgery? What if your house was terribly damaged or even destroyed in a natural disaster? What if you were badly injured and unable to work again? What if you became chronically ill? What if your spouse died? What if you died? I do not pose these questions to scare you; I don't believe that fear is a very effective teacher in the long run. I ask these questions because they are real possibilities in your life, and I want you to be financially prepared for them. Remember, Financial Greatness depends on taking care of what you can control. You can't predict what will happen to you or when, so you have to do all that you can to prepare for "what if" before it happens.

I call these personal catastrophes Financially Fatal Falls (such as major accidents, chronic illnesses, unexpected disabilities, premature death, and property-destroying disasters.) Many financial planners refer to them as Economic Deaths or Unexpected Life Events. By nature, these experiences are typically too costly for most families to survive, financially speaking. That is why I call them *Financially Fatal:* unless you are ready for them before they strike, these events can wipe out your financial plans and kill your chances of reaching Financial Greatness.

Working with many people who have reached Financial Greatness over the years, I have noticed that they are not afraid to speak about "what if." In fact, quite the opposite is true—people with a *Financial Greatness*

*Mindset* are constantly asking themselves "what if" and preparing for it. Not only do they ask difficult questions about potential threats to their finances, they aggressively shore up their financial defenses until they are fully prepared for every "what if." Because they have connected their financial plans to their deepest values, they want to do everything they can to protect their plans from disaster. Once they have answered all of their "what if" questions and prepared for them, there is nothing more they need to do. They don't need to worry or wonder about "what if," and that peace of mind itself yields immense value in their lives.

When I was in high school, someone told me that "worrying is like trying to get someplace by running on a treadmill; you end up exhausted in the same spot you started." If you find yourself worrying about "what if," it's time to stop spinning your wheels. Instead, start asking "What can I DO about it?" When you are DOING everything that you can do to prepare for "what if," you won't need to worry about it.

Those who reach Financial Greatness do not pour their energy into worrying. Remember that negative feelings, thoughts, and words decrease financial momentum like friction slows a moving object. Positive feelings, thoughts, and words increase momentum and amplify financial results. However, those who do not properly plan for "what if" should worry. Worrying serves one useful purpose: it can motivate us to take ACTION. Those who reach Financial Greatness are doers—they have moved past worrying and have begun doing. They take care of what they can control now so that they are prepared for what they cannot control in the future.

Pillar Four is about having the confidence that you have silenced your "what if" questions. To do so, you need to understand two fundamental keys to financial risk management: insurance and estate planning. Once you have grasped the core principles involved, you need to take action. Taking care of "what if" now will help you focus on your values and achieve your financial goals much more effectively.

## INSURANCE: YOUR SAFETY NET

I am grateful for insurance. I like knowing that I can utilize insurance companies to move financial risks away from my family. Essentially, that is what insurance does: transfers risk. I exchange the risk of a catastrophic event that would decimate my family financially for a known and manageable premium cost. The insurance company pools the premiums of many people to cover the "what ifs" of the unfortunate few who have to file claims. In this way, insurance acts like a safety net, protecting financial plans from Financially Fatal Falls.

## The Greatness Gap™

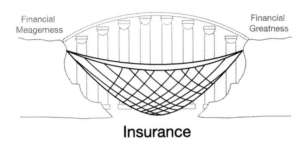

Financial
Meagerness

Financial
Greatness

## Insurance

Many people do not share my positive view of insurance. In fact, I frequently meet people who completely despise insurance. They believe that I am blind to its pitfalls and negative aspects. Let me assure you that my gratitude for insurance does not result from blind ignorance. Like many of you, I have found myself stuck in a room with a pushy insurance agent trying to sell me a product that I did not need. I understand the unpleasant aspects of insurance and recognize that some insurance companies and agents sell junk policies filled with gimmicks and high fees.

Naturally I don't get excited about paying insurance premiums, but I recognize them as necessary costs because I understand the benefits of being insured. A friend of mine is fond of saying that insurance is like a toilet plunger—you don't buy it because you hope to use it; you buy it in case you have to. In Chapter Two, I shared with you some of my values such as safety, security, and freedom for my family. Insurance helps me protect these values.

Not only does insurance provide real financial security for my values, it also gives me a deeper level of psychological security. When I am properly insured, I am more confident about my financial plan. I have a greater *feeling* of security and safety. This allows me to experience a *present* benefit from insurance whether "what if" occurs or not. The peace of mind I have when I am properly insured adds value to my life even if I never experience any Financially Fatal Falls.

I manage the downsides of insurance through the power of education. The more I understand about insurance and the companies that provide coverage, the more control I gain over the process. I view insurance as a risk transfer tool and nothing more. I find it interesting that most people who tell me they do not like insurance aren't using it properly. It is easy to blame the tool for not working when the fault actually lies with the user not knowing how to utilize it.

Many people simply do not have the proper types or amounts of insurance coverage. These individuals are often convinced that insurance is a "rip off" and either choose not to have it at all or pay as little as possible for virtually worthless coverage. In most cases, these individuals continue to worry about "what if."

On the other hand, some people have too much insurance and use it too often. They have insurance for everything possible and own insurance policies that they do not need. Usually they experience buyer's remorse every month when they pay their premiums. Further, many of these individuals have extremely low deductibles and become reliant on insurance companies for even very small claims. Low deductibles equal high premiums. Using insurance to protect against every little financial hiccup (rather than just protecting against Financially Fatal Falls) costs people more than it is worth in benefit.

I want to be clear about this: over-insuring is no better than consumer debt for your financial health. At the beginning of this section, I stated "insurance acts like a safety net, protecting financial plans from Financially *Fatal* Falls." I use the word *fatal* for a very specific reason. You do not need insurance for financial bumps and scratches. I have a well-funded *Financial Confidence Account*™ for occasions when I take smaller falls (falls that cost me $1,000 - $4,000). In fact, I could survive a $10,000-$15,000 out-of-pocket fall if push came to shove. I only need insurance for potentially *fatal* falls, and so I choose to transfer only my *major* financial risks to insurance companies. I call this the *Financially Fatal Rule*™ of insurance.

> The *Financially Fatal Rule*™ of insurance: To reach Financial Greatness, you should only insure yourself against *fatal* financial falls that you could not recover from without the insurance.

Every insurance policy you purchase should be able to pass the *Financially Fatal Rule*™. For example, if I get a serious disease and need major medical help, I could not afford a $250,000 medical bill. Therefore, I transfer this risk to a solid health insurance company with an appropriate policy. On the other hand, when my wife comes down with the flu and needs to see a doctor and fill a prescription, I can afford to cover the $75-$150 costs out of pocket. The flu is not a major financial risk for my family, so we don't need a health insurance policy with low deductibles and high premiums.

The same holds true for our auto insurance policy. If I get into a little fender bender, I am prepared to pay $700 out of pocket to fix my car. Fixing minor damage to my car is not financially fatal because I am prepared with a *Financial Confidence Account*™. On the other hand, getting sued for $300,000 after a major car accident would result in our immediate financial coronary without our insurance policy in place.

I follow this principle with every type of insurance I own. However, please note that to safely apply the rule, you first need a fully funded *Financial Confidence Account*™. This is one more reason why I put Pillar One first out of *The 8 Pillars*™. Once you have completed part one AND part two of Pillar One, you can raise your insurance deductibles and pay for financial bumps and scratches out of pocket. Higher deductibles translate into reduced premiums, money saved, and momentum gained. Usually your premiums will also remain lower due to the absence of numerous small claims. People who have low deductibles and use their insurance for small claims eventually end up paying for these small claims through increasing premiums.

## REDUCE YOUR INSURANCE DEPENDENCE

I have noticed that as people take more responsibility for minor financial setbacks (rather than becoming overly dependent on insurance companies) something very interesting takes place. Self-reliant people actually become less likely to need insurance at all, even for fatal falls! This effect has two parts.

**1. First, when people become more conscious of paying small amounts of money out of pocket, they live their lives with a higher degree of cost consciousness.**

For example, when you pay for doctor visits out of pocket, you tend to become more aware of your health. You become more conscious of the benefits of taking better care of yourself and your family (perhaps by improving hygiene, eating healthier foods, drinking more water, exercising regularly, and getting the right amount of sleep). You become more cognizant of the price of medical care, desiring to utilize it less often but to have high quality care when you need it. Cost consciousness can have a huge impact on your values over the long run, leading not just to lower insurance expenses but also to better health.

Consider another example: driving. When you know that small expenses will be out of pocket, you tend to drive with a higher degree of safety consciousness. You literally learn very quickly what it means to "PAY" for your own mistakes. Taking financial responsibility for your actions is an essential attribute of the *Financial Greatness Mindset*.

I teach my children from a very young age that they need to take responsibility for their own mistakes. This may be as simple as picking up all of the individual Cheerios that have fallen on the kitchen floor. As they get older, their mistakes become larger, but they will learn to understand that there are financial consequences to their actions (positive and negative). The money spent paying for a mistake can be a great teacher for us and our adult children. By living your life with a higher degree of cost consciousness, you will intuitively begin to repel unwanted consequences by making more informed choices.

**2. The second part of insurance independence comes about when you no longer need certain types of insurance at all.**

This is called "self-insuring," and many people I know who have achieved Financial Greatness accumulate enough assets to insure against risks without relying on an insurance company. In a way, self-insurance simply means having a larger *Financial Confidence Account™*. It allows people to consider the cost of insurance in terms of risk versus return, rather than having "what ifs" to protect against.

For example, when you purchase life insurance, you are insuring against the risk of leaving your dependents without income or with debts and costs they cannot pay. When you no longer have dependents, your death no longer represents the same financial risks (since the "what if" concerns are greatly reduced). You can begin to evaluate your life insurance needs based on other factors such as tax benefits, estate planning considerations, final expenses, and so on. This changes the amounts and types of life insurance coverage you might consider, and in some cases, you may find no benefit to continuing to pay for life insurance at all.

## SAY *YES* TO EDUCATION AND *NO* TO SALES PITCHES

Just like every other principle in this book, education is the keystone to properly insuring against the "what ifs" in our lives. We need to learn what types of insurance are necessary so that we can act wisely rather than being preyed upon by the insurance industry. My clients on the road to Financial Greatness do not wait for pushy agents to tell them what types of insurance they need. Instead, they ask the important "what if" questions and then do their homework to find solutions.

**My clients follow a simple 3-step insurance process:**

1. They learn what types of insurance are essential for their particular financial situation.

2. They determine the level of coverage they need for each type of essential insurance.

3. They obtain multiple insurance quotes from solid, reputable insurance companies to make sure they are getting the best deal possible. Through this process, they also look for an insurance agent with the heart of an educator—not just the polish of a salesman.

When the time comes to sit down with an insurance agent, there is no sales pitch needed because they have completed the 3-step process. The tone of the meeting is set by the clients, not the agent. They are prepared to tell the agent what types of insurance they need, how much, and for what.

This does not mean that my clients do not learn or take counsel from their insurance agents. A trusted agent with a reputable company who has the heart of an educator can be a great resource to an educated customer. Remember, the more you know, the more valuable your advisors will become to you. When you meet with your agent be prepared to ask intelligent questions and get needed clarification. This will allow the agent to spend more time educating and less time selling. Your meetings will be discussions rather than sales pitches, and you will spend less time to accomplish better results.

## GET WHAT YOU NEED AND FORGET WHAT YOU DON'T

Because this book is designed for people of all ages, lifestyles, and income levels, it is difficult to give specific advice regarding insurance. My first goal in this chapter was to raise your awareness of the *need* to be properly insured. My second goal is to provide you with valuable *guiding principles* that will apply no matter what your specific financial situation may be.

Rather than overwhelm or bore you with a barrage of information you may not need, I will simply list the *Fundamental Insurance Types* and the types of *Insurance to Scrutinize*. Insurance regulations, policy designs, features, and riders are constantly changing, so I would be doing a disservice to my readers if I made specific insurance recommendations. Further, without knowing your particular plans and situation, I cannot assess your true insurance needs.

Insurance is one of those areas of the financial jungle where professional advice becomes essential and valuable. A good specialist or agent will help you determine which types and amounts of insurance coverage figure (or don't figure) into your journey along the road to Financial Greatness. The list below will give you an educational starting point and foundation on which to construct an assessment of your specific insurance needs.

## Fundamental Insurance Types:

I    Property, Casualty, & Liability Insurance:
- Auto Insurance
- Homeowners Insurance
- Umbrella Insurance Policy (if your net worth exceeds $200,000)

I    Health Insurance

I    Life Insurance (Term)

I    Long-Term Disability Insurance (if you are not retired)

I    Long-Term Care Insurance (if you are over 55 years old and
     unable to self-insure)

I    Business Insurance (if you own a business)

Each of the fundamental insurance types transfers the risk of a major
economic disaster away from you and onto an insurance company. Some
coverage such as auto, home, and some types of business insurance are
mandated by law. Because of the extremely high costs associated with
major medical expenses and premature death, you should consider health
and life insurance mandatory as well. Keep in mind the importance of not
relying too heavily on insurance. It is usually better to opt for a higher
deductible with lower premiums whenever applicable.

You are statistically more likely to experience a work-affecting
disability or long-term care need in your lifetime than any of the other
risks insured against above. This means that insurers must charge more
in premiums to offer these types of insurance. Because of the higher cost,
you should not keep disability coverage any longer than you need it—
which means the need ends when you retire or you no longer have anyone
else depending on your working income. Long-term care needs are most
ideally insured through reserve assets or dual-use life insurance (which
allows access to some of the death benefit for terminal illnesses or long-
term care expenses *before* death). However, if you are over 55 years old
and do not know how you would afford an extended nursing home stay,
you need to consider long-term care insurance.

A few words about life insurance: there are several types of life insurance
available but they break into two basic categories, *term* and *permanent*.

**Term life insurance is best for transferring the risks of premature
death**. This type of life insurance is simple and very inexpensive compared
to permanent insurance. When insuring the life of a breadwinner, term
insurance should be used in almost every circumstance. It is called *term*
because the premium only stays level for a certain "term" or period of

time. For most families, the major risks of premature death are temporary and are therefore only needed during a specific "term" or number of years. When the children have moved out and the mortgage has been mostly paid off, the financial consequences of a breadwinner dying are greatly reduced. If you need life insurance, nine out of ten times I would recommend an inexpensive, plain-vanilla term policy.

**Permanent insurance is not recommended for transferring the risk of premature death.** This type of insurance is very complicated and comes in many forms such as Whole Life, Universal Life, and Variable Universal Life (sometimes called a VUL). Permanent insurance is very expensive if used for only transferring risk. You also should know that this type of insurance normally pays large commissions to the agent. In contrast, term insurance pays a very small commission to the agent. Because of the commission structure of permanent insurance, the product is often oversold and inappropriately used.

While warning you of the pitfalls, complexity, and expensive nature of permanent insurance, I also believe it can be beneficial for certain clients when used properly. Before considering permanent insurance, you need to follow and act on all of the steps outlined in Pillars One through Four. In addition, you need to consistently max out all of your available retirement vehicles including your 401(k) and Roth IRAs. Further, it is important to know that investing in a permanent life insurance policy is a long-term endeavor. Because of the high costs and many fees, it only makes sense to get involved with permanent insurance for a minimum of six to eight years. Because of the complexity and long-term nature of the product, it is advisable to be careful before investing.

I think of permanent insurance as an investment and tax planning tool rather than a true insurance product. For strictly insurance purposes, permanent insurance is too expensive. Permanent insurance builds cash value and can help to create wealth through a tax-advantaged automatic savings plan. Permanent insurance is better suited to protecting assets and estates from taxes and inflation rather than transferring pure risk. Permanent life insurance should be part of your overall investment and asset protection strategy rather than your "what if" analysis.

## Insurance to Scrutinize:

- **ɪ**   Mortgage Protection Insurance

- **ɪ**   Variable Life Insurance (including VUL)

- **ɪ**   Cancer Insurance

- **ɪ**   Product Replacement Insurance (including most extended
     warranties unless the product is very expensive and you rely on it
     for your livelihood)

Each of the insurance types on this list typically covers a risk that can be better prepared for or insured against in a more effective way. If an advisor or agent recommends any of these types of policies to you, be very careful. Get a second opinion, do some research, and put your guard up—that agent is likely more worried about selling a high-commission product than providing value for a fair premium. Be particularly wary of anyone who advises you to use your life savings or home equity to "invest" in a Variable Life policy. This strategy is inappropriate and downright dangerous in all but a tiny percentage of situations.

## GUIDING PRINCIPLES FOR THE INSURANCE JUNGLE

In an effort to recap the major points of this chapter and coach you through the complicated and ever-changing world of insurance, I have provided you with the following *guiding principles*:

- **ɪ**   **Continue to educate yourself about insurance.** Proactively
     follow the Learn-Do-Become process of *The Greatness
     Continuum™*. Utilize resources like *8 Pillars University™* to
     investigate particular types of insurance.

- **ɪ**   **Work with only highly rated, reputable insurance companies.**
     Do your homework before purchasing a policy. Insurance
     guarantees are only as strong as the insuring company. Always

obtain multiple quotes and review the fine print of any coverage you are considering.

I   **Find an insurance agent with the heart of an educator.** Don't work with agents or advisors who use manipulative sales tactics or who don't spend time educating you about your options. A trustworthy agent can be invaluable to you, so do business with people you trust and feel comfortable with. Never buy insurance out of fear, under pressure, or when you are feeling rushed by a pushy insurance salesperson.

I   **Consolidate.** Once you are comfortable with an insurance company and agent, you may want to place the majority of your policies there. Most insurance companies offer a "multiple lines" discount that can save you money; this also helps simplify your financial life for billing, record keeping, dealing with customer service, and filing claims.

I   **Always ASK insurers for available discounts.** Remember, you are responsible for learning as much as possible and asking intelligent questions. Many insurance companies offer discounts for good grades, a safe driving record, multiple lines, automatic payment, good claims history, good credit, and so on.

I   **Once you have a fully funded *Financial Confidence Account*™, raise your deductibles.** For health and auto insurance, the more you cover out of pocket the lower your premiums will be. Disability and long-term care insurance use a time deductible called a waiting period. The longer you can cover the expenses yourself before filing for insurance benefits, the lower your premiums will be.

I   **Use the *Financially Fatal Rule*™ of insurance.** Buy insurance to transfer MAJOR risks, not to cover minor financial stumbles.

I   **Be extremely careful before buying insurance on the "Insurance to Scrutinize" list.** These should raise immediate red flags for you.

I **Live your life with a high degree of financial consciousness.**
Reduce the risks you are insuring against—drive safely, and live
a healthy lifestyle. Don't erase the benefits of lower premiums
and peace of mind by speeding or smoking. These two behaviors
alone drastically increase several of your major life risks and will
ultimately cost you untold amounts in direct costs and in extra
insurance expenses.

I **Teach your children to take financial responsibility for their
own mistakes.** Your children should understand your liability
for them as minors before they are 18 years old (legal adults).
More specifically, your children should understand the financial
consequences of speeding, reckless behavior, and unhealthy
choices like smoking, drinking, and doing drugs.

I **Reevaluate your insurance needs regularly.** If you have
never created an insurance plan, it's time to find a good agent
and put one together. If you have not reviewed your plan for
three years, you need to make sure you still have the right types
and amounts in place and are not overpaying. Any time you
experience a major life event (birth or death in the family, job
change, retirement, relocation, etc.) you should also review your
insurance coverage.

The bottom line on insurance is that you need appropriate coverage
if you want to achieve Financial Greatness. Having a safety net for the
major "what ifs" in your life gives you protection and peace of mind. Do
your best to reduce your dependence on insurance over your life—yet be
grateful for the protection it provides. Keep in mind the guiding principles
above, but remember that everyone's insurance needs are different. Work
with a trustworthy insurance professional to assess your true needs and put
the appropriate coverage in place.

**Thoughts, Feelings, and Ideas** – What are some of the thoughts or feelings you had while reading Chapter Twelve? What insights occurred to you while reading? Did any particular action ideas pop into your mind as you read?

_____

_____

_____

_____

_____

_____

_____

_____

Can you see how financially preparing for "what if" by being properly insured will improve your life?

How will your life specifically improve as you use insurance to manage your major financial risks?

_____

_____

_____

_____

_____

_____

_____

_____

_____

_____

## DOER CHECKLIST – CHAPTER 12

☐     I have all of the *Fundamental Insurance Types* in place that
        apply to my situation.

☐     If I do not have all of the insurance I should, I have a plan to
        follow the 3-step process to obtain the needed insurance
        policies to protect my financial plan from *fatal* falls.

☐     I am committed to being very careful about the types of
        *Insurance to Scrutinize.*  I will never purchase insurance
        too quickly or out of fear or from a pushy insurance
        salesperson.

☐     Once I have a fully funded *Financial Confidence Account*™, I
        will raise my deductibles to save premium costs where
        appropriate.

## CHAPTER 13

# ESTATE PLANNING:
# WHERE THERE'S A WILL, THERE'S A *WILL*

If you ever have trouble falling asleep at night, I have found a cure better than counting sheep: start reading a long book about estate planning. Unless you are an estate planning attorney, this subject will probably beat the best prescription sleep aid on the market. Unfortunately, it is a subject that everyone who wants to reach Financial Greatness needs to address.

## MORE THAN A CURE FOR INSOMNIA

Before completing my Masters Program, I thought I understood a lot about estate planning. I was wrong. The more I have learned, the less I feel like I know about the subject. I now realize how big and complicated the realm of estate planning can be. Estate Planning is an area of personal finance that is the product of numerous laws and tax regulations. Attorneys and politicians seem to find ways to complicate even the simplest issues, so imagine how convoluted things get when you mix the legal system with the IRS Tax Code. To make matters worse, the rules and laws that surround estate planning are always in flux. All of this explains why many personal finance books today do not even touch on estate planning. This chapter will present the essentials of estate planning simply and help you prepare for "what if" so you can sleep at night *without* having to read tomes of tax code.

Many people do not think they need to do any estate planning because they do not believe they have an estate to plan for. *Estate* seems like a fancy word that would only apply to the wealthiest class of people.

However, if you own ANYTHING (such as a car, home, wedding ring, or stamp collection) you already have an estate. In this sense, "estate" is just a sophisticated code word for *stuff* (property, money, and ownership rights). Your estate also encompasses your debts, dependents, and other financial liabilities. These are also left behind and must be reconciled upon your death. The more stuff you own relative to your liabilities, the larger your estate. If you follow the principles outlined in *The 8 Pillars*™, your estate will grow over time and so will your need for a proper estate plan.

Forget about the boring aspects of estate planning and think for a moment about the people who will be affected by your death. As unpleasant as it is to imagine, suppose you died in a tragic accident tomorrow morning. If you have children, pretend that they are now left without a living parent. Think of all of the "what ifs" for them and for the rest of your family. Insurance can ensure they are taken care of financially, but what happens to all of the other "stuff" you have accumulated? How will your debts be settled, your estate taxes paid, your possessions sold or distributed, and your insurance proceeds meted out? Who will be responsible for the dependent children that survive you?

Now imagine that all of these unpleasant questions have already been answered in advance. You have guardians appointed for your children in case something happens to you. The settlement of your estate is laid out on paper, and you have a capable executor assigned to ensure your wishes are followed. Your debts, taxes, and responsibilities are all paid for, and there are no loose ends left to burden your family. They are able to deal with their grief and move on without lingering consequences, grateful for your forethought.

Legalese aside, do you want to make your death easier for your loved ones or overwhelmingly difficult for months or years afterward? Remember, Financial Greatness means controlling what you CAN control financially in the service of what (or who) matters most to you. Taking the time to plan for your estate now gives you peace of mind in the present and eases the burden on your survivors in the future.

## WHERE THERE'S A WILL, THERE'S A *WILL*

The number one estate planning document that every person needs is a WILL. In fact, you have one whether you have a formalized document or not. If you die without having created a personal WILL, the state that you live in has a set of rules that *will* determine how your property is distributed (and possibly taxed before distribution). This type of WILL is called *intestate*—the legal term for dying without a written WILL.

It is a very satisfying feeling to know that when you die your property will go to the exact individuals you intended. Yet, a properly constructed WILL does more than just list who should receive your "stuff" at the time of your death. A good WILL should include the following elements:

**Financial Inventory** – A simple list of your assets including personal belongings, financial accounts, insurance policies, and valuables. Included with this list should be the corresponding contact information of each financial institution or the location of personal property.

**Funeral Arrangements and Specific Wishes** – Leaving your heirs any specific instructions you would like them to know and follow in the event of your death. If written correctly, this can be a very important section of your WILL.

**Named Guardians** – The person(s) who will take care of and raise your children should you die before they are legal adults (this is one of the most vital aspects of your WILL).

**General Power of Attorney** – A legal document that allows you to name a person to act on your behalf in legal matters. You may want to specify this individual as a *"Springing"* Power of Attorney (one that only has power when you become incapacitated). On the other hand, a *"Durable"* Power of Attorney has power immediately and can sign your name on legal papers as soon as the document is in force. You can get more specific and name a "*Financial*" Power of Attorney or a "*Medical*" Power of Attorney (sometimes called a Healthcare Proxy) to stipulate more specific authority.

**Living Will** (sometimes called an Advanced Medical Directive) – A legal document that explains which life-prolonging measures you do or do not want pursued if you become incapacitated, terminally ill, or unable to communicate.

**Named Executor** – A person of your choice who is responsible to carry out the written instructions specified in your WILL.

Don't burden yourself with trying to memorize all of the various estate-planning terms. I encourage you to understand the essential need for estate planning but not to get too caught up with the details. I would much rather see you get these estate planning tools in place without understanding all of the jargon than have you get bogged down in endless details. More important than remembering the exact terms is simply getting your estate plan complete. Remember to keep a copy of your WILL in your fire/water-proof safe and give your named executor the key or combination and the location of the safe. I'll explain more about *how* to create a WILL later in the chapter.

## THE BENEFITS OF BENEFICIARIES

One of the simplest and most effective estate planning steps you can take is to properly name beneficiaries on your financial accounts and insurance policies. You should ensure that your spouse is named as primary beneficiary for any life insurance policies or retirement accounts. If you have other banking or investment accounts that are not jointly owned, make your spouse or children the beneficiaries on those accounts as well.

Naming beneficiaries typically avoids probate, makes it easier for your heirs to access the assets held in the account, and often provides them with more flexibility at distribution than they would have otherwise.

## COMMUNICATION CAN GO A LONG WAY

A key part of the estate planning process is taking the surprise out of "what if" for your loved ones. Speak with your spouse and children about what would happen in the event of your early death. Communicate with your aging parents to ensure their affairs are in order. Keep the named executor of your estate up to date on changes you make to your WILL and any other estate planning you do. Make sure your beneficiaries know what institutions they need to contact when you die and where to find the account numbers. Unexpected complications are the last thing anyone grieving your loss will want to deal with, so a little communication now will go a long way if something happens to you.

## ENLIST HELP – AN ESTATE PLANNING ATTORNEY

Even though you can create a legal WILL on your own, I recommend enlisting the services of an estate planning attorney. People with the *Financial Greatness Mindset* understand the importance of doing things right the first time and see the value in paying for expert advice. Most estate planning attorneys will charge between $300 - $1,000 for a WILL and the other corresponding documents listed above. The cost is normally determined by the complexity of your estate. For example, if you have a former spouse, step children, a high net worth, or a disabled child, you may need more work to be completed and thus it could cost you more. Having an attorney assist you ensures that your WILL complies with your state's laws, which protects your wishes in case the WILL is contested.

Follow the same principles when choosing an attorney as you would when selecting any other financial professional. First, make sure they have the heart of an educator; second, remember that the more you know about estate planning, the better your lawyer will serve you. Clearly explain what estate planning documents you need and request a written price quote. Make sure that the attorney understands that they are to not exceed the quoted price without your written permission—this will help you to stay within your budget. Make sure that the attorney you select is well trusted in your community, is reputable, and works for a well established law firm.

# A QUESTION OF TRUST

Do you need to form a trust as part of your estate planning? Trusts have some benefits that a WILL alone does not provide, but they are not for everyone. Primarily, trusts are created to protect larger estates from lawsuits and excess taxes. Without overloading you with massive amounts of detail, the following list explains the major reasons why you may want to consider setting up a trust as your estate grows:

I  **More Privacy.** The process of distributing your property through a WILL is called *probate*, and the proceedings become public information. Trust distributions are not typically public knowledge. If you are well known in your community or have other reasons for protecting your family's privacy, you may want to use a trust.

I  **Less Red Tape.** Assets held in trust are not subject to probate, and thus the process of distributing your property can be streamlined. This can potentially save your heirs (particularly the executor of your estate) some time, hassle, and expense.

I  **Greater Control.** With a trust, you have more control of your distribution wishes than with a WILL. If you do not want your heirs to receive your property immediately after your death, you can specify time frames and certain conditions for them to receive it. For example, you may want your children to receive the inheritance in two separate payments at certain ages set by you. Possibly, you will require that your children graduate from college or any number of other stipulations before they receive funds from the trust. If you do not want all of your assets to go directly to your spouse, a trust can specify your exact wishes. If you want your estate to provide for someone's maintenance and have the remainder donated to charity, a trust can be set up to handle these types of funds.

I  **Asset Protection.** Trusts may help you protect your assets from lawsuits and creditors. This aspect of trusts can be complicated and tricky, so make sure you consult an expert estate planning attorney for specific advice.

**I Tax Reduction.** Even a modest estate can quickly become very large when you include your life insurance death benefits. Trusts can be set up to maximize the amount your beneficiaries will receive after taxes, or to simply ensure that taxes and other debts are paid at your death. Again, this is an extremely complicated and ever-changing aspect of trusts, and you should always consult with a tax professional or tax attorney regarding your specific situation.

There are too many different types of trusts (designed for specific results) for me to cover in this book. As your net worth increases and your estate grows, so will your need for a more complex estate plan that may include the proper use of trusts. As you continue to implement *The 8 Pillars*™ and you begin to accumulate wealth, a skilled estate planning attorney can become increasingly important.

However, do not be caught up in financial fads—just because you *could* set up a trust does not mean you should. I have seen a trend towards the overuse of trusts brought on by so-called financial "gurus" who want to sell you trusts. Once your current net worth surpasses $500,000, a trust is almost always advisable. Until then, the extra costs to create and update a trust may not be worth it. Along with the possible restrictions and difficulties trusts create in managing your money, you will typically pay several times as much for a trust as you would for a WILL. When your net worth warrants it, you will rely on trusts to help protect assets not only at your death but also while you are alive. Remember: do not take advice in the area of estate planning from anyone other than a trusted estate planning attorney.

## BREATHE EASY – "WHAT IF" HAS BEEN PLANNED FOR

Once you have a properly constructed WILL and other important estate documents completed, you can rest assured that you have taken the essential steps within your control to prepare for "what if."

Usually, my clients find that thinking about "what if" becomes easier and more comfortable the more they practice it. Once they have proper insurance in place, they feel more prepared to think about the actual details of their death, funeral, and estate. When they create a solid WILL, they sometimes report to me a feeling like a huge weight was lifted from their shoulders that they never knew was there. They gain more confidence to plan for less final "what ifs" like college for their children, retirement income, and taking care of their own parents. Everything I teach in *The 8 Pillars*™ will always have an impact on the things you value, as long as you remember *why* you are implementing each pillar.

When you have completed the doer checklists for the first four pillars, take a deep breath and pat yourself on the back. You are well on your way to Financial Greatness and you have built a foundation of financial preparedness. You can move forward boldly with the more exciting parts of your financial plans (Pillars Five through Eight) because you have solidified your values and taken steps to protect them. Let's review what you should have accomplished if you have been doing more than just casually reading this book.

First, you funded a *Financial Confidence Account*™ to prepare for the unexpected. Second, you organized your finances and records around a values-based blueprint and put your goals on autopilot. Next, you began to declare your financial freedom from the bondage of consumer debt, poor credit, and financial ignorance. Finally, you are protecting your financial plans and your loved ones through proper insurance and estate planning.

Although these are fundamental pillars for anyone who wants to protect his or her family and achieve Financial Greatness, a very small percentage of people ever come this far. Breathe easy—you are doing an exceptional thing.

**Thoughts, Feelings, and Ideas** – What are some of the thoughts or feelings you had while reading Chapter Thirteen? What insights occurred to you while reading? Did any particular action ideas pop into your mind as you read?

_____

_____

_____

_____

_____

_____

_____

_____

_____

Can you see how financially preparing for "what if" by having a completed estate plan will improve your life?

How will your life specifically improve after you have created a solid WILL?

_____

_____

_____

_____

_____

_____

_____

_____

_____

_____

_____

## DOER CHECKLIST – CHAPTER 13

☐   I have a properly constructed written WILL, along with the necessary corresponding estate planning documents.

☐   I have updated and checked the accuracy of my named beneficiaries on all of my financial accounts and insurance policies.

☐   If I am near or above $500,000 in net worth, I have discussed the need for a trust with my estate planning attorney.

☐   I can rest assured that I have done all that I can do to financially prepare for "what if."

# PILLAR FIVE

*Invest for Happiness Now and in the Future*

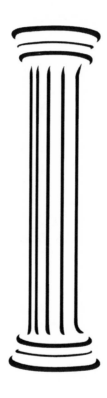

## CHAPTER 14

# INVESTING: THE DEFINITION AND FIRST THINGS FIRST

Before I can teach you anything meaningful about investing, you need to revisit your values. Unless you have clearly defined what matters most to you, Pillar Five (like each of the other pillars) will have little power to improve your life. Too many people skim over this principle so that they can "get on with making more money"—but that approach does not lead to Financial Greatness. I fervently believe that lasting happiness springs from devotion to our deepest values, not from the mere accumulation of money.

## DON'T LEAVE YOUR VALUES TO CHANCE

I have seen countless people (including some close friends) attempt to begin their financial trek by "investing" right out of the gate. Because they lack a *Financial Greatness Mindset*, these individuals believe investing should have been the first pillar of my book. In fact, they are convinced that investing is the *only* pillar they need! Given a choice between this book and one entitled, "The Ultra Secret Magic of Insanely Wealthy Investors," they would choose the latter. While it sounds a bit silly, these types of book titles do seem to fly off the shelves.

Most people possess an incomplete definition of investing, which leads them to vacillate between investing out of greed and not investing due to fear. You are different; by investing *for happiness*, you will put yourself well down the road to true Financial Greatness. True investing always has a purpose. Unless you are investing *for* something beyond profit itself, you aren't really investing. Let me illustrate with a personal story.

When I was in college, I asked one of my close friends what he planned to do when he graduated. I was surprised by his answer. He stated very plainly, "I want to be an investor." At first I was impressed and wanted to know more about his specific plans. But the more we discussed his plans, the more I realized that *he had none*. I came to see that his definition of an investor was very different from mine.

My college friend had an incomplete understanding of investing. He knew that when you invest, you use money or capital to get more money—that's the "return" part of investment, and he grasped that concept just fine. However, he did not have time for the fundamental principles of personal finance. My friend was not concerned about the importance of saving or living by a budget. He was not interested in the difference between a use asset and an asset that appreciates over time. Staying away from consumer debt and truly paying the price to learn from real investors were not priorities for him.

He had just finished reading a very popular book on becoming RICH and was convinced that "traditional" personal finance and education was completely wrong. Because of this book, he no longer wanted to stay in school but was sure that the only true way to wealth was through owning his own business. Becoming affluent became his number one goal, since he could no longer imagine himself happy or content until he truly struck it rich.

This single book completely changed my friend's life. One day he announced to his bride of less than a year that he had dropped out of college. He wanted to start his own company and become an "investor." Unfortunately, my friend had confused investing with *speculation* (a fancy word for gambling). He soon realized that business and investing can be extremely difficult and fraught with risks. After early failures and losses, he felt that he had fallen behind financially. In an effort to "catch up," he continued to gamble his money in high risk "investments" rather than applying the time-tested financial principles I will share in Pillar Five. He soon divorced, and to this day he struggles financially.

Stories like this one are not rare. I constantly see people beginning to "invest" without a clue about how money works or the ability to save. Most of these individuals purchase a book or attend a seminar on how to invest in stock options, foreign currency, or real estate—then pay hundreds or thousands of dollars (financed, of course) to jump right in. Instead of asking financially intelligent questions, they completely buy into and trust the system being sold to them.

Recently I happened upon an intriguing infomercial selling a book that claims to teach regular people how to make money with amazing real estate tactics. The author boasted that one of his clients had made $300,000 using his program—and until now that client had never been able to save even $3,000 his entire life! Some people find this impressive, but I am not one of those people. I can tell you from experience that for an individual who does not understand his values enough to save money, no amount of financial success will bring about long-term happiness.

In an attempt to get rich quickly, countless people buy into false promises of easy cash. Let me be very clear: that is not investing—it is speculation, plain and simple. If a speculator happens to get lucky and time the market correctly, they might indeed make a lot of money overnight. Yet, without a solid foundation to support their financial house, it inevitably falls. I wish this were not true. I do not like to see people fail. But I cannot change reality: gambling and investing do not mix well. If you try to invest without clearly defined values, you are leaving your happiness up to chance.


## INVESTING DEFINED

I have made several references so far to what people erroneously call "investing." Before we can go forward, we need to accurately define the term. Let's first be clear about what investing is NOT. Investments are never gimmicks, schemes, speculative gambles, lucky breaks, or criminal activities. When it comes to investing, the old maxim entirely applies:

**If it seems too good to be true, it probably is.**

I call this pillar *Investing for Happiness Now and In the Future*™ very deliberately. The word "invest" means more than just hoping for a nice return on your money. To invest means to commit your money for a desired purpose. Usually this commitment is long-term, meaning you accept some wait time and some potential risks to your funds before you will be compensated for your investment. There are many types of investment risk, and without them you could not expect a meaningful return on your money. By taking calculated risks and delaying your returns, you effectively <u>devote</u> your money to the desired investment goal. This is why having values-based goals comes before investing. You'll rely on that deeper devotion to keep you committed in difficult times.

Let me give you another illustration that has helped me connect my investment objectives to my values. One meaning of "invest" is to <u>endow</u> something or someone with a certain quality or ability. Many universities possess large endowments donated by generous alumni who wish to further the work of their alma mater. These funds allow the university to secure the best faculty, facilities, and students possible—effectively increasing the school's ability to impact society. Your investments should do the same thing for your goals and values. Calling my kids' college savings money "The Ford Endowment for Higher Education" conveys a sense of what investing means to me. I call our retirement vehicles "Freedom Accounts" to further connect our values with our long-term goals.

Let's get very specific about the significant differences between investing and speculating before we proceed:

**Speculating** is betting money on highly unpredictable economic ventures and vehicles. Speculators gamble funds in hopes of making a quick and very large profit, often taking risky positions that are not based on adequate information or a systematic approach.

**Investing** is putting money to work for a specific purpose involving a measured level of risk and a corresponding expected return or profit. An investment cannot be deemed gambling or betting if it meets these criteria:

**Investments are well-researched.**
1. You know what specific results you want from the investment.
2. The investment fits into your long-term strategy.
3. You understand how the investment vehicle works.
4. You understand the risks involved in making the investment.

**Investments are not left to chance.**
5. You take a systematic approach to managing the investment.
6. You do not base investment decisions on emotions, such as greed or fear.

7. The investment is not motivated by addiction or entertainment.
8. The odds of positive and consistent results are favorable to your purposes.

In a nutshell, speculators bet on *predictions* while investors follow time-tested *principles*.

## INVEST WITH BOTH EYES OPEN

I live by a simple but unbreakable investing rule:

> **I don't invest in things I don't understand.**

A friend of mine once wanted me to get involved with his real estate investment company. At the time, he was making roughly $85,000 <u>per month</u> using a proprietary investment strategy he had developed. That's over $1,000,000 per year in income! Based on his earnings alone, he had my attention. But beyond the income potential I saw, I was excited to better understand how his investing strategy generated such great returns.

He took me out to lunch in his brand new Ferrari, and during a three-hour conversation he explained how his real estate system worked. I asked as many questions as I could without being annoying. I was impressed, to say the least. His system was very complicated, involving multiple companies and many detailed steps throughout the investing process.

After our lunch, I went home and discussed the meeting with my wife, MeKette. She knows this particular friend well because we have been on double dates together in the past. I told her how much money our friend was making, and she too was impressed. After we spoke about the opportunity for a time, she could sense that I was not planning on investing in his company. I could tell she was confused by my disinterest in the strategy. Finally she asked me, "Why are you not going to get involved?" My response completely stunned my wife. I simply said, "*I don't get it.*" There are very few investment strategies that I do not understand. I went on to explain to MeKette that after having the entire system unfolded to me in great detail, including the opportunity to ask all of my questions, I still did not fully understand how my friend was generating such staggering returns. It seemed too good to be true.

I did not get involved in the opportunity because I did not adequately understand the investment. As the months rolled by, I continued investigating my friend's real estate process but never could quite figure it out—somehow it just did not add up for me. Over a two-year period, I watched (from the sidelines) as close to thirty investors became very wealthy using this investment strategy, and not once did I question my decision. I don't invest in things I don't understand.

A few months later, this real estate investment system started unraveling. It began with officers of the company not returning phone calls and investors not getting paid. Next, the real estate investment company's assets were frozen, the Ferraris were sold, and the entire operation came under investigation by the FBI. The returns were indeed too good to be true—in fact the whole operation was plagued with fraud and speculation. This is just one example of how my simple rule of not investing in things that I don't understand has kept me from financial disaster.

## FIRST THINGS FIRST

One of my greatest joys in life is to watch people thrive and realize their dreams. My desire to see you succeed motivates me to write this book. I have very good reasons for placing Pillar Five fifth rather than first as my friend thought it should be. Completing Pillars One through Four before beginning Pillar Five sets your investment plans up for success. Whether you invest for retirement, a new business, your children's college education, or a real estate deal, having the strong foundation outlined in Pillars One through Four will be vital to your long-term investment strategy. Let's take a moment to briefly review what you should have accomplished before beginning to invest.

**Pillar One:**

I   Do you have three months of living expenses in a no-touch *Financial Confidence Account*™?

**Pillar Two:**

I   Do you know your net worth?
I   Are you financially organized?
I   Do you have a working budget?

**Pillar Three:**

I   Are you completely free of consumer debt?
I   Are your "acceptable" forms of debt appropriate for your
    income?
I   Are you building a credit score of 720 or higher?
I   Are you committed to increasing your financial knowledge?

**Pillar Four:**

I   Are you properly insured for the fundamental "what ifs" in your
    life?
I   Do you have an up-to-date will?

If you can answer yes to these questions, you are ready to implement the
four crucial steps to *Invest for Happiness Now and In the Future*™.

**Step ONE**: Become a Saver
**Step TWO**: Research Opportunities
**Step THREE**: Take Action
**Step FOUR:** Set *The Five Mousetraps of Investing*™

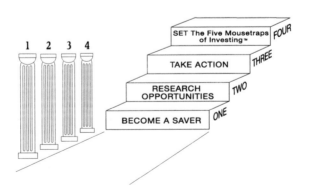

**Thoughts, Feelings, and Ideas** – What are some of the thoughts or feelings you had while reading Chapter Fourteen? What insights occurred to you while reading? Did any particular action ideas pop into your mind as you read?

_____

_____

_____

_____

_____

_____

_____

_____

_____

_____

_____

Can you see why it is so important to avoid speculation and have a strong financial foundation before you invest?

How will your life specifically improve when you invest _after_ implementing important principles taught in Pillars One through Four?

_____

_____

_____

_____

_____

_____

_____

## DOER CHECKLIST – CHAPTER 14

☐   I have clearly defined values and long-term investment goals centered on those values.

☐   I understand the difference between speculation and investing.

☐   I will not invest in something that I do not understand.

☐   I have completed the Doer Checklists from Pillars One through Four including fully funding a *Financial Confidence Account™*.

## CHAPTER 15

# SAVE, RESEARCH, AND TAKE ACTION

## STEP ONE OF INVESTING:
### BECOME A SAVER

The very definition of investing includes a measured amount of risk. If you do not expose your money to some form of risk, you are *saving* rather than investing. Although saving and investing are not the same, I am convinced that in order for you to be a wise investor, you first need to become a consistent saver. My conviction comes from countless experiences with numerous successful investors. In almost every instance, I find that good investors are first excellent savers.

BECOME A SAVER  ONE

People with a *Financial Greatness Mindset* are not just good at saving, they love doing it! They enjoy watching their money accumulate because they understand that money can help them live their values and accomplish their dreams. They are more emotionally connected to saving than they are to spending. Saving comes naturally for them, while spending money on items that do not truly add value to their lives feels worse to them than having teeth pulled. Rather than saving only with their heads (logically), they also save with their hearts. They literally picture themselves fulfilling their dreams, and they understand the role that saved money can play in that picture.

Let me ask you an important question:

## Are you a Saver?

Be careful how you answer. How you identify and label yourself can have a powerful impact on your future. The way you see yourself, and thus project yourself to others, unconsciously gives people permission to treat you in certain ways, thus reinforcing how you act. I call this process the *Self Projection Reinforcement Model*™ as illustrated below.

**Self Projection Reinforcement Model ™**

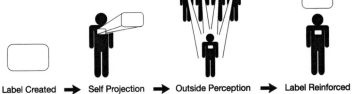

Label Created ➡ Self Projection ➡ Outside Perception ➡ Label Reinforced

*Self Projection Reinforcement Model*™ – Poor Saving Example:

1. You think or say, "I'm not disciplined with saving money" (**Label Created**).

2. You behave in ways that fit the label, like rarely saving (**Self Projection**).

3. Other people see you as a poor saver (**Outside Perceptions**).

4. People treat you accordingly, as a person who cannot save (**Label Reinforced**).

Have you ever met someone who identifies themselves as healthy or athletic? Their habits and the way they speak about themselves project fitness and a balanced diet. In turn, people treat them as though they are healthy and thus reinforce the "healthy" label. Amazingly, such people almost always stay healthy and in shape!

In Chapter Two, I stated that every person *is* unique and amazing. I believe that you have wonderful gifts that you are meant to develop and share. When life slows down, and you have the opportunity for reflection, do you ever have the feeling that you are not in complete harmony with who you really are deep inside? If so, you are not alone. This feeling is your *best* self urging you on to greatness. It is not uncommon to get off track on your journey to greatness; the important thing is that you do not lose sight of your potential. Your ultimate results begin with how you view yourself.

I want you to start identifying yourself as a saver or someone who enjoys saving. If this is not currently one of your labels, you have the power to adopt it. One of the fundamental principles in this book is the fact that <u>you have the ability to change</u> and become the person you want. Who you are right now reflects the sum of YOUR thoughts and actions up to this point in your life. Take responsibility for your actions and realize that you are where you are because of the choices you have made. Start noticing and choosing the labels you give yourself, and you will realize that you hold the power to be the person that you want to be.

How can you turn the *Self Projection Reinforcement Model*™ to your advantage?

I    First, change your thoughts about yourself.
I    Second, change your behavior.

The most effective way to communicate your new label to others (such as a spouse, parent, or child) is to change the way you act. Be a person who speaks less and does more. Please don't misunderstand me; I am not advocating less communication. Effective communication in our relationships is vital. I am simply saying that if you ARE something, represented by your actions, it is difficult to argue the contrary. As your behavior changes, you will notice that people will begin to view and treat you differently. Remember, this process is called *"<u>SELF</u>" Projection Reinforcement.* In most instances, <u>YOU</u> are the origin of the label.

Unfortunately, becoming a person who consistently saves takes more than an understanding of psychology! In an effort to help you become a saver, let me share with you the number one secret to saving. This saving secret has been passed down for thousands of years from one successful saver to another. Believe it or not, the saving secret works every time. Are you ready? The saving secret is:

## SAVE FIRST!

I know what some of you are thinking—"That's no secret; I already know that!" Fair enough, but remember that *to know how to do something* and *to do it* are two very different things. If you understand this principle but are not applying it, you are no better off than those who do not know the secret to saving at all. Are you DOING what you know will work? Are you saving first? Do you save a portion of your income automatically before handling your fixed and variable expenses?

> **To reach Financial Greatness, you need to pay yourself first by saving and investing at least 10-15% of your income for long-term goals.**

If this habit is new to you, *saving first* will require some effort and discipline. You will find the strength to save first when you understand what you are saving for. As you emotionally connect yourself to what you value most, saving will become a priority. Consistently saving will lead to a habit of paying yourself first. The word habit is very powerful, as captured in the following quotation:

### Who Am I?

I am your constant companion;
I am your greatest helper or your heaviest burden.
I will push you onward or drag you down to failure;
I am at your command.

I am easily managed;
You must merely be firm with me.
Show me exactly how you want something done
And after a few lessons I will do it automatically.
I am the servant of all great people and
Alas! Of all failures as well.
Those who are great I have made great;
Those who are failures I have made failures.

I am not a machine, but I work with the precision
Of a machine and the intelligence of a person.
Now, you may run me for profit or
You may run me for ruin;
It makes no difference to me.
Take me, train me, be firm with me,
And I will lay the world at your feet.
Be easy with me and I will destroy you.

**Who am I?  I am Habit.**

- Author unknown

Those with a *Financial Greatness Mindset* do not wake up every morning searching for the motivation to save and invest. They have trained themselves in the <u>habit</u> of saving. You will need the discipline such habits provide in order to *Invest for Happiness Now and in the Future™*. In a powerful sense, positive savings habits become the fuel for every financial goal you place on autopilot. And the money you accumulate through saving becomes the capital for all of your investments.

## STEP TWO OF INVESTING:
## RESEARCH OPPORTUNITIES

With substantial amounts of accumulated cash, successful savers are prepared to take advantage of investment opportunities. Most of the investments you will make aren't going to fall into your lap accompanied by user's manuals. Deciding how to invest your savings takes research and knowledge. Remember what sets a true investment apart from a speculative gamble: investments are **well-researched** and **not left to chance**. In investing, it's usually what you *don't* know that ends up hurting you the most.

The best investors are those with the best information about their investments. Before making any investment, you need to understand how the investment vehicle works, what specific results you expect from it, how it fits into your long-term strategy, and what risks are involved. Entire volumes could be (and have been) written about investment strategies and types, but what I want to provide you with for now is a conceptual framework for analyzing potential investments. Keep in mind that your success depends upon your willingness to gain knowledge and do a little homework. Learning to save is your first investing lesson, but before you convert savings into any investment, you need to research some specifics about it.

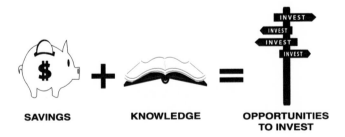

I still read books on investing regularly. They don't all agree or teach the same ideas, but the more I read, the better I become at recognizing the basic principles that work for anyone with a *Financial Greatness Mindset*. There are volumes of information out there on economics, markets, investing strategies, investment types, and money matters in general. You can't know everything, but you can inform your decisions with an ample reservoir of solid information. This section will give you some fundamentals to build on.

## Know the Two Basic Categories of Investments

When it comes right down to it, there are only two ways to put your investment dollars to work. You can either seek to profit through *owning* a performing asset, or you can earn returns by *loaning* your money for interest. The first thing I do when analyzing an investment is to determine whether I would benefit from it as an owner, as a lender, or both. Determining this helps me to better understand the risks and opportunities presented by the investment. Ownership investments usually involve greater uncertainty and less consistent returns than loan investments, but they also provide the opportunity for much higher long-term profits. Here are some examples of investments in each category:

| Examples of **"Own"** Investments | Examples of **"Loan"** Investments |
|---|---|
| Stocks<br>Equity Mutual Funds<br>REIT's<br>Real Estate<br>Exchange Traded Funds<br>Options<br>Precious Metals<br>Art, Jewlery, and Collectibles<br>Commodities and Futures<br>Variable Annuities<br>Some Permanent Life Insurance | Certificates of Deposit<br>Treasury Bills and Notes<br>Fixed Annuities<br>Bonds (Government, Municipal,<br>Corporate, Zero-coupon)<br>Bond Mutual Funds<br>CMO's<br>Mortgage-backed Securities<br>Unit Investment Trusts<br>Commercial Paper<br>Private Loans<br>Trust Deeds and Tax Lien Paper |

With either type of investment, you can profit in two fundamental ways: *growth* and *income*. In other words, your investment returns come either as appreciation in the asset's value or as payments you receive while you hold the asset. Ownership generally favors growth, while loaning usually leads to interest income. A few common investments do offer both types of returns; two examples to help clarify this point are stocks and real estate. Many stocks pay quarterly dividends (income), as well as carrying the potential to increase in value over time (growth). A rental property can provide current income from rent, as well as long-term appreciation in the value of the home.

Keep in mind that, in a sense, even your savings accounts and money market funds operate like loan investments. The bank pays you interest because they "borrow" your deposited funds to make a profit. If the bank had to keep one hundred percent of your deposit in their vault at all times, they would charge you a management fee instead of paying interest! But rather than holding all of your money, they keep a portion on reserve and loan the rest out to other borrowers. Because they always lend at higher rates than they pay you in interest, they profit from the difference.

**Know Your Risks**

Loan and ownership investments carry different types and levels of risk. You need to find out all of the risks involved before making any investment; *generally* ownership involves more risk than lending does. The security of loan investments depends on the ability of the borrower to pay income and return principal at maturity. If you are investing in instruments guaranteed by the government, then you have effectively no risk to your principal. Ownership investments depend on a variety of factors like company profits, supply and demand, and other market forces. You have no guarantees as an owner, just the potential for greater rewards in the long run.

I remember once seeing a sign in the window of a barbershop that read:

GOOD    CHEAP    FAST

(PICK TWO)

Remember the first investment principle I taught you? *If it seems too good to be true, it probably is.* As the barber's sign so pointedly acknowledged, there are tradeoffs involved in everything we do in life. All investments involve tradeoffs between three areas: safety, liquidity, and rate of return. By safety, I mean the security of your principal, or the likelihood that you will not lose what you have invested. Liquidity refers to your access to the investment—how much you can take out, how soon you can take it, and whether there are risks or penalties for doing so. Any time you increase the safety or liquidity of an investment, you decrease the potential returns involved.

RATE OF RETURN

INVESTING TRADEOFFS

SAFETY                    LIQUIDITY

It is essential to match your particular investment goals (what you expect the money to do for you long-term) with the appropriate types of investments. You must determine your time horizon, risk tolerance, need for access, and exit strategy for each individual investment you make. For example, if you need to supplement your retirement income from your investment portfolio, you will have to use investment vehicles that offer income and liquidity rather than a great potential rate of return. Understanding the tradeoffs involved in investing will help you find the right balance between risks and results.

I don't classify my savings accounts as investments because the expected return is too low. Saving accumulates cash, which becomes the capital I need in order to make an investment. Precisely because I can take my money out at any time (full liquidity) or leave it there at virtually no risk (complete safety via FDIC insurance), my savings accounts can offer me very little interest. At the other end of the risk spectrum would be owning stock in a fledgling company in a volatile industry. Such an investment would give me limited liquidity, since I would have to sell it at whatever price the market will pay me. I would also have to wait a few days for my trade to clear before I could use the proceeds of a stock sale. Where safety is concerned, I couldn't even be sure of the company's survival from quarter to quarter. Because of the high risk and low liquidity, investing in a small company commands the potential for very high returns.

## Know Your Account Options

Investments can be broken into categories and sorted by their levels of safety, liquidity, and potential return. But it also makes a difference *where* you hold those investments—meaning the *type of account* they are titled in. Many ownership and loan investments (such as mutual funds or bond funds) can be purchased "inside" company-sponsored retirement plans.

**For Example:** Making investments under the account umbrella of a 401(k) gives you some tax advantages to your funds but also attaches some restrictions on withdrawals.

You can purchase many investments (most often mutual funds) within specialized accounts such as:

- **Individual Retirement Accounts** (Traditional or Roth IRAs)
- **401(k) or 403(b) Accounts** (Traditional or Roth)
- **Health Savings Accounts** (HSAs)
- **College Savings Plans** (529 Plans)

Of course you can always title investments in *your name* (or the name of a trust or other entity) but you will not enjoy the tax advantages that these specialized accounts have. Whether or not you want to invest inside a specialized account (like a Roth IRA) depends on the *purpose* of your investment. Tax advantages associated with these accounts come with a price—you need to be sure that you can commit your funds for the intended purpose (such as retirement, college, or medical expenses) and the required duration specified for each account type. This makes investing *for* your values even more applicable when using these specialized accounts. While I will not attempt to give you an exhaustive review of the laws and terms of each account type here, I do want to explain the major purposes of the four most useful types of specialized accounts.

A **Traditional IRA** provides an account for investing retirement money on a pre-tax basis. Earnings in the account remain tax-deferred until you withdraw them. Contributions are limited to a certain amount each year and access to funds is limited until age 59 ½. If you take money out before then, you will most likely incur a 10% IRS tax penalty on the amount of the withdrawal. The best use for a Traditional IRA is to consolidate and gain control of funds you originally invested in a company retirement plan. Everything from securities to real estate to gold can be purchased inside an IRA, so once you roll over your 401(k) or other company plan, you expand your control over how the money is invested. One drawback to investing in a Traditional IRA is that minimum distributions (withdrawals) become required each year starting at age 70. Thus, deferred taxes eventually have to be paid whether you need the funds or not.

A **Roth IRA** is another specialized account designed for <u>retirement</u>. The Roth IRA has the same 59 ½ rule as a Traditional IRA, but no forced withdrawals at age 70. Contributions to a Roth must be from money that has already been taxed, and there is no associated tax deduction. However, money inside a Roth grows and can be withdrawn completely tax free, no matter how long you leave it in or how much it appreciates. For this reason, everyone who has ten years or more for their investments to work should be taking advantage of Roth IRAs. You do have to show earned income in order to contribute, but one working spouse can fully fund two Roth IRAs if he or she is married.

A **Health Savings Account** (HSA) is a specialized account for <u>qualified medical expenses</u>. HSAs work in conjunction with a High Deductible Health Plan, allowing you to make pre-tax or tax-deductible contributions that can be invested or earn interest. When you withdraw funds for qualified medical expenses, you pay no taxes. You can only fund a HSA up to age 65, at which point you can withdraw funds for any purpose without paying taxes (just like a Roth IRA). Because it enables you to pay for medical expenses with pre-tax money while potentially saving for retirement at the same time, a Health Savings Account can be a powerful tool in your investment and insurance plans.

A **529 College Savings Plan** is a specialized account for saving for <u>college</u>. A 529 Plan works like a college ROTH. Money that has already been taxed can be contributed by parents, grandparents, or anyone else who wants to help fund a particular beneficiary's higher education. The only investment option for these plans is mutual funds, and the only qualified withdrawals are for expenses at an accredited college or university. Money for school (including room and board) can be withdrawn tax-free, but any other withdrawals incur a 10% IRS tax penalty. If one beneficiary does not use the entire fund, it can be reassigned to another family member. The main purpose for these accounts is obviously to fund education, but a secondary purpose involves gift taxes. A 529 Plan allows contributors to accelerate five years of the normal gift tax exclusion at once—meaning you can shift large portions of your taxable estate into a tax-free account and direct that money to your relatives instead of Uncle Sam.

When using specialized accounts, I recommend researching the many "exceptions" and other provisions they carry so that you are fully informed before investing inside them. Just one example is that the 10% tax penalty on a Roth IRA withdrawal is waived when the funds are used for a first-time home purchase. There are many such complicated provisions, and I highly recommend consulting with a reputable financial advisor who will educate you and help you decide how to use these specialized account types.

## Know Yourself

The largest single obstacle to most investment success is the investor—by that I mean you and me. Making uninformed decisions, acting out of fear or greed, and following the herd can lead us into more investing blunders than any amount of bad luck. Recognize your own limitations—don't invest in something you don't understand, or something that will keep you from sleeping at night. Don't be afraid to seek professional advice, but don't let salespeople push you into investing in ways you aren't comfortable with. Ultimately, you have to rely on your own knowledge, research, and good judgment to make your investment decisions.

The best investments you will ever make will be in yourself. Nothing can protect you from losses and mistakes like knowledge. I have spent $15 on books that taught me thousands of dollars' worth of information. The fuller your investment understanding becomes, the better investments you will make. Living *The 8 Pillars of Financial Greatness* gives you the potential to earn huge dividends—not just financially, but also in overall happiness. The whole concept of greatness revolves around what you *become* when you follow the principles represented by these pillars. Further resources for continuing to develop your financial knowledge can be found on my website—www.8pillars.com. Specifically, check out *8 Pillars University*™, my flagship financial education program.

## STEP THREE OF INVESTING:
## TAKE ACTION

One of the fundamental themes throughout *The 8 Pillars*™ is the need to be a doer. Investing is no exception. While it is important to complete Pillars One through Four, become a saver, and research investment opportunities, please do not misunderstand me:

**I want you to begin investing!**

You can only learn so much by reading, speaking to professionals, or attending classes. Hands-on experience is the best teacher—we learn best by *doing.*

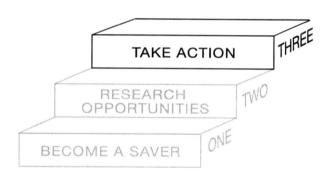

Conducting exhaustive in-depth research before investing is critical for serious, full-time investors. However, most people have no desire to become full-time investors. Even with my love of personal finance, I would not consider myself a professional investor. Like most of you, I use investments to grow my money, outpace inflation, and reach my long-term financial goals. I put the powers of compound interest and time to work for me, so that I can achieve important milestones in my life. Investing becomes a financial means to many very important and personal ends, such as retirement, my children's college educations, my business, and a more secure future for my family.

Do not put off investing altogether because of the fear of risk or the fear of not knowing enough. There comes a point when you need to jump in and get started. By reading this book, you have proven that you are a person who values learning. Please keep learning, but do not over-analyze investments to the point of inaction. Stick to the framework I gave you in the previous step when doing investment research and don't get bogged down in irrelevant information. You will learn more in a month of owning an investment than in six months of research on it.

Taking action will mean different things to different people. Only you can determine where you are and what you need to do next. As you are reading this chapter, I am sure that constructive ideas and thoughts will come to you. Remember to write these down as they occur. From such notes, you can set more specific goals and begin immediately to execute an investment plan.

For some of you, taking action literally means investing for the first time. If you have never invested before, read the short section below entitled, "For First Time Investors" to help you get your feet wet.

The majority of you are already investing—most likely for retirement in a 401(k), 403(b), or IRA. For you, taking action may require understanding your investments better and becoming more involved in managing them. It may mean reviewing *The Five Mousetraps of Investing*™ and applying a particular strategy in order to maximize your gains. Or, getting started may mean beginning to invest for other goals and in other ways. Remember, most people will have to save and invest 10-15% of their income for long-term goals in order to reach Financial Greatness. Perhaps for you, "taking action" means setting more money aside for investments.

Some of you may already be down the investing road many miles. Perhaps you have a solid investment foundation and feel that there is nothing more to be done; you already max out your 401(k), have your Roth IRA on autopilot, and have 529 plans for each of your children. You have a diversified stock and bond portfolio and a rental property or two. If this describes your situation, you should be commended—great job! Congratulations notwithstanding, there is always more to learn and do to keep your investment plan on track. Unconnected to your values, your investments won't bring happiness; left unattended, they will eventually get off track.

If you still have dreams and values that need to be funded, then you have more action to take and more investments to make. Even if you are a seasoned investor, you will always need to keep an eye out for further investment opportunities. Those who are serious about reaching Financial Greatness sooner rather than later usually save and invest 20% of their incomes. Could you stretch yourself a little more in order to reach your dreams sooner? You should never stop learning about investment opportunities or give up on growing your money. Set investment goals that will take you to the next level and take action!

## FOR FIRST TIME INVESTORS

My advice to first time investors depends on your situation. I will first provide some direction to working adults (typically between the ages of 18-50 years old). Then I will address a second group comprised of those who are retired or near retirement. Regardless of your age, make sure you read about *The Five Mousetraps of Investing*™ (the final step to investing, covered in the next chapter) before you take too much action. As a new investor, you will want to understand these core investing principles *before* you put your hard-earned savings to work and at risk.

### Group 1: Working Adults

First of all, you should be very proud of yourself for reading *The 8 Pillars of Financial Greatness*. Whether you are still in school or well into a career, taking time to further your financial education demonstrates good sense. By applying what you learn in this book now, you will benefit tremendously in every aspect of your life. Not only will you be ahead of the curve financially, you will also discover improvements in your relationships, health, and confidence.

I am convinced that understanding financial principles at a young age can help people to make better choices in life, including who they marry and what job training they receive. I made my first investment, with my own money, when I was in the ninth grade at the age of fifteen. A large part of who I am can be traced back to my early desire to understand how money affects my deepest values. By learning to manage money and establishing good financial habits in my youth, I developed into a responsible and prepared adult.

One of my favorite opportunities is speaking at high schools and universities. I love teaching young adults because I can see that starting their careers already knowing *The 8 Pillars™* is much easier than learning them later in life. Sadly, the older we get, the more we tend to resist change (another testament to the power of habits). No matter how young or experienced you are, the sooner you start investing wisely the better.

Before you take the step to become an investor, I want you to wholeheartedly embrace three qualifying principles. I have already emphasized and reemphasized all three of these principles previously in *The 8 Pillars™*. I mention them again because they are so important to potential investors, yet so easy to cheat on. These principles are the sort of unglamorous, but essential, nuts and bolts of Financial Greatness that you have to implement if you ever want to succeed financially:

**1. Spend less money than you earn.**
**2. Stay away from consumer debt, especially credit card debt.**
**3. Save before you invest.**

If you live these three principles, you have qualified yourself to become an investor. Here are the best things you can do to get your feet wet in the big ocean of investing:

I    Start with a small amount. If your *Financial Confidence Account™* is fully funded and you have accumulated another $5,000 in extra savings, invest half of that ($2,500) for now.

I    Begin by funding a **Roth IRA** (Individual Retirement Account) held at an online brokerage company. This will give you long-term tax advantages for retirement but also allow you to access the money for a first-time home purchase if you are not yet a homeowner. Funding the IRA simply moves the money from savings into the account; it does not mean you have invested anything yet. Until you purchase an investment, your money will typically earn money market interest rates.

I    If you have a **401(k) or other retirement plan** at work, begin to make automatic pre-tax contributions from each paycheck. If your company matches part of your contribution, try to deposit the maximum that they will match each year. If your job does not have this benefit, contribute the maximum allowed by the IRS to your Roth IRA each year (and do the same for your spouse's IRA if you are married).

I    Do some research on the major market indices (like the S&P 500®) and look at their volatility. Read about the ways volatility (ups and downs) is measured, such as beta and standard deviation. Select a stock index to invest in based on your tolerance for financial roller coaster rides. Then find out which **index mutual funds** and **exchange-traded funds** are available in your Roth IRA and company retirement plan to let you "buy" into that index.

I    Finally, if you think you may be tapping into this account to buy your first home in the next few years, take half of your investment and purchase a **balanced managed mutual fund** with low expenses. Purchase the stock index fund with the other half. If you already own a home, put your entire initial investment into the index fund.

I    Try to fully fund your retirement accounts and do your own research each year. As your account value grows, you will need to manage the investment mix and apply *The Five Mousetraps of Investing*™. You will also want to start funding other investment goals. Don't be afraid to seek out a professional advisor, even as your confidence grows—remember, the more you know, the more a good advisor can do for you.

**Group 2: Retired or Retiring Soon**

If you are late in your career and have never invested in anything beyond certificates of deposit or savings and money market accounts, I commend you for taking the right steps to get started. It is never too late to begin making the right financial decisions. The only way to change destinations is to start doing things differently now. Allow me to be very straight forward in stressing to you that NOW is the time for you to get serious and become a doer. The following steps should be taken immediately for you to get on track to reaching Financial Greatness.

**I**    Because retirement is looming (or already attained), and inflation will plague your buying power for the rest of your life, you need to evaluate your income needs first. Make sure you fully understand how social security and any pensions you receive will work (or do work). Determine if you will need to take income from your savings and investments in order to maintain your standard of living throughout a long retirement.

**I**    If you foresee supplemental income needs early in retirement (within the first few years), you need to find a well-qualified financial advisor who specializes in or has solid experience with income planning. Don't try to do this on your own.

**I**    If you do not have impending income needs, then you can start investing in conservative instruments that match your needs for liquidity and safety. Research balanced mutual funds, fixed annuities, municipal bonds, and REITs (Real Estate Investment Trusts). Investing in a combination of these basic loan and ownership securities will help you master *The Five Mousetraps of Investing*™ while providing you with a balanced portfolio producing both growth and income. This combination also provides some tax advantages and greater tax control, which becomes more important as your assets grow. Once you have done your homework, find a good financial advisor who can help you purchase the investments in a low-cost brokerage account with as few fees as possible.

## A NOTE ABOUT RECOMMENDATIONS

I am often asked for recommendations about specific investments, brokerage companies, and other financial resources. I do not address these here. The object of this book is to teach <u>timeless</u> principles—not deal with passing and changing financial issues.

One of the main benefits of *8 Pillars University*™ is having access to a host of current and specific resources and recommendations. Through the members-only online portal, students and alumni receive quality, up-to-date financial information such as my favorite financial websites and books along with evaluations of insurance and investment companies. As a student of *8 Pillars University*™ you will have access to more specific tools that will help you reach Financial Greatness. Visit www.8pillars.com to learn more.

**Thoughts, Feelings, and Ideas** – What are some of the thoughts or feelings you had while reading Chapter Fifteen? What insights occurred to you while reading? Did any particular action ideas pop into your mind as you read?

_____

_____

_____

_____

_____

_____

Can you see how saving and investing will allow you to reach your long-term goals?

How will your life specifically improve when you are saving and investing?

_____

_____

_____

_____

_____

_____

## DOER CHECKLIST – CHAPTER 15

☐ I have established the habit of saving 10-15% of my income for long-term goals.

☐ I know my own risk tolerance and what investment tradeoffs I can live with.

☐ If this is my first time investing, I have begun implementing the appropriate advice from the "First Time Investors" section relative to my situation.

## CHAPTER 16

# SET THE FIVE MOUSETRAPS OF INVESTING

## STEP FOUR OF INVESTING:
### SET *THE FIVE MOUSETRAPS OF INVESTING* ™

Rather than overwhelm you up front, I decided to <u>close</u> Pillar Five with my meatiest investing principles. To explain where I came up with the mousetrap analogy, I have to share a story with you. I have a dear friend that told me of an experience with his family that to this day makes me laugh. He and his wife have four boys. One day they realized that a furry little critter had made its way into their home—they had an unwelcome mouse in the house. My friend and his sons determined to catch this elusive creature.

They put their heads together and began to brainstorm ideas for the best invention they could create to catch this mouse. After much deliberation, they agreed to take a piece of paper and with a razor blade, carefully cut many little slits across it. They fastened the piece of paper over a bucket. Finally, they put a tiny chunk of cheese on the middle of the paper. They were confident that their brilliant idea was foolproof. The mouse would crawl onto the paper to get the cheese and then fall into the bucket when the sliced-up paper tore. After testing the invention to their satisfaction, they set it up in a strategic place before going to bed.

The next morning they were excited to see that the cheese was gone and the paper was torn in half. They quickly looked into the bucket, expecting to see their prisoner. No mouse! Their trap had sprung, but it was empty. They soon realized that they had a world champion high-jumping mouse on their hands! After some careful thought, they agreed to modify their invention and try again. This time they would pour water into the bucket in order to stop their impressive leaper from escaping.

That night, they set up the trap with the added water. The following day, as if it were Christmas morning, the boys bounded out of bed. They ran downstairs to check the trap. The paper had been broken again! This time they were certain of their success. But when they looked into the bucket, the cheese was gone and no mouse could be found. This little critter had not only mastered the high-jump, but he was apparently a first-rate swimmer as well!

The boys and their father decided that further modifications to their invention were necessary. They needed more supplies and decided to wait a couple of days before proceeding. In the meantime, my friend's wife became impatient that the pest remained free to roam her house. That night she went to the store, purchased a good-old-fashioned mousetrap and set it up without the boys knowing. The next morning the family discovered the athletic mouse had been caught in the simple old-fashioned mousetrap—his impressive agility notwithstanding. To this day, they laugh about this story and use it within their family to teach a very valuable lesson: **<u>you don't need to reinvent something that already works!</u>**

After carefully studying successful investors, I want to share with you five principles that really work. *The Five Mousetraps of Investing*™ may seem simple, but they are time-tested and proven by the experience of thousands of investors. The best thing about these investing strategies is that you don't have to reinvent the wheel or rewrite the book in order to have success. These principles hold the keys to managing investment risk. Remember that all investing involves some level of risk; by managing your risks, you increase the likelihood that you will reach your investment goals. Implementing *The Five Mousetraps of Investing*™ helps ensure that you don't leave your values to chance.

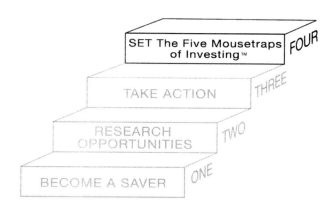

**Note:** It is important to keep in mind that *The Five Mousetraps of Investing*™ are good—you want to implement each one of them. Despite the little story of my friend and his four boys, people may be confused and think of traps with negative connotations. These traps are positive, time-tested principles that will <u>help you</u> to become a more effective investor. As you *set* these mousetraps, you are more likely to *catch* better returns.

## MOUSETRAP ONE:
## TAKE A LONG-TERM VIEW OF YOUR INVESTMENTS

When it comes to investing, "short-term" means anything five years or less. The biggest mistake most people make with their investments is worrying too much about short-term volatility. It can be very hard to watch your investments fluctuate in value, but taking a long-term view of their performance will settle your stomach somewhat. Almost every good investment will experience ups and downs, but very rarely does a good investment take longer than five years to produce acceptable overall results. The higher the risk (and potential return) involved, the longer you need to set your sights.

The media does not generally take a long-term view of anything. Media feeds us *news*—new information, the latest trends, the most recent headlines. The fact is that long-term investments are boring to follow and too slow to watch. Investor panic, record market gains and losses, and economic extremes all catch our interest quicker than "long-term investors stay put." Relying on the media for financial information will make you more worried and less committed to your investment plans. Take the long-term view and distance yourself from the financial graffiti that thrives on television, in newspapers, and on the Internet.

One of the major enemies of all investment portfolios is what I call **"The Stealth Tax"**—the value-eroding culprit called *inflation*. Inflation occurs when the prices of goods and services increase over time. There have been very few periods in the history of the free world when inflation was not at work. Because of inflation, the real value of money (meaning what you can buy with it) keeps decreasing. The $10 that once filled your gas tank now buys only a couple of gallons of fuel. In the long run, none of us can avoid the effects of inflation.

Inflation affects your investment strategy in two important ways. First, it demands that you take enough risk to allow your investments to outpace it over time. If inflation averages 4% per year, your invested funds are not growing in *real* value unless they average *better* than 4% returns. Second, inflation requires you to keep your money working even when you need current income. For example, to maintain your current standard of living in retirement, your income will need to keep up with inflation. Factoring in estimated inflation rates increases the amount of assets you will need in order to retire comfortably. This makes it more difficult to balance your needs for growth and current income, safety, and return. Only by taking a long-term view can you both plan for and combat the eroding "tax" of inflation on your retirement lifestyle.

In addition to preventing bad decisions and fighting inflation, taking a long-term view will benefit your investments in other ways. It will allow your investments to work the way they are meant to by giving them time to even out market cycles. It will keep you from investing on whims or following the latest fad—which almost always leads to poor investment returns. However, a long-term approach does not mean doing nothing for five years at a time. You should still review your goals, evaluate your portfolio mix, and assess your investment returns once each year, rebalancing as necessary.

## MOUSETRAP TWO: DIVERSIFY

The best way to hedge against most forms of investment risk is to fund many different types of investments. Diversification simply means to spread your money around and allocate your investment dollars into vehicles that work differently. As you diversify your assets, you decrease your overall investment risk. If one type of investment fails, only a part of your portfolio is affected.

No serious investor questions the principle of diversification, but speculators will try to tell you that no one ever gets rich by diversifying. The reality is that almost no one ever gets rich *over night* by diversifying—

or by implementing any other investment strategy for that matter!
Speculators only care about the chance to get rich quick. People with a
*Financial Greatness Mindset* invest based on their deepest values. They
view riches in the fullest sense of the word and *Invest for Happiness*, not
just for material wealth.

Diversification is like putting a variety of vehicles at your disposal.
To get to some destinations, you drive a car. For others, you can ride a
bike or just walk. Some locations are exotic enough that you need to take
a plane or boat to reach them. Others you can get to by train, car, or plane
with pros and cons to each option. At different times in our lives, most of
us end up using nearly every form of travel available. The same holds true
for investing—most of us will utilize many types of investments to get us
where we want to go. The mix of "vehicles" will change as our goals and
means change, but it should *always* be a mix.

If you already have a portfolio of stocks, mutual funds, and bonds, it
may be time for you to further diversify into precious metals, annuities, and
real estate. You may even want to look into investing in a small business
or collecting art. Diversify wisely, always matching your goals and values
to your investments.

It is also essential to diversify further within the types of investments
you own. I don't have space in this book to delve into more specific
portfolio allocation strategies, but once you understand the principle
of diversification, you need only apply it consistently at each level of
investment.

## MOUSETRAP THREE:
## IMPLEMENT SYSTEMATIC STRATEGIES

Looking at the big picture, your emotions play an important role in
saving and investing. As mentioned previously, connecting emotionally
to your values and goals will give you tremendous motivation to save and
invest for them. Having said this, beyond driving you to take action, your

emotions should play a very *small* role in *specific investment decisions*. Most emotional investment decisions are quite bluntly <u>bad</u> ones. Especially if your investments summon either of the two anti-investment monsters: **fear** and **greed**. Investing for the long term tempers many causes of fear and keeps greedy impulses in check. Diversifying protects you from large losses in one type of investment, preventing the panic that would ensue if your entire portfolio crashed at once. Diversification also keeps your money from becoming too concentrated in high-risk vehicles that stoke greed when they are performing their best.

Beyond diversifying and thinking long-term, you can also eliminate emotions from your specific decisions by investing systematically. Remember from Pillar Two that a *system* is the methods and procedures you follow to accomplish a task or produce a result. Relying on predetermined methods to automatically grow and rebalance your portfolio removes the temptation to invest emotionally.

In fact, your investment choices should be relatively boring. Your investment portfolio is not the place to seek thrills or take gambles. If you want to speculate because it seems like an exciting hobby, set aside some "play" money each year and don't feed your infatuation any more than that (even if you get lucky and have wildly successful results). Playing with your money in risky securities is not much different than gambling at a casino—you get the rush that you pay for and rarely much else. Investing systematically isn't exciting or exhilarating, but it works—especially as part of a diversified, long-term portfolio strategy.

Two specific strategies warrant explanation here, although there are countless others out there for you to research and evaluate. Putting these two strategies on autopilot will build you a solid platform from which to implement other disciplined investment strategies.

First on my list is **Dollar Cost Averaging**. This method of investing can be applied to any security whose value fluctuates daily (such as stocks and mutual funds). When you Dollar Cost Average, you invest a fixed amount of money in the same security at set intervals (such as monthly or quarterly). When the shares of the security are higher in value, your fixed dollars buy fewer shares. When the shares drop in price, the same dollar amount buys more shares. The net effect is that over time, you typically accumulate more shares at a lower average cost than if you invested all at once. You take the guesswork (and hence most of the emotion) out of the equation, which is the main benefit of this strategy.

Dollar Cost Averaging does protect you against sudden drops in the market after a large investment. However, it does so at a price. You also give up potential market gains by spreading your investment out over a longer period. My rule of thumb on Dollar Cost Averaging is this: don't delay investing accumulated cash *just so you can Dollar Cost Average.* If you have a goal that needs funding and the required funds are all there sitting on the sidelines, get that money in the game. Don't skip any steps, but don't think that lower average share prices are going to be better in the long run than investing when you have money ready. Dollar Cost Average when you don't have large blocks of money to invest at one time.

The easiest way to incorporate Dollar Cost Averaging into your plan is to implement it within your retirement accounts. Most 401(k) plans allow you to automatically have contributions deducted from your paycheck and invested into preselected mutual funds. Just be sure that you change investments within the account every 6-18 months so that your regular investment amount does not all end up in the same place. Diversify *while* you Dollar Cost Average and keep emotions out of it!

The second strategy to implement is called **Income Cross-Reinvestment**. This method can be used with securities that pay out regular dividends or interest. The central principle at work is *compounding*, where your interest earns interest. Unlike a simple compound savings account, however, you are putting your interest to work in a *different* vehicle than the investment that generated it.

Let me give you an example of how this could work for a hypothetical investor named Chad Smith. Chad purchases $100,000 of a bond that promises to return his principal in ten years and pay him a 6% fixed income in the meantime. He receives a monthly check for $500 from this investment. Instead of spending that interest or stashing it in savings, Chad immediately reinvests it into shares of a growth mutual fund each month. By Cross Reinvesting his interest into another investment vehicle, Chad further diversifies his portfolio, creates an automatic Dollar Cost Average plan, and completely circumvents any chances for emotional decision making.

Income Cross-Reinvestment can be adapted to almost any type of goal, portfolio, or level of risk tolerance. The key is to keep your money moving automatically and quickly, so that it works for you constantly and systematically. However you implement this strategy, recognize that without a long-term view, it will be impossible to gauge your progress accurately. Compounding impacts your results most when given time to do its work. Be creative but be consistent and you can accelerate the effects of compounding through Income Cross-Reinvestment.

The more I learn about investing, the more convinced I become that serious investors follow disciplined, systematic, principle-based strategies to grow and protect their money. As you progress toward Financial Greatness, keep learning new methods for investing systematically—the mousetraps have already been built for the very mice you will deal with in your future. You just need to find them and set them in place properly.

## MOUSETRAP FOUR:
## UTILIZE TAX-ADVANTAGED INVESTMENT VEHICLES

In Chapter Two, I shared with you the importance of fighting against the friction of negative thoughts, words, and behaviors. Investments also have to fight their own versions of friction—primarily inflation and taxes. Every return on investment eventually faces depreciation due to taxes. Taxes on dividends, interest income, and capital gains erode the real return on your investment and need to be minimized and planned for in advance so that you can meet your goals.

Investment taxation concerns could fill thousands of books, and my purpose here is not to take the place of a qualified tax advisor. Any time you are dealing with issues of taxation or litigation, you should seek the guidance of a trustworthy professional. What I will point out for now is that many great mousetraps are already available to help you minimize the friction of taxes on your investments. You can take advantage of them by researching some of the appropriate pre-tax, tax-deferred, and tax-free investment vehicles from the following sections.

**Tax-Free Investments**

Two ways for your money to work tax-free are investing inside Roth IRAs and investing in Municipal Bonds. **Roth IRAs** (including Roth 401(k) plans) do not offer an up-front tax deduction on your contributions, nor can they accept pre-tax dollars. But when it comes time to tap into your nest egg, everything you earn inside a Roth IRA comes out completely tax-free. Your investment can do all of the growing and compounding it wants and Uncle Sam won't get a dime of those returns. This is one reason I recommend a Roth IRA to every qualified first-time investor.

**Municipal Bonds** are loan investments where the borrower happens to be a municipal government entity (such as a school district, a county, an airport, or even a state). Because the funds borrowed are intended for the public good, you get a tax break for lending your money to the cause. Typically, the interest you earn will be paid semiannually and will be exempt from Federal taxes, State and local taxes, or both. You can purchase these bonds directly for income (they typically are very safe but have long terms such as 20 or 30 years) or indirectly through municipal bond mutual funds. Because of the relative safety and the tax-free payouts, reinvesting the dividends from such a mutual fund by buying more shares can have great results. Many conservative investors employ this strategy as an important vehicle in their armada for beating inflation and fighting taxes without being too aggressive on the risk scale.

**Pre-Tax Investments**

Because the IRS limits the amount you can contribute to a Roth IRA, you will likely want to invest additional retirement funds pre-tax. Pre-tax specifically refers to *income taxes,* meaning you contribute to the account from your gross pay prior to taxes being assessed. The two primary vehicles for pre-tax investing are **company retirement plans** (such as 401(k) plans, SEPs, 403(b) plans, and Money Purchase Pension Plans) and **Traditional IRAs**. Although you may not be able to contribute to a Traditional IRA directly from your gross paycheck, your contributions are deducted from your income when you file your income taxes for the year. Please note that any contributions you make to a Roth IRA will reduce the amount you can add to a Traditional IRA in a given year.

The main benefit of pre-tax investing is that you are paying yourself first—before taxes, before bills, before any discretionary spending. Your funds go right to work, then grow and compound *without the friction of taxes* until you need them (i.e., in retirement). The main drawback to pre-tax retirement accounts comes when you start taking those withdrawals. Every penny you remove is then taxed as ordinary income—so the income you deducted thirty years ago is now returned to you, along with any gains, and taxed at your retirement tax rate. Far be it from me to predict what that will be for you—tax rates do change at times, and so will your income levels. If you stay on the path to Financial Greatness, ideally your income will continue to increase in retirement to keep pace with inflation and maintain (or improve!) your standard of living.

But even if you end up giving back some of your untaxed-profits later in life, you still have the advantages of lower taxes now, a systematic way to invest, and a larger account balance to owe taxes on in retirement. I've never been upset about a large tax bill; I know when I write that check out to the IRS, it means I earned a good income.

## Tax-Deferred Investments

One oft-maligned but sometimes very useful investment vehicle is the **tax-deferred annuity**. These come in two major varieties—*variable annuities* (which I don't recommend for most investors due to high fees and restrictive features) and *fixed annuities* (which range from investor-friendly to buyer-beware depending on the contract). Drawing on our analogy of different types of vehicles, there are as many variations of annuities to choose from as there are makes and models of cars. The term annuity gets a bad reputation sometimes, precisely because there are so many lemons among the group. For this reason, be very careful when dealing with annuity contracts. But a good fixed annuity can provide an attractive combination of safety, liquidity, and tax-deferred returns for a variety of investment goals.

Annuities are deposit contracts issued by insurance companies. I see annuities as intermediate-term, tax-deferred alternatives to many loan-type investments. They are designed to provide income and tax control options in retirement, so until you are well into your career, you probably don't need to even think about annuities. The key to finding a good contract is to work with an experienced insurance or financial advisor who can explain several options from a few highly rated and well-established companies. Find out specifically how the surrender penalties work and what other access you have to your money in case of emergency, sickness, or income shortage. If fixed annuities can help you reach specific investment goals better than other vehicles, don't avoid them just because someone told you they were no good. You don't stop driving cars altogether just because your neighbor had a bad experience with a complete lemon. Do your research and make your own decisions based on your values and goals, and you'll be happy regardless of what the bewildered masses think.

Annuities have special tax implications which you should discuss with your tax advisor. Gains are taxed as ordinary income when the owner accesses the account, but stay with the policy without a step up in cost basis when the owner passes away. Unlike life insurance death benefits, the amount inherited from an annuity will not pass on to heirs tax-free. These features make it wise to consult a tax professional and an estate planning attorney when adding annuity contracts to your investment portfolio.

## MOUSETRAP FIVE:
### KEEP EXPENSES LOW

The final mousetrap I want you to know about is pretty simple. It is so simple that people often ignore it completely, inventing elaborate ways to "catch mice" (beat the investing averages) that drain more energy and profit than they could ever make up for in style points. The fact is *you don't get to keep what you pay in fees*. While I encourage my clients and readers to seek professional advice, I also acknowledge that when it comes to the world of brokers, insurance agents, financial planners, and asset managers, you don't always get what you pay for.

Let's use an example to make this point as vividly as possible. Suppose Wanda B. Rich invests $100,000 in a mutual fund sold to her by a financial advisor named Lem E. Gogh. Because Lem makes his living selling investments, he will earn a commission on this sale. Wanda can choose to have that commission deducted all at once or over several years. At Lem's advice, she chooses the former option and a 5% sales charge is deducted from her new account. That means only 95% of her money goes to work for her.

$100,000 investment – 5% sales charge = $95,000 at work

Now, when Lem sold her the mutual fund, he showed her how well it had performed in the past. Although he admitted that past returns do not guarantee future results, he was certain the fund was well-managed and would outperform all of its benchmarks. Let's assume that this fund does indeed do slightly better than its benchmark index, the S&P 500 Composite Index®. In the first year, Wanda earns a 5% return while the index only gained 4.2%. Where does Wanda stand now?

$95,000 at work x 5% return in year 1 = $99,750 value of investment

After a full year and a five percent return, Wanda still has less than what she started with. Why? Fees ate her profits. If she had chosen to spread the sales charge across several years, the end results would not have fared much better. Sales charges, management fees, and other investment expenses markedly diminish your results over time. You need to find the right balance between quality advice, smart investment vehicles, and low fees. As the sign in the barber shop window points out, you will have to make some tradeoffs at times. Just remember that you don't get to keep what you pay in investment fees.

## INVESTING FOR HAPPINESS

I sincerely hope that after studying Pillar Five, you understand why I focus so much on investing *for* meaningful goals that make you happier and better for reaching them. Too many people get caught up in the excitement of investing itself and forget that in the context of Financial Greatness, it isn't a game. You can certainly "play with" investment vehicles if you want to, but that is called speculating rather than *investing*. Real investments always have a purpose and a plan behind them and a foundation of solid principles beneath them.

I know that I have done little more than whet your appetite on this subject, but I urge you to continue learning and become an informed investor. Follow the four steps to investing and help your money work as hard for you as you worked for it.

**Step ONE**: Become a Saver
**Step TWO**: Research Opportunities
**Step THREE**: Take Action
**Step FOUR:** Set *The Five Mousetraps of Investing*™

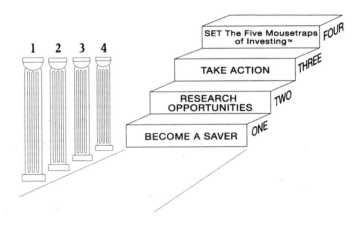

**Thoughts, Feelings, and Ideas** – What are some of the thoughts or feelings you had while reading Chapter Sixteen? What insights occurred to you while reading? Did any particular action ideas pop into your mind as you read?

_____

_____

_____

_____

_____

Can you see how saving and investing will allow you to reach your long-term goals?

How will your life specifically improve when you are saving and investing?

_____

_____

_____

_____

## DOER CHECKLIST – CHAPTER 16

☐     I am committed to setting _The Five Mousetraps of Investing_™.

I will:

- o   Take a long-term view of my investments
- o   Diversify
- o   Implement systematic strategies
- o   Utilize tax-advantaged investment vehicles
- o   Keep expenses low

☐     I have a trusted financial advisor or have interviewed at least two potential advisors.

# PILLAR SIX

*Make Your Home the Heart of Money Matters*

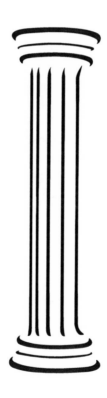

## CHAPTER 17

# HOME IS WHERE THE HEART IS
## (In more ways than one)

Calling a place *home* imbues it with special meaning. A home provides more than just shelter from the elements or a host of convenient amenities. The word *home* embodies a sense of security, comfort, stewardship, and responsibility. Homes are held dear to most of us, whether in the cherished memories of a beloved childhood house or the proud satisfaction of the first home we buy on our own. As the saying goes, home is where your heart is. When it comes to your personal finances, your home can play a central part in helping you achieve (or fail to achieve) Financial Greatness. Hence, Pillar Six will teach you to put your home at the heart of your financial matters.

The relationship between home ownership and achieving Financial Greatness unfolds in two ways:

**First** and foremost, your home should provide a nurturing environment for living your values. The place you live affects your career, your schedule, your quality of life, your ability to raise a family, and your wealth. Home ownership can create feelings of security and a sense of stability for an individual, couple, or family. Every home becomes a place to build memories and pursue the goals and dreams you value most.

**Second**, real estate is very likely to appreciate over time, allowing you to substantially increase your net worth by owning a home.

The home you live in can either be an area of great enjoyment and financial reward or a source of ongoing headaches and grief. Pillar Six will help you make your home a wonderful and enriching aspect of your life.

## SHOULD YOU RENT OR BUY?

Financial talking heads often tell us that renting a home is "like flushing your money down the toilet." We have been programmed by our relatively wealthy society to feel that if we rent a house, condo, or apartment, we are somehow inferior to those who own. While I do believe that owning real estate will be an important step for anyone who wants to reach Financial Greatness, I also know that this type of "renting is bad" mentality gets a lot of people in trouble. Buying real estate is a serious financial commitment involving a number of factors. Although I place mortgages on my list of "acceptable" forms of debt, not all mortgages are acceptable! In some situations, it makes more sense to rent than to own, and you need to be wise with your housing decisions. Many people purchase a home when they should be renting, and too many of these buyers end up bankrupt.

Ask yourself the following key questions *before* you buy a home or any other real estate. If you cannot honestly answer YES to each of these questions, you need to seriously consider renting a while longer.

I   Will you live in the home for at least 3-4 years?

I   Is your credit score high enough to get a competitive interest rate?

I   Can you easily afford the total monthly payment in addition to any other debts you may have?

I   In addition to your monthly principal and interest payment, have you factored in the cost of insurance, utilities, maintenance, private mortgage insurance (PMI), and any homeowners association fees?

I   Are you confident that your job position and current income are stable?

I   If you lost your job, could you continue to make your monthly payment for a minimum of 3-4 months?

I   Do you have at least 10% for a down payment?

I    Besides money for the down payment, do you have additional
     funds to cover the applicable closing costs?
I    Are you free of consumer debt?

Remember: it is okay to rent while preparing for home ownership. You
will be better off waiting than jumping into the responsibilities of a house
before you are financially and mentally prepared.

After my wife and I graduated from college, we watched many of our
friends begin buying homes right away. Our friends were convinced that
renting was no different than throwing away money and that the real estate
market only goes up. My wife and I did not agree with that philosophy.
Given our income level and understanding of personal finance, our friends
were confused that we chose to continue renting.

What our friends did not understand is the fact that my wife and I
make financial decisions based on OUR VALUES and not what other
people think or say. We wanted to make sure we were completely ready
before we purchased our first home. MeKette and I set a goal to save 20%
for a down payment. Because of this goal, we did not purchase our first
home for another four years.

I can tell you from personal experience and from working with
numerous clients that buying a home when you are financially ready
makes a big difference in the way you feel about your home. Many people
today are "house poor" and struggle to make their payment every month.
Because of the financial strain, they often complain about their homes and
consider downsizing to free themselves of the financial stress. Owning a
home should be a wonderful and satisfying experience. Before purchasing
a home, take a deep breath and make some sound decisions based on what
is best for you and your family. Forget about what other people are telling
you and ground your decisions about home ownership on YOUR values.

Although renting is perfectly acceptable for a few years (especially
when you are just starting out), it does not excuse anyone from working
diligently towards home ownership. If you are currently renting, you need
to set goals, save up, and prepare for buying your own home. There is
a strong correlation between owning real estate and achieving Financial
Greatness. Renting for an extended period of time (more than five or six
years) does not mesh with the *Financial Greatness Mindset*. If you follow
*The 8 Pillars*™ you will be headed for home ownership sooner rather than
later.

## IS YOUR HOME AN INVESTMENT?

In much of today's financial press, we read opposing views regarding home ownership. Some financial gurus strongly state, "Your home is not an investment—it is only a place to live." Conversely, many finance authors are adamant that your home is the "largest" and possibly the "best" investment you will ever make. Both sides have strong, persuasive arguments to prove their points. After studying what it takes to not only achieve Financial Greatness but also to become a great *person*, I am convinced that we can benefit from both viewpoints.

Should you consider your home an investment? Absolutely! Treat your home as both a financial asset and something more. To start with, your home is a place to live your values—to raise a family, pursue hobbies and dreams, and build enduring friendships and memories. Your home should match your values and goals. The neighborhood you choose determines who your children will grow up with and where they will attend school. It impacts the friends you will make, the security of your property, your peace of mind, the safety of your family, and the distance you will travel to work and play. From this perspective, your home is a crucial investment in your overall quality of life. It is important to always keep this aspect of your home as your primary focus. Your family's well-being should be your first priority. Many people who view their homes as purely financial investments neglect these important value considerations.

Beyond the quality-of-life benefits, home ownership provides a powerful investment opportunity. Your home may be the largest single purchase you make in your lifetime. There are considerable upfront costs to consider and critical financial principles to follow when purchasing a home. A home usually demands around 30% of your monthly income and there are multiple elements of risk at play when you carry a mortgage. However, your home also has the potential to increase in value over time, sometimes significantly. From this perspective your home is a very real financial investment—an investment that requires as much research and careful management as any other, if not more.

Let's take a look at our definition of investing from Pillar Five. As you review this definition, think about what it takes to locate, buy, finance, maintain, and sell a home.

**Investing** is putting money to work for a specific purpose involving a measured level of risk and a corresponding expected return or profit. An investment cannot be deemed gambling or betting if it meets these criteria:

**Investments are well-researched.**
    1. You know what specific results you want from the investment.
    2. The investment fits into your long-term strategy.
    3. You understand how the investment vehicle works.
    4. You understand the risks involved in making the investment.

**Investments are not left to chance.**
    5. You take a systematic approach to managing the investment.
    6. You do not base investment decisions on emotions such as greed or fear.
    7. The investment is not motivated by addiction or entertainment.
    8. The odds of positive and consistent results are favorable to your purposes.

So a home, if purchased properly, surely fits our definition of an investment. It also provides us with a place to live out our values. Is it too much to ask that we use both criteria when evaluating our homes? I believe that we are savvy enough to make decisions from both a <u>values-oriented perspective,</u> as well as a <u>financial perspective</u>. In fact, the two viewpoints prove mutually beneficial. Most of the criteria used to purchase a home for the benefit of your family and values will in turn make your home a better investment. People with a *Financial Greatness Mindset* understand how to view their home both ways. They learn to manage both perspectives at the same time and do it effectively. In order to reach Financial Greatness, you need to strike a balance between viewing your home as the heart of your values and as the heart of your investment portfolio.

## WHY PILLAR SIX MATTERS MORE
## NOW THAN EVER BEFORE

In Pillar Five, I taught that having a long-term investment strategy is important. You can decrease your market risk by having a longer investment timeframe. This is due to the effects of market volatility—a fancy word to describe how financial markets, including housing markets, constantly go up and down. The longer the view you take on an investment, the less difference short-term volatility makes to you. When you can ride out the inevitable ups and downs over time, you give the investment a chance to even out and hit its typical average rate of return.

Why is volatility important with respect to home ownership? Because there is a national trend taking place that makes many of us more susceptible to normal volatility in housing markets: people are living in their homes for a shorter period of time. Young homeowners today live in a more mobile society than previous generations did. Workers are now more likely to change careers, jobs, or companies than they used to be and many end up relocating with greater frequency than their parents. Statistics show that the average person today lives in their home for 7-8 years. This trend is significant.

Minimizing your risk and maximizing your return takes a lot more effort over a 7-8 year period than if you have 14-15 years like previous workforces averaged. You must be armed with more financial education than your parents had if you want to succeed as a homeowner. For you to see a positive return on your home investment, you need to develop the ability to manage the many complexities of home ownership.

We will delve further into managing your home as a financial investment in the next chapter. For now, remember that just as with every other type of investment, your key to success will be educating yourself and working with the right professionals. This is truer in today's complex housing market than ever before in the history of real estate.

**Thoughts, Feelings, and Ideas** – What are some of the thoughts or feelings you had while reading Chapter Seventeen? What insights occurred to you while reading? Did any particular action ideas pop into your mind as you read?

_____

_____

_____

_____

_____

_____

Can you see why it is important to find a balance between viewing your home as a place to pursue your values and seeing it as a financial investment?

How will balancing a <u>values-oriented perspective</u> with a <u>financial perspective</u> help you achieve Financial Greatness and become a great person at the same time?

_____

_____

_____

_____

## DOER CHECKLIST – CHAPTER 17

☐    I view my home as an investment. I understand that my home is first and foremost an investment in my values and my everyday quality of life. Second, my home is a true financial investment with the potential to appreciate over time.

☐    If I am currently renting, I have set specific goals to save and prepare for buying my own home.

## CHAPTER 18

# THE MAGIC NUMBER

## WHAT IS THE MAGIC NUMBER?

Most people cannot pay upfront and in full for the homes they live in. If you are like me, and you needed to borrow money in order to purchase a home, then you probably realize that the lender owns the majority of your house. The number that represents YOUR portion of the home is a very important figure. I call it the *magic number*.

Once you subtract the outstanding loan or mortgage amount from the market value of your home, you arrive at your home equity. For example, if you could sell your home today for $425,000 and your outstanding mortgage was $300,000, your equity would come to $125,000 ($425,000 - $300,000 = $125,000). Your home equity is the *magic number* in home ownership and you need to safeguard it well. Your home equity likely contains a significant portion of your true wealth and actual net worth.

We discussed the importance of your net worth in Pillar Two. I stated in Chapter Six that "many people who own expensive cars, nice boats, designer clothes, luxury homes, and opulent jewelry may appear to be wealthy when in reality they are not. In fact, some of the wealthiest looking people in your area may actually have a negative net worth!" The same principle applies to home equity.

Just because someone lives in an expensive and beautiful home does not mean they are wealthy. The home's appearance tells us nothing about how much debt the "owner" has on the property or how much equity they've built (their *true ownership*). In fact, someone in a very modest home may have more equity than a person living in a mansion. This is an important distinction to understand. Those with a *Financial Greatness Mindset* manage and grow their home equity just as intensely as they do their other assets. They understand that their home equity can greatly affect their net worth. The *magic number* has very little to do with the price of your home and everything to do with your home equity.

There are two primary ways to build your home equity:

      1. Payments toward principal (including down payments)
      2. Appreciation in value (including home improvements)

One of the reasons I call home equity "magic" is because both points 1 and 2 normally occur as if by magic just by living in a home and paying the mortgage bill over time. The remainder of this chapter will be dedicated to helping you grow your home equity by *managing* the variables that drive these two equity components—making some of your own magic.

## I. PAYMENTS TOWARD PRINCIPAL

Excluding taxes and insurance, when you make your monthly house payment, your money is split into two main categories: principal and interest. The amount of money going toward principal is the portion of the payment that you keep—it remains *your* money because it goes straight to home equity! Your monthly payments toward mortgage principal work as a powerful automatic savings plan. As your loan balance goes down, your true ownership in the home goes up each month, building equity slowly but steadily.

The two main variables affecting your payment toward principal are the type of mortgage you select and the interest rate you qualify for.

## MORTGAGE TYPES

The type of home loan you select can have a large impact on the amount of equity you build through your payments toward principal. There are many different types of mortgages to choose from, but almost all loans fall into one of three general categories: Fixed-Rate Loans, Adjustable-Rate Loans, and Creative Loans. I will briefly explain each type of loan here and discuss when (if ever) a particular kind of mortgage might be a good choice.

### Category One: Fixed-Rate Loans

Mortgages with a fixed-rate are very common, simple, and predictable. Your monthly payment stays the same over the life of the loan because principal and interest have been amortized (spread out) across the term. The shorter the term (how many years the payments are spread across), the higher your monthly payment will be. The three most common fixed-rate loans are the 15-Year Fixed, 30-Year Fixed, and 40-Year Fixed mortgages.

Although your monthly payment will be more for a 15-year Fixed mortgage than for a 30- or 40-year option, more of your payment will go toward principal and you will pay less interest over the course of the loan. Conversely, a 40-year mortgage will have a lower monthly payment because less money goes toward principal (and therefore home equity) each month. Assuming you make only your regular loan payments, you will grow the *magic number* more quickly with a 15-year fixed loan than with a 30- or 40-year fixed mortgage.

| Fixed-Rate Loan Term | Interest Rate Used | Loan Amount | Monthly Payment | Total Interest Paid Over Time |
|---|---|---|---|---|
| 15 Year | 6% | $250,000 | $2,109 | $129,736 |
| 30 Year | 6.50% | $250,000 | $1,580 | $318,861 |
| 40 Year | 6.75% | $250,000 | $1,508 | $474,028 |

## When to Use a Fixed-Rate Loan

**For the vast majority of situations, I recommend a fixed-rate home loan.** They are simple, and in the mortgage industry, simplicity is good. Fixed-rate loans make even more sense when you plan to stay in your home for a longer period of time (5-10 years or more).

**A 15-year fixed mortgage can be a good choice** if you have a strong source of steady income and can afford the higher monthly payments. Fifteen-year fixed loans typically offer a lower interest rate than other fixed-rate mortgages. When you put a lower rate together with a more aggressive payoff schedule, a 15-year fixed loan is like being on the "fast-track" to growing the *magic number.*

If you choose a 15-year loan, having a well-funded *Financial Confidence Account*™ becomes crucial, so that the larger payment does not become burdensome if your income is temporarily interrupted. You need money set aside for your mortgage because lenders do not take long to foreclose on homes where payments are not being made. Don't rely on your home's equity to bail you out either, because you can never predict when refinancing may be difficult, unwise or even impossible. Even existing home equity lines can usually be frozen or closed at any time at the lender's discretion, so you should never substitute home equity for a *Financial Confidence Account*™.

**My favorite mortgage is the 30-year fixed.** The vast majority of my clients use a 30-year fixed mortgage on their primary residence. Are you surprised that most of my clients are not on the "fast-track" using a 15-year fixed loan? They often still are on that fast-track! Let me explain.

People with a *Financial Greatness Mindset* want to maximize their financial control as well as the *magic number* (their home equity). I teach them to use a 30-year fixed loan but make extra payments every month as if they have a shorter-term fixed loan. As they continue to pay extra payments, they increase the *magic number* at tremendous speed and put themselves on pace to be mortgage-free a lot sooner.

At the same time, they maintain some flexibility and control over their mortgage payments. If something happens to lower or interrupt their income, they can always drop down to their "actual" lower monthly payment for a few months until they get back on track. This allows them to be on the "fast-track" while not sacrificing too much flexibility. It also allows people in many housing markets to buy the house they need rather than settling too much just to get a 15-year term.

Finally, for my more disciplined clients a 30-year mortgage frees up cash flow to invest in assets that have the potential to appreciate better than their home. In order to maximize your control, you need to be certain that your loan does not have a pre-payment penalty. I do not recommend any type of loan with a pre-payment penalty.

Be warned: paying extra payments toward principal or dedicating money every month to investing can be difficult. There are endless things and people competing for every dollar you earn. These strategies require a tremendous amount of self-discipline. If you have a strong, reliable source of income, a fully funded *Financial Confidence Account*™, and can comfortably afford a higher monthly payment, you may want to shoot for the true "fast-track" loan and use a 15-year fixed mortgage to effectively *force* yourself into investing more.

**I do not recommend using a 40-year fixed loan.** You simply pay too much money in interest and do not build equity fast enough. Your interest rate will likely be higher on such a loan, and your payment will not be that much lower than on a 30-year fixed mortgage. If you cannot afford the monthly payments on a 30-year fixed loan, you are probably not ready for home ownership. Consider looking for a less expensive home or continuing to save while you rent. Please review the questions found in the previous chapter before purchasing real estate.

**Category Two: Adjustable-Rate Loans**

Adjustable-Rate Mortgages, often referred to as ARMs, have a fixed interest rate for a set period of time after which the rate becomes adjustable. The amount of time the interest rate stays fixed depends on the type of ARM and can last for as little as one month or as long as ten years. Why would you want a mortgage with a potentially adjustable rate? Because these types of loans typically offer a lower *initial* interest rate than traditional 15-year or 30-year fixed mortgages. The downside is that once the fixed rate period ends, your rate and monthly payments will begin changing. This can cause serious financial difficulties if rates have risen or start to go up.

The most common types of adjustable-rate mortgages are the 5/1 ARM and the 7/1 ARM. The 5 and 7 represent how long the rate will remain fixed before adjusting. After the fixed term is over, the rate normally adjusts annually (but not always). The amount the rate can adjust depends on changes to a named index; adjustable rates are calculated as an index plus a certain margin (or spread) added to it. There are limits on how much the interest rate can adjust, but these limits offer only small protections over time. Maximum rates can be very high on ARMs. In addition, ARMs are much more likely to have extra fees, pre-payment penalties, and other complicating factors that can end up costing you money.

Are you beginning to see why adjustable-rate loans are not as simple as fixed-rate loans? There are many more variables to manage and keep track of with an ARM, and the number of "unknowns" is far greater. As the complexity of a loan increases, so does your risk. It is important to remember that Financial Greatness comes down to taking care of what you can control. The more variables and possible outcomes, the less control you have.

### When to Use an Adjustable-Rate Loan

**I rarely recommend adjustable-rate loans.** The only time an ARM may make sense is when you are absolutely certain that you will be in the home for a *shorter* period of time than the rate adjustment. For example, a 7/1 ARM may make sense if you *know* you will be moving in 5-6 years. Even in this example, you need to factor in the time it could take to sell your home in a possible down market. I do not recommend any type of loan where your rate (and consequently your payment) will adjust sooner than 5 years. Remember, if you are planning to live in your home for less than 3-4 years, you may be better off renting than buying due to the amount of money you will pay in closing costs and other fees.

If you definitely will be moving before the ARM would adjust, you still need to make certain that the interest rate works to your advantage. To make it worth the complexity and risk, the ARM initial rate would need to be at least a half percent lower than a traditional fixed-rate loan. For example, if 30-year fixed loans are currently at 6.5%, then a 5/1 ARM needs to be at 6% or lower before you consider it. Keep in mind that you are making tradeoffs in order to get a *lower initial interest rate.* I have seen 30-year fixed loans with lower interest rates than ARMs; choosing an ARM in such a case would be crazy! It makes absolutely no sense to use a more complicated loan with the risk of an adjusting rate if you cannot get significant savings out of it.

In addition to the financial considerations, adjustable-rate loans are often in conflict with our first criteria of a home as a place to pursue your values. I have seen friends forced to move their family because their adjustable-rate mortgage adjusted. As interest rates increased, so did their monthly payment until, eventually they were forced to sell or lose the house. Never go into an ARM planning to refinance before it adjusts. If interest rates go up, your income goes down, or lending practices change, you could end up worse off than before and left with fewer options. The last thing you want your home to do is become a burden to your family and your values. For these reasons, I rarely recommend adjustable-rate loans.

### Category Three: Creative Loans

In an effort to sell more loans, mortgage companies have become very creative at luring buyers who normally would not qualify for a traditional loan. Their creativity tends to be irresponsibility disguised as generosity. By "helping" consumers get into homes using creative loan designs, the lenders cover up facts that would typically prohibit people from purchasing real estate. A few of these loans would include Interest-Only mortgages, No Closing Cost mortgages, Negatively Amortizing loans, Hard Money loans or Sub-Prime mortgages. In order to continually sell these loans, the lenders will no doubt call them by different names as time goes by. Do not be quick to use a "new" type of mortgage. Following the mortgage industry's latest fad or trend usually hurts the homebuyer. Rather than examining the endless variety of Creative Loans one by one, let's look into the root causes for their existence.

What kind of customer necessitates the need for Creative Loans? A lender will try to brush the following facts under the rug by utilizing a more creative mortgage type:

I   Bad credit scores
I   High levels of debt relative to income
I   Not enough income for a traditional payment
I   Bankruptcy
I   Needing to close on a property very quickly
I   No available cash for a down payment

As a general rule, if you cannot qualify for or afford the payment on a traditional fixed-rate mortgage at a competitive interest rate, there is a good reason why. Loans that pretend to help such buyers are almost never good for the consumer.

People who are struggling with one or more of the factors above are less likely to discuss their personal finances with other people. They usually ask fewer questions than a more qualified buyer would. Hence, many lenders will take advantage of their situations and pretend they are doing the consumer a favor by allowing them to purchase real estate when they probably should be renting. To make matters worse, many of these Creative Loans carry incredibly high interest rates, prohibitive pre-payment penalties, and hidden costs that take advantage of less-qualified buyers.

### When to Use a Creative Loan

**I do not recommend using any form of Creative Loan to buy real estate.** If you find yourself unable to qualify for the standard 30-year fixed mortgage, you would be better off to first take care of the underlying reasons why. This may mean renting for another six to twelve months (or more in the case of a previous bankruptcy). This is okay. After you have removed the obstacles (bad credit, inadequate cash flow, etc.) you should qualify for a more traditional loan with a competitive interest rate and no hidden surprises or complications.

## INTEREST RATE

Your rate is the second variable that affects how quickly your principal goes down. The type of loan you select will affect your interest rate, which is why you need to determine the variety of mortgage first; but then you need to find the best interest rate you can on that loan. Mortgage brokers and loan officers will try to get you to focus on the monthly payment rather than on the interest rate, especially with some of the Creative Loans. Don't be tempted into a bad mortgage by a low monthly payment. Remember, you want to increase your equity over time, and paying interest slows that process down. If you have low levels of debt, a good credit score, and cash at your disposal (as previous pillars teach you to), you ought to qualify for the most competitive interest rates available. Make sure you shop around at different lenders and brokers to be sure you get the best possible rate and loan terms.

If you already have a mortgage, should you refinance in order to lower your interest rate? That depends on how much lower you can go, as well as how much longer you will live in the home. Assuming reasonable closing costs and loan origination fees, you need to plan to be there at least a few more years and get a new rate at least one percentage point lower. If your time horizon is short, your fees high, or your rate decrease negligible, refinancing probably won't be worth your while.

## II. APPRECIATION

Appreciation is the second way to grow the *magic number* of home equity. Appreciation works very differently than payments toward principal. While payments come out of your pocket and rely solely on your efforts, most home appreciation occurs due to market forces beyond your control. Normally, in the long run homes do appreciate or go up in value. However, I want to be very clear that home values can be unpredictable and do go down, even for extended periods of time. Remember, your home qualifies as a true financial investment, and investing always involves some element of risk or uncertainty. Often during extended cycles of home appreciation, people forget that their homes can depreciate; such thinking has brought devastating financial losses to many families. The reality you must never ignore is that housing markets fluctuate just as other financial markets do. There are many factors that affect how and if your home will appreciate. In this section, we will examine the areas you *can* control: purchasing, maintaining, and selling a home.

## PURCHASING A HOME

How you purchase your home can dramatically affect its long-term potential for appreciation. When purchasing a home, you want to consider how much you can afford, the location, the resale potential, and the actual purchasing process itself.

## How Much Home Can You Really Afford?

I cannot overemphasize the importance of knowing how much home
you can actually afford. Every situation is unique, but the rule of thumb
for my clients is to never spend more than 30% of their gross income on
housing expenses. For example, an individual who makes $75,000 a year
should not spend more than $1,875 per month in housing expenses (30%
of $75,000 is $22,500 divided by 12 months = $1,875).

When using the 30% rule of thumb, you need to keep a couple of key
points in mind. First, I base my rule of thumb on using a conventional 30-
year fixed loan. Remember, you can use a number of Creative Loans to
squeeze your purchase price into an affordable monthly payment, but that
doesn't mean you can really afford the home. As I mentioned earlier, be
extremely cautious about using Creative Loans. Second, your total monthly
housing costs include more than just your monthly payment for principal
and interest. You need to take into consideration all of your housing costs
including insurance, utilities, maintenance, private mortgage insurance
(PMI), and any homeowners association fees. Depending on the age and
condition of your home, maintenance alone usually costs between 1-3% of
the total purchase price every year. The 30% rule of thumb includes all of
these expenses—your *total* housing costs.

Another important topic related to buying, owning, and selling a home
is taxation. Property taxes and capital gains taxes both have to be factored
into the true cost of home ownership. You should familiarize yourself
with local property tax rates so that you understand the full costs of being
a homeowner in your area. You can obtain detailed information online
or from your county and city offices about current and future property
tax rates and policies. When you sell a primary residence, a part of the
proceeds are free from capital gains taxes. At the date of this publication
the current exemption for a married couple who file their income taxes
jointly is the first $500,000. Talk to a qualified tax professional before you
sell any property or real estate to make sure you know your potential tax
liability from the sale.

Home ownership also typically offers a significant income tax
deduction. This applies to interest you pay over the course of the year
in your payments, as well as any interest paid to a lender when closing
on a loan that year. This benefit lets you put more of your earned income
to work instead of toward taxes. Although any tax break feels great and

helps financially, don't get caught up in basing your real estate investment decisions solely on tax benefits. I have seen too many people fail to pay off high-rate mortgages or home equity loans because they were worried about losing the tax deductions. People with a *Financial Greatness Mindset* do not want to pay thousands of dollars in extra annual interest just to save a few hundred in taxes each year.

## Location, Location, Location

Perhaps no variable plays a bigger role than *location* when it comes to growing the *magic number* through home appreciation. Unfortunately, predicting the best neighborhoods and properties to invest in for the long term can be difficult. The good news is that viewing your home through the lens of your values tends to vastly improve your home's appreciation potential. The following criteria form some general guidelines about what makes a great location. A neighborhood that offers these features appeals to some of the most commonly held values for homebuyers and therefore puts homes in that area in greater demand:

- Quality schools for children and a family-friendly neighborhood
- Within a relatively short commute to multiple employers
- Close to parks or other recreational areas
- Secluded enough to be quiet and safe with low levels of crime
- In a neighborhood that is clean and well-maintained
- Convenient access to shopping, medical facilities, airports, and so on

While you may not be able to find or afford a home that meets all of these criteria (and you may view others as equally important for your values), the more of them you have, the better the demand for a house like yours. Ultimately, demand for housing drives most of the appreciation in real estate values over time. Living in a place where more people want to live amplifies the potential increases in your home's value.

## Resale Potential

Although a good location sells a home more quickly than anything else, you also need to evaluate a potential home to make sure it does not have negative factors that will make it hard to sell. Even if you never plan to move, you cannot predict the future of your career, health, or family needs, so you need to be objective about your home's appeal to other buyers. For example, some people don't mind living near railroad lines and actually enjoy the frequent train whistles and rumbling of rail cars at all hours of the day and night. If you love trains, you wouldn't think that nearby tracks would make your home harder to sell (and thus affect its value over time). But most people see train tracks within a quarter mile of a home and keep right on looking somewhere else. Some people want a really big house, and some want a smaller home—look at the demographics in your area to get an idea of what size or style of houses will stay in the highest demand.

Countless factors can affect the eventual resale potential of a home, and of course it will be impossible to anticipate all of them. However, you can give your home a better chance at staying in high demand by considering the following areas before you buy:

I    Are the other homes and yards nearby attractive and well-maintained?

I    Is the home subject to noise from railroad tracks, freeways, airport routes, etc.?

I    Are there any nearby sources of strong odor, pollution, and so on?

I    Does the home have any layout quirks, like bedrooms without closets, wasted space, shortage of storage or bathrooms, too many stairs, and the like?

I    Are there any zoning ordinances or other rules restricting remodeling, building additions, landscaping, pets, and so on?

I    Does the home have potentially nice curb appeal?

I    Are there any structural concerns in the home? Will it require any major repairs?

I    Does the home have amenities like a garage, a good-sized yard, central heating and air, vaulted ceilings, fireplaces, and such that would be difficult to retrofit?

I    How big is the market for homes this size and with this layout?

## The Purchasing Process

Purchasing the right home usually requires hard work, time, patience, and eventually making a few necessary tradeoffs in order to stay in your price range. But finding a home you want to buy is only half the battle. You then have to make an offer on it, have the offer accepted, finalize your financing, close with a title company, and fit all of these meetings into your already busy life with precision timing. How does this process affect the potential appreciation in your home?

First, it affects the initial *value* of your purchase. When you get a "good deal" on something, you feel like you bought it for a good price. In this sense, the starting price of your home has a lot to do with its *initial value*—if you are buying at a high price, you have less room for subsequent appreciation. The principle of taking care of the things you can control applies here. You can't move the housing market on your own, but you can keep tabs on prices and be prepared to buy when values are lower. When you find the house you want, you need to be ready to make an offer and negotiate for the best value you can get. In other words, don't pay too much for a home out of ignorance.

Second, the purchasing process affects your ability to actually complete a home purchase. When you have home financing already lined up before you begin searching for homes, you can negotiate price and timing with more authority. You will also be given priority by agents and sellers over buyers with sketchy or no financing. Another benefit to starting this process before you shop for a home is that you will have a much clearer picture of your total house payments and what you can really afford. This will not only help you negotiate with sellers, it will help you search for appropriate homes more effectively.

Third, what you do during the purchasing process can literally keep you from being suckered into a bad deal. Once you close on a home, there is no changing your mind. You are stuck with any problems the home or the mortgage have, so you need to be exceptionally thorough when purchasing real estate.

So what can you do to get a better buy, give yourself more negotiating power, and eliminate the possibility of bad deals?

1.  Shop for lenders based on the rates they will offer you and the level of attention they will give to seeing the

loan through to a timely closing. Often there is room for negotiation on the rate if your credit score or down payment is high enough. When you have narrowed your list down to two or three lenders **ask for a written "Good Faith Estimate"** before making your final choice. This will allow you to compare the total costs of each loan. Also, find out if you have any say in which title company will be used. You can follow the same pattern there, shopping first for price and then asking for a detailed estimate before making your final choice.

2.      **Become preapproved** with your lender, or at the very least prequalified. *Preapproval* means the lender agrees in advance to lend you up to a certain amount of money for a home purchase, subject to some basic conditions being met and an offer being made on a house within a set period of time. *Prequalification* means the lender believes that you are credit-worthy and will most likely be approved for a home loan should you apply there. However, no underwriting or in-depth assessment has been done, so being prequalified does not impress sellers as much as being preapproved. Always get the preapproval or prequalification in writing from the lender, so you can bring it with you to the negotiating table.

3.      **Watch the home market** in your area for at least three months (and ideally six or more) before you start the buying process. Essentially, you want to "curb shop" homes in neighborhoods where you might consider buying and track their price fluctuations. You can do this on the Internet or with a good real estate agent or just by calling the numbers on "For Sale" signs. This will help you get a feel for what kind of trend the market is in, how many homes are on the market, how fast homes are selling, and where you want to focus your search. This also helps when you are in the final purchasing phase because

you will have seen plenty of other homes to compare
to when you are negotiating and evaluating the home
you do buy.

4.        You should *always* have a thorough **professional
          home inspection** done before closing on any real
          estate purchase. Then if a major problem with the
          home is discovered, you can back out with minimal
          cost rather than finding yourself in a living nightmare
          later on with no way out. Having a full inspection
          also provides you with more leverage when you are
          negotiating final price. You may also want to order a
          full walk-through appraisal of the home, as this can
          identify further opportunities to negotiate a better
          deal.

5.        Ask for a copy of the **HUD-1 settlement statement**
          from your mortgage broker or lender and review it
          *before* the actual closing. This will allow you to verify
          that nothing has been altered and that the loan costs
          and conditions are exactly as agreed on. If the lender
          has made any errors or changes, catching them before
          you sign your name may save you big time down the
          road. Pay careful attention to any possible hidden
          fees and avoid all prepayment penalties—these can
          be elusive but they will be in the HUD-1 if you look
          closely.

6.        **Slow down!** The most costly home-buying mistakes
          are usually made when the buyer feels rushed or
          pressured. Prepare mentally and follow the steps
          above so that you can be sure about the decisions you
          make during the purchasing process.

A note about refinancing an existing mortgage: the same underlying
principles apply as in a purchase situation. Steps 1, 5, and 6 above are just
as important when refinancing as when buying a new home.

## HOME MAINTENANCE and IMPROVEMENTS

Keeping a well-maintained home and yard is important for your quality of life, as well as for realizing positive appreciation in your home's value. If you let your home fall into disrepair, it can lose a surprising amount of market value. The worse state your home is in, the less money potential buyers would be willing to pay for it (and the more it will cost you in time and money to fix it up again). By staying on top of maintenance issues, you will protect your home as an investment while enjoying greater comfort and peace in your home as a residence. Every homeowner needs to budget and set aside an appropriate amount each month towards repairs, deep cleaning, and other maintenance costs.

Upgrades and home improvements can be another way to inject value into your home. However, such projects need to strike a balance between adding value to your everyday quality of life and getting a decent return on your investment. In other words, you need to be realistic about how much value an upgrade might bring to your home's price versus how much you spend on the upgrade. Will installing a swimming pool and hot tub that cost you $40,000 increase your home's market value by $40,000? Typically not even close. Generally speaking, you get the best return on your investment when improving your kitchen, remodeling bathrooms, adding bedrooms, or enhancing curb appeal (how the house appears from the street). Fifty-dollar shutters and a new paint job may end up improving demand for your home more effectively than building a new deck or sun room. Do your homework about the real costs of any upgrades you are considering and find out if buyers in your area usually put a premium on such improvements—and do it *before* you get halfway into the project!

### Should I Finance A Home Improvement?

I am often asked whether borrowing money for a home improvement is okay. Opinions vary widely on the topic, but my answer depends (as usual) on the facts as they relate to your core values. Let me use an example of what I mean.

Suppose the Jones family realizes their home has gone up a good deal in value and they are receiving offers from their bank to take out a special-rate home improvement loan. They have wanted to put hardwood flooring on the main floor and finish the basement for some time but they have not been able to save much for these projects. The loan payments would be manageable and they have a fully funded *Financial Confidence Account*™. They could put off the projects, but it would take at least three years before they could save enough to pay for them outright. Would this home improvement loan fall into the "acceptable" debt category?

The answer in this case depends on two things: how much the improvements will enhance the Joneses' quality of life (the present value received) and how much they will increase their home's value. In this case, finishing the basement will add a family game room and two bedrooms, greatly relieving the crowded upstairs sleeping arrangements and giving the older kids their own rooms. The flooring in the kitchen and dining room would replace worn out linoleum that never looks clean anymore and just feels disgusting to live with. The Joneses would receive immediate, ongoing, and highly enjoyable benefits by implementing both of these projects. The additional rooms and the improvement to the look and feel of the kitchen would definitely add market value to the home immediately. And since the Joneses will be able to make extra payments on the loan, they can pay it off in less than four years.

Having considered all of the factors in this example, my advice to the Joneses would be to go ahead and make the improvements but don't get carried away. If they stick to the principles we have been discussing, evaluating the real costs and the real potential benefits and returns, they will be making a calculated investment in their home and their lives.

One other example will illustrate what I DON'T want to see you do with your home equity. The Green family across the street from the Joneses has also seen their home go up in value. They really like what the Jones family did to their home and decide they need to keep up with their neighbors. They go to their bank to apply for a home equity loan, but because they aren't sure how much they will need for their projects, they take out an equity line as well. Unfortunately, their credit is below average and both the loan and line of credit carry fairly high rates. Now, the Greens have no children left at home, so they won't really benefit from having extra bedrooms. Instead, they install a home theatre room, an exercise room, and a hobby room in their basement. Upstairs they have the finest (and most expensive) hardwood flooring put in to really impress the neighbors. When all is said and done, they are much more in debt on the projects than they thought they would be. Mr. Green takes on a night job to keep up with the payments, so he never gets to enjoy his home theatre. Mrs. Green succumbs to the temptation of the open credit line and adds to their debt with pricey additions to her wardrobe.

I think you can guess what my advice to the Greens would have been: don't bother with the home improvements—they won't improve your life or your home as an investment enough to make them worth it. I would also have told them that their poor credit indicated that they had discipline issues and therefore should save up and pay cash for all of their major purchases whenever possible.

## Home Improvement Financing Options

If you determine that borrowing money to improve your home will be a worthy and affordable investment for you, the best way to finance the project is usually to borrow *against* the equity in your home. Securing the loan with your home's value will get you a better rate than with an unsecured loan, and the interest you pay will usually be tax deductible. I also find that my clients take the whole process more seriously when their home is on the line, and that leads to better and more careful decisions about how much to borrow, what type of financing to use, and which projects to complete.

There are three basic ways to borrow against your home's equity for upgrades and improvements:

1. **Home Equity Loans**: Essentially these loans operate like a second mortgage, amortizing the principal and interest over a set term from 5-25 years. They usually carry a fixed rate 1-3% above the prime lending rate. These are ideal for relatively large projects where you are fairly certain of the amount of money you will need. If you find you can't afford the loan payments unless you stretch them fifteen years or more, you should probably rethink your improvement plans and save up for them instead. The higher rate will be hard to overcome through appreciation, so you have to be very careful not to overextend yourself just because you really want something.

2.  **Cash Out Refinancing**: This involves refinancing your existing
    mortgage but for a higher amount than you currently owe. You
    receive cash for the additional amount of the loan and start over
    with a new amortized term. Sometimes I see people employ this
    strategy as an alternative to the higher rate of a Home Equity
    Loan. Instead of borrowing $20,000 for 25 years in a 9% Home
    Equity Loan, they refinance their mortgage for $20,000 extra at
    6% for 30 years. This sounds like the better option, but you need
    to keep two things in mind. First, the refinance will probably
    cost several thousand dollars in loan origination fees, closing
    costs, and so forth. The Home Equity Loan likely has minimal
    fees, if any. Second, spreading a home improvement loan over
    so many years indicates to me that you really can't afford the
    loan right now. You basically erase a huge chunk of your equity
    and start the *magic number* over again when you borrow more
    than you should or for too long. There are two situations where a
    Cash Out Refinance makes sense: when your alternative to home
    improvements would be moving and buying a new house, or
    when you are leveraging the equity in an investment property. In
    most other cases, my advice would be to avoid this type of loan.

3.  **Home Equity Lines of Credit (HELOC):** Unlike the first two
    options, a HELOC does not have an amortized term. Interest is
    paid on the average outstanding balance of a variable rate line
    of credit. A HELOC has two advantages for home improvement
    funding. First, you can borrow only what you actually need when
    you actually need it. This means less loan balance to owe interest
    on. Second, when you pay off the balance on a HELOC it
    becomes available for use again. This means you can attack your
    projects in stages, only borrowing what you can pay back in a
    reasonably short period, and not have to get a new loan for each
    project. Normally, you don't want to use a HELOC to fund a
    larger home improvement like a remodel or addition, because the
    variable rate represents too much risk should rates rise suddenly.
    The other drawback to a line of credit is the temptation to use
    it for things you don't need. You can get yourself into financial
    trouble using a HELOC inappropriately. I often recommend that
    many of my clients set up a HELOC as a backup emergency

account but I also caution them to be very careful with this
strategy. If they are not disciplined or if they are tempted to
borrow money for consumer items, they would be better off
without one.

# SELLING A HOME

For most people, the equity they build in their homes doesn't greatly affect
their lives until they sell the home and the *magic number* is suddenly
handed to them. The average person has only a vague idea what their home
might sell for, and usually they are way off the mark. While people do
tap into their home equity for business investments, home improvements,
sending kids to college, and other uses, most often the appreciation in
one home goes towards the purchase of the next one. Regardless of what
you do with your home equity, you don't want to lose potential equity
by selling your home for less than you could. Making some preliminary
selling preparations will help you maximize the price your home fetches.
What can you do?

The first step is usually to enlist a good Realtor® who will work with
you to prepare your home for selling. Your real estate agent will be well-
paid when your home sells, so don't be afraid to demand a lot from him or
her. They should be able to help you enhance the curb appeal of your home,
simplify your interior decorating to help buyers see themselves living in
the home, and determine an appropriate asking price. If your Realtor®
does not have the experience, knowledge, or time to give you this level of
service, get a new agent. If your agent pushes you to set a price that you
know is too low, then they are more interested in a quick and easy sale (and
commission) than in your best interests. A good agent will also work with
you to make sure that buyers can be shown the home at almost any time,
and even put on open houses if necessary.

If you are in no rush to sell your home but instead can wait as long as
you need to, you could consider listing your home "For Sale by Owner."
You risk settling for a lower price due to a lack of interested buyers, but
if you feel qualified to prepare your home for showings, maximize the
curb appeal, and market the home to a decent pool of buyers, you could
save some money by not paying a real estate agent's commission. In my
experience, the majority of people greatly overestimate their ability to do

better selling on their own than they could with a Realtor®.

The same rules apply when enlisting the services of a real estate agent or mortgage broker as when finding a good financial advisor. These professionals can be valuable members of your financial team if used properly. The more knowledge and education you have regarding the process of finding, financing, improving, and selling homes, the better job a good real estate agent can do for you.

## GUARD THE MAGIC NUMBER

If you follow the principles outlined in Pillar Six, you will increase your net worth by increasing your equity. Statistics show that a large portion of most people's wealth resides in their home equity. Interestingly, this is not so much due to the performance of real estate as it is to the *nature* of real estate. Home ownership *forces* people to implement some of the fundamental principles of Financial Greatness—usually without even knowing it!

For example, simply by paying their mortgage every month, people are applying a long-term strategic investment strategy, putting their savings on autopilot, and investing in an appreciating asset. Paying a mortgage every month is one of the most common automatic savings plans that people participate in. That is the "magic" in the *magic number*.

Another reason why a large portion of people's wealth is in their home equity is the difficulty involved in accessing it. It used to be almost impossible to tap into your home equity, but it has become much easier in recent years. While still more difficult to access than a regular savings or checking account, Home Equity Loans and Lines of Credit are readily available to decrease your *magic number*. Be very cautious about using your home equity. Like the money invested in your retirement accounts, I encourage you to view home equity as off limits. Give your *magic number* a chance to grow over time.

> **You need to be much more careful with your home equity than your parents were with theirs.**

Financial institutions and retailers are getting smarter and more aggressive at coming after your home equity. Banks, credit card companies, and retail stores are acutely aware of your *magic number* and they want you to use it! Banks and credit card companies want you to borrow against your home equity, so that you can pay them more interest. Retail stores want to free up your home equity so you can purchase more "stuff" than you could afford without the equity.

Those who walk the path to Financial Greatness <u>almost never</u> borrow against their home equity. There are only two exceptions to this rule and we need to be careful even with these exceptions. The only two exceptions are for a home improvement project that will increase the value of your home or for an extreme financial emergency. Money borrowed from your home's equity should *never* be used to purchase consumer items—*<u>EVER.</u>* The Greens from our earlier example broke this rule repeatedly, blowing their home equity on theatre equipment and luxury items. Don't fall into the consumer trap: guard your *magic number* and only use your home equity as a last resort.

I hope that by now you understand better why I want you to view your home as the heart of your values as well as the heart of your investing. One additional benefit to this dual perspective is that it prepares you to become a more effective real estate investor overall. Thousands of books have been written about real estate investing, but none of them can teach you as much about the subject as actually turning the home in which you live into a successful investment. Pillar Six perfectly exemplifies the symbolism of an architectural pillar: enhancing your quality of life (like a pillar adds to the beauty of the structure) while building your net worth (like a pillar supports the entire building).

If the principles I am teaching you in this book haven't fully clicked for you yet, now is a good time to go back and work on the doer checklists. Pillar Six should make sense to anyone with a *Financial Greatness Mindset*, and the best way to adopt that outlook is to apply what I present to you. If you HAVE been taking action as you've been reading, great work! Only two more pillars to go and you will be well on your way to Financial Greatness!

**Thoughts, Feelings, and Ideas** – What are some of the thoughts or feelings you had while reading Chapter Eighteen? What insights occurred to you while reading? Did any particular action ideas pop into your mind as you read?

_____

_____

_____

_____

_____

_____

_____

_____

_____

_____

_____

Can you see why it is important to grow and safeguard the *magic number*?

How will growing and safeguarding your home's equity specifically help you reach Financial Greatness?

_____

_____

_____

_____

_____

_____

## DOER CHECKLIST – CHAPTER 18

☐    I am committed to growing and guarding my home's equity.

☐    When purchasing or refinancing a home, I will use a simple fixed-rate loan that I completely understand unless I have a very good, sound reason to do otherwise.

☐    Because I have applied my knowledge from Pillars One, Two, and Three by having adequate cash, low levels of debt, and a credit score of 720 or higher, I am committed to getting the most competitive interest rate available.

☐    I will purchase a home that does not cost me more than 30% of my gross income to pay for and maintain.

☐    I will increase my home's chances for appreciation by always applying what I have learned about finding, buying, maintaining, and selling homes.

☐    I will be very careful about tapping into my *magic number* for any reason.

# PILLAR SEVEN

## *Maximize Your Money-Making Machine*

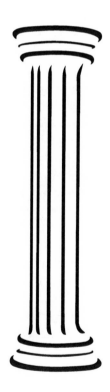

## CHAPTER 19

# CREATING VALUE

Each of the first six pillars focused on how to manage your money with a *Financial Greatness Mindset*. Pillar Seven will now take a step beyond *managing* the money you make and focus on helping you *make more money*.

If you are like me, you probably work to earn a living. Whether self-employed or working for an organization, the money you receive from your occupation funds your investments, pays for your lifestyle, and buys the insurance that protects you. In this way, your "earned" income is the engine that powers your financial plans. I believe that the *size* of your paycheck (or the bottom line from your business) matters <u>less</u> than the proper *management* of that income. However, your ability to reach Financial Greatness does depend on increasing and safeguarding your income over time.

The central purpose of investing is to get your *money working for you*. When your money makes additional money your economic engine gains horsepower. But usually before you have anything to invest, you have to *work for money*.

Your money-making potential over the course of your career represents one of your single largest assets. A twenty-five year-old person who earns $50,000 per year for forty years has made $2 million in his or her career. Assuming pay raises that keep pace with a 5% inflation rate, such a worker will earn $6,039,989 during his or her lifetime. Here is the real kicker: these figures do not calculate the *present value* of this worker's future earnings. If you were to insure this worker's future earnings potential in full (right now) for the next forty years, it would require a death benefit of $4,492,320 (based on a $50,000 salary and a 6% investment return). Paying the premium on that policy would take most people's entire paycheck!

Ultimately, the income from your economic engine depends on how effective you are at _creating value for others._ You have the potential to generate far more than $50,000 per year for the rest of your career. People earn what the market is willing to pay them; those who create the most value in the market are consistently rewarded financially. Usually, the more risks you take with your vocation (i.e., the more entrepreneurial you are), the higher your potential earnings from your work. Whether your working market is a specific company, an industry, a government, or the mass of consumers, you make money by creating value that others are willing to pay for. Creating value is exactly what I mean by working _for_ money.

Every time I mention working for money, I want you to think of what money really means to you and your family. The idea of becoming "rich" has infected society with an epidemic case of what John Stossel calls "affluenza." People have become so fixated on the pursuit of wealth for wealth's sake that they frequently fail to find satisfaction financially.

Money is only worth what you value it for. You can value money for the roof it keeps over your head, the food it puts on your table, the comforts and conveniences it provides, or the memories and experiences it affords you. You can enjoy the peace of mind that comes from having your finances under control, your loved ones protected from hardship, and your economic freedom secured. But valuing money for money's sake does not yield true enjoyment. If you work only to amass wealth, you may end up "rich" but you will have completely missed the Financial Greatness boat. By working to _create value for others_, you generate income to fund your own values without missing the point of what money really means to you.

How can you create the kind of value for others that will fuel your economic engine? The answer is simple. Invest in your greatest financial asset and most important money-making machine: **YOU**. Maximizing your money-making machine requires you to view yourself with a _Financial Greatness Mindset._ This means putting as much forethought, time, effort, and care into managing your career (income sources) as you do to managing the rest of your financial health. It also means maintaining a balance between _making money_ and _enjoying money._ Just as you should invest _for_ happiness and not just for asset growth, you need to work _for_ the values that money represents to you and not just to be affluent. Income management really comes down to developing your capacity to create value for others while working to secure your own values.

## THE IMPORTANCE OF PILLAR SEVEN

Your earning potential has no limits, so from the standpoint of possible ROI (Return on Investment), the principles in Pillar Seven can have more financial impact than all of the other pillars combined. Managing your career should be an important aspect to your overall financial plan. Pillar Seven can have a multiplying effect on the rest of your financial goals. Increasing your income magnifies your ability to live each of the other pillars. Funding a *Financial Confidence Account™,* saving for specific goals, breaking the bonds of debt, paying for insurance, funding investments, and home ownership all require income sources. The higher your income goes, the faster you can implement *The 8 Pillars™.*

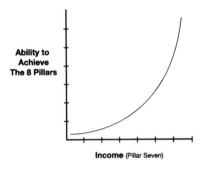

**Income** (Pillar Seven)

Of course, *knowing* what you should do with increased income and actually *doing it* are two very different things. Most people allow their budget to immediately expand and consume every little bonus, raise, or new income source that comes their way. This is why <u>each</u> of *The 8 Pillars™* is so important and interrelated.

## THE VALUE CREATION MATRIX ™

What kinds of investments in yourself will help you manage your career and increase your income? Pillar Seven introduces you to *The Value Creation Matrix™,* a powerful tool that teaches you how to gain greater rewards from the marketplace. It shows the relationship between the *Type of Work* you do and the *Value Created* by your efforts. This relationship determines where you fall on the matrix (Wage, Opportunity, Profit, Excellence, or

Greatness) and usually corresponds with how much income you generate. The matrix is designed to help an individual move from <u>Wage</u> to <u>Greatness</u>. Let's take a closer look at *The Value Creation Matrix*™ and discuss how this tool can help you achieve Financial Greatness.

### The Value Creation Matrix ™

Value Created

|  | Labor | Ideas | Leadership |
|---|---|---|---|
| **Work for Employer** | *Wage* | *Opportunity* | *Profit* |
| **Work for Self** | *Opportunity* | *Profit* | *Excellence* |
| **Work for a Cause** | *Profit* | *Excellence* | *Greatness* |

*(Type of Work)*

*The Value Creation Matrix*™ illustrates that the results you merit depend on the *Type of Work* you do and the *Value Created* in the workplace. As you study and further understand the matrix, *The Five Levels of Financial Merit*™ will emerge.

### *The Five Levels of Financial Merit*™ are:

1. Wage
2. Opportunity
3. Profit
4. Excellence
5. Greatness

Take a moment to review the matrix and how the *Type of Work* you do and the *Value Created* by your efforts determine one of *The Five Levels of Financial Merit*™. For example: if you <u>Work for an Employer</u> by using your <u>Labor</u>, you earn a **Wage**. In contrast, if you <u>Work for a Cause</u> using <u>Leadership</u>, you will achieve **Greatness**.

# THREE <u>TYPES OF WORK</u>

Listed on the left side of the matrix, you will find the three basic <u>Types of Work</u>.

1.  You can **Work for an Employer**. This would include a government, public or private company, non-profit organization, small business, or any other entity that pays you to do a job. Employers have to pay employment taxes, follow labor laws, and compete for the best workers by offering benefits, competitive wages, good working conditions, and so on. The employer also withholds your income taxes for you (not that they are doing you a favor—this is simply how the IRS has automated their income tax system!) and has a high degree of control over how you do your job.

2.  You can **Work for Yourself.** This would include owning your own business or professional practice, contracting as a business to do work for other entities, actively investing your money for a living, and any other for-profit ventures you put your energy and resources into. Working for yourself can have significant tax advantages versus working for an employer and can also give you greater income potential (naturally accompanied by an increased risk of financial loss). Most self-employed people also cite the advantages of having greater control and autonomy over their work than employees do.

3.   You can **Work for a Cause** that you are passionate about. Whether you are paid for it right away or not, you do this kind of work because you believe in a cause larger than yourself. You can work for a cause as an employee, as an independent consultant, as a business owner, or as a volunteer for the sake of the cause alone. The amazing thing about working for a cause is that even if the immediate financial rewards are minimal, the work you do for the purposes you most care about tends to yield better long-term results than any other work you will do. Income follows those who pursue what they are most passionate about in their vocations.

## THREE WAYS <u>VALUE IS CREATED</u>

Across the top of the matrix are listed the three ways <u>Value is Created</u>.

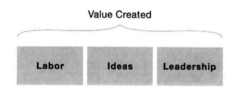

1.   <u>**Labor:**</u> You can create value through personal time and effort—what I call *labor*. Not all labor has to be drudgery, but it does require hard work to create value through labor. Working an hourly job or a set schedule always involves labor at a minimum, though you can create value in the other two ways *while* laboring to earn a living. Investing long hours into getting a new business off the ground or handling the day-to-day management of your own business practice would also fall into the labor category. No one can deny the positive results from the many forms of labor we all participate in. The marketplace will always pay the most skilled or specialized workers with the highest financial rewards.

2. **Ideas:** You can create value by contributing *ideas*, advances, and innovations to the marketplace. Rather than drawing mainly on your time and physical energy, ideas spring from creative thinking, problem solving, and cooperation with others. The market puts a high premium on good ideas and inventive thinking, so working at the level of ideas carries a lot of earning potential. However, unless you can find a way to capitalize on your ideas by turning them into opportunities, they may never materialize into career advancement, business success, and so on.

3. **Leadership:** You can create value by providing *leadership* in your sphere of influence. Perhaps no quality is more in demand in our society than effective leadership. The marketplace consistently rewards leaders in every field and every industry. Leaders excel at creating and seizing opportunities for their organizations and inspire those they work with to strive for greatness. Every person no matter what his or her vocation or temperament has the potential to become a leader in some aspect of their life. Even if this does not *directly* increase a person's financial rewards, leadership characteristics impact and spill over into the other work that a person may do. Labor could be called working hard. Contributing Ideas could be termed working smart. In contrast, *Leadership* can be viewed as getting *others* to work harder and smarter.

The goal of *The Value Creation Matrix*™ is not to persuade you to quit your day job and become an entrepreneur. Financial Greatness does not depend solely on the type of work you do. Many popular books on personal finance and most real-estate investing gurus constantly chant the mantra that you will never get rich as an employee—I disagree. Further, you do not need to become "rich" in order to achieve Financial Greatness. While business ownership does provide excellent opportunities (perhaps even the most and the best opportunities) to build personal wealth, not everyone has the desire, aptitude, or outlook necessary to succeed in business. Nor could our economy survive without the millions of employees who work in a host of dynamic industries. Likewise, most people lack the desire, ability, or stomach to become a full-time, professional investor.

With that said, you will see from *The Value Creation Matrix*™ that financial excellence and greatness usually don't stem from working only for employers. Most people who reach Financial Greatness as employees have something else going "on the side" or retire early from their corporate careers to pursue more independent work.

The potential tax benefits alone of working for yourself usually make that route to Financial Greatness faster than the employee path. In addition, everyone who wants to succeed financially needs to learn to invest, even if they don't do so full time. Having your money work for you makes true Financial Greatness possible.

No matter what type of work you do or *want* to do, I firmly believe in the value of education—both formal and informal. Education can open doors and unearth resources you would not have discovered otherwise. Higher education and specialized training have value in the marketplace, and so increase your ability to earn income while creating value for others. Continuous self-education is crucial for anyone with a career, business, or cause to advance.

So, how then does the intersection of the *Types of Work* you do and the *Value Created* by your efforts impact your income? The rest of this chapter will take you through *The Five Levels of Financial Merit*™ (Wage, Opportunity, Profit, Excellence, and Greatness) and what they mean to your money making machine.

## LEVEL ONE: WAGE

Everyone who has ever held a job or worked for a hard day's pay has experienced the first level of Financial Merit. Earning a wage requires only an *employer* willing to pay and a *laborer* willing to work. The variety of jobs performed for wages has no limit, and the amount paid in wages differs dramatically from one job to the next. Through diligent effort, networking, training, education, and experience, you can increase your wage level many times over throughout your life.

Value Created

| | Labor | Ideas | Leadership |
|---|---|---|---|
| **Work for Employer** | Wage | Opportunity | Profit |
| **Work for Self** | Opportunity | Profit | Excellence |
| **Work for a Cause** | Profit | Excellence | Greatness |

*Type of Work*

Wage earners have one major problem: if they stop working, they stop making money. Their income has very little if any residual properties. Their work can be interrupted or made obsolete by industry changes, company restructuring, economic slowdowns, technological advances, disability or chronic illness, and a host of other causes. Losing your wage is the primary risk at this level of Financial Merit. Since almost everyone starts out at this level and most people stay there for the majority of their careers, proper insurance is crucial to protect against the "what ifs" of wage loss.

Again, I want to emphasize that earning wages, working for a paycheck, and being an employee DO have value. Wage earners turn the gears of society, the economy, and the world. Unfortunately, there is very little security in being a wage earner. If you ever want to *stop* working or achieve Financial Greatness, you need to *start* meriting income from additional sources—ideally, sources that don't depend solely on the hours you put in at work.

## LEVEL TWO: <u>OPPORTUNITY</u>

How do you take the first step beyond toiling year after year for a wage? You seek additional *income opportunities*. Income opportunities result from either doing a different type of work or creating value in a different way than you do now. If we look at *The Value Creation Matrix*™, we see that the second level of merit results from your creative <u>*Ideas*</u> at work or from <u>*Working for Yourself.*</u>

Value Created

| Type of Work | | Labor | Ideas | Leadership |
|---|---|---|---|---|
| | **Work for Employer** | Wage | **Opportunity** | Profit |
| | **Work for Self** | **Opportunity** | Profit | Excellence |
| | **Work for a Cause** | Profit | Excellence | Greatness |

Let's look at two hypothetical examples. Anne M. Ployee works for the Kash Korporation. She works hard and earns an average hourly wage. One day she has a bright idea that ends up making her 25% more effective at her job. Anne's supervisor asks her to train the others on her team to implement her ideas, and soon the team becomes number one in the region. In due course, Anne's supervisor gets promoted, and guess who moves into the vacant position? Anne does, and she continues to create value by innovating in her new role. Before long, a competing company comes knocking at her door with a great offer to come work for them. You get the idea—Anne has created value beyond her ordinary job description and her money making opportunities keep growing as a result.

For our second example, let's introduce Andre Prenure. Andre grew tired of selling products he didn't believe in for a boss he didn't agree with, and decided to go into business for himself. At first he had to work more hours than he ever did at his old job, and he wasn't earning as much or as stable an income as before. But he could see the potential in his market and knew the opportunity was there to make an attractive income. Andre labored in his own enterprise because he knew he was priming his money-making machine for peak performance in the future.

In each of these examples, an individual moved from the level of *earning a wage* to the level of *opportunity*. This does not happen by itself, or without some risks; any time you give up something known and comfortable for something unknown and new, you have an element of risk. Anne has no guarantees that changing companies will benefit her career or work out better than staying where she is. Andre has no assurance that his business will succeed or even stay viable long-term. But opportunities for better income resulted from managing the way each worker created value. The opportunities from *creating value through creative ideas* for an employer and from *laboring for yourself* instead of an employer tend to outweigh the risks. A shift in either direction can unlock new potential income for anyone who feels stuck in the "meaningless job" rut.

A note on business ownership: starting a business *always* involves some form of risk.There are no sure things in business, and even a skilled and experienced professional has to work very hard to compete for customers and stay profitable in today's marketplace. In my experience, self-employed individuals and small business owners work harder than anyone else and have little financial reward to show for it at first. In the beginning of most entrepreneurial ventures, all you really have is an *opportunity*. Keep in mind that the risks of business failure and financial loss are real and need to be prepared for. However, the potential risks of business ownership are matched by tremendous income opportunities.

## LEVEL THREE: <u>PROFIT</u>

You can turn your opportunities into what I call *profit* when you make another shift to the next level of merit. By profit, I mean income that does not rely so much on your immediate efforts. How can you receive this kind of income? Let's go back to our example of Andre and see what he did. After struggling for two years, he came up with a breakthrough way to market his business and revenues took off, kicking Andre's money-making machine into high gear. What changed from the early days of his business? He shifted from creating value by his own <u>Labor</u> to creating value through his <u>Ideas</u>.

| | | Value Created | | |
|---|---|---|---|---|
| | | **Labor** | **Ideas** | **Leadership** |
| Type of Work | **Work for Employer** | Wage | Opportunity | **Profit** |
| | **Work for Self** | Opportunity | **Profit** | Excellence |
| | **Work for a Cause** | **Profit** | Excellence | Greatness |

When you work for yourself, you work not for a simple wage but for potential profits. You take on more risk by having a stake in these profits, since profits can be a fickle thing to maintain. But greater risk does allow for greater returns, and there are hundreds of thousands of successful and profitable small businesses in this country that prove it every year. Building a business that achieves long-term success takes more than just hard work. Business owners need to constantly reinvent and innovate to keep up with changing demands, competition, and economic cycles. In other words, they need to create value by relentlessly infusing their businesses with the right _Ideas_ and creative thinking. A restaurant owner may go work the kitchen from time to time, but he doesn't make his money by cooking— his income springs from the profits of the restaurant. If he only owned the restaurant so he could have an hourly job to work, he would be taking unnecessary risk and missing out on the real returns. A business owner needs to work smarter, not more hours, to see his venture succeed.

But what if you really don't want to go into business at all? Is it possible to make profits as an employee? Yes, you can earn profits from your employer but not usually through simple labor or even good ideas. No matter how hard you work for your boss or how many great ideas you come up with for your company, you are probably only earning your keep and hopefully furthering your career there. However, you can create more value by obtaining a _Leadership_ position in a company. Company leaders are generally treated and compensated as de facto owners. They share in the profits of their organization through limited partnerships, profit-sharing plans, stock options, profit-based bonuses, and the like. The corporate ladder can take years to climb, but essentially it has three rungs: laborers at the bottom, managers (idea workers) in the middle, and leaders at the top. And the leaders of companies can certainly make impressive, profit-based incomes.

## Corporate Ladder

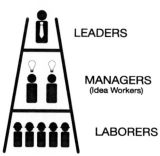

LEADERS

MANAGERS
(Idea Workers)

LABORERS

Let's return to the example of Anne M. Ployee, where we find that she has worked her way into management and has done very well for several years. While continuing to put in plenty of hours (labor) and make innovative changes (ideas) at her company, Anne's real career goal is to be an executive with the firm. What does she most need in order to reach this goal? The attribute of leadership. Leaders don't just manage other people, they inspire them. Leaders know how to get the most effective efforts out of those they lead. Leaders take ownership in their work and think like owners in their day-to-day decisions. If Anne can demonstrate these qualities, over time she may achieve her goal to be a company executive.

So we have seen what a shift to the right on the matrix means for an employee and for a business owner, but those are not the only options for reaping profits. Many business leaders (both owners and executives) eventually grow tired of corporate pressures and the constant struggle to stay competitive. Often they turn to causes more important to them than money and devote their experience and knowledge to work they are truly passionate about.

One of the greatest enigmas about income is that it often increases the most when you are least focused on it. When you are laboring for a cause you believe in, every hour you spend and every victory won count as profit for you. Even if you labor for no pay in the service of a worthwhile cause, income will somehow find you. Though not always in the short term, over time the world best rewards those who create the most value for others. Hence, a shift *down* the matrix will also land you at the profit-making level, even if you are only giving your spare time (labor) to a worthy cause.

## LEVEL FOUR: <u>EXCELLENCE</u>

Excellence in the type of work you do literally means taking it to another level. To excel is to surpass or outdo, and to move to this level of merit requires a shift towards providing superior value to your marketplace. When working for yourself or a cause you prize, you can achieve this level of merit by shifting to the right on the matrix. The result of moving from a busy, creative, self-employed individual to a business leader who gets others to work harder and smarter for him or her is *excellence*. The result of putting not just your time and energy into a worthy cause but your ideas and creativity into it as well accomplishes the same shift—to a level of excellence that mere labor cannot match.

| | Value Created | | |
|---|---|---|---|
| **Type of Work** | **Labor** | **Ideas** | **Leadership** |
| **Work for Employer** | Wage | Opportunity | Profit |
| **Work for Self** | Opportunity | Profit | **Excellence** |
| **Work for a Cause** | Profit | **Excellence** | Greatness |

Does this mean that you cannot achieve Excellence if you work for an employer? Absolutely not. Remember, you can do more than one type of work at the same time. Excellence flows out of passion, personal commitment, and character. When you obtain a level of excellence in any organization, it feeds on itself in a self-reinforcing cycle. Excellence opens up further opportunities, which create greater profits, which fuel more excellence and opportunities for success.

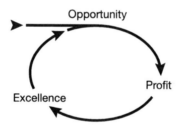

This cycle applies to employees as much as it does to business owners; however, I rarely see excellence in companies whose employees do not fully believe in the mission of the company. When a company creates compelling value through its products and services, people working for that company can simultaneously work for the causes it represents *and* for their paychecks. Companies that do not have this higher sense of purpose may still be very profitable financially, but they will never attain the income and profits merited by companies who reach the level of true excellence. The same principle applies to individuals—it takes a healthy dose of purpose and passion to achieve excellence in your field, company, business, practice, or life.

## LEVEL FIVE: <u>GREATNESS</u>

The seeds of Financial Greatness are being sown when you feel compelled by a cause greater than yourself to blaze new trails, set new standards, raise the bar, or change the world! Greatness comes when the work you engage in means more than the income itself. Greatness occurs when you become a <u>*Leader*</u> in a <u>*Cause*</u> greater than yourself. When income becomes secondary to the value you create for others, Greatness is achieved.

Value Created

|  |  | Labor | Ideas | Leadership |
|---|---|---|---|---|
| Type of Work | Work for Employer | Wage | Opportunity | Profit |
|  | Work for Self | Opportunity | Profit | Excellence |
|  | Work for a Cause | Profit | Excellence | Greatness |

Please don't misunderstand *The Value Creation Matrix*™: Excellence and Greatness do not necessarily indicate a person who earns more money. As I have said before, Financial Greatness can be reached no matter what your current income or net worth. The key to Financial Greatness will always be connecting your deepest values to your money. The ways you earn and merit income are no exception.

Notably, we cannot measure Financial Greatness by whether someone works as an employee or owns their own business. We cannot assess Financial Greatness by balance sheets or income statements or any other objective means. Remember, our financial life does not happen to us objectively. Financial Greatness will mean different things to different people thanks to the countless different causes we work for, different styles of leadership we employ, and different strengths and weaknesses we all bring to the mix. This is what makes building your financial house with *The 8 Pillars*™ so effective—they rely on a solid foundation of clearly defined but unique values.

Moving through the *Five Levels of Financial Merit*™ can take a few months or it can take a lifetime. The central principle I want you to grasp from this chapter is that no matter what the source of your income right now, you have the power to expand and improve your money-making machine. In the next chapter we will look at some specific ways to create more value and generate better income.

**Thoughts, Feelings, and Ideas** – What are some of the thoughts or feelings you had while reading Chapter Nineteen? What insights occurred to you while reading? Did any particular action ideas pop into your mind as you read?

_____

_____

_____

_____

_____

_____

_____

_____

_____

Can you see how the _type of work_ you do and the way you _create value_ in your vocation affect your income over time?

How will the _type of work_ you do and the way you _create value_ in your vocation affect your income over time?

_____

_____

_____

_____

_____

_____

_____

_____

_____

_____

# DOER CHECKLIST – CHAPTER 19

☐    I understand that the principles in Pillar Seven can have more financial impact than all of the other pillars combined. I know that managing my career and income should be an important aspect of my overall financial plan.

☐    I have located where my current occupation and income sources fit into *The Value Creation Matrix™*.

☐    Circle where your current occupation falls within the *Five Levels of Financial Merit™* :

        1. Wage
        2. Opportunity
        3. Profit
        4. Excellence
        5. Greatness

☐    I am committed to creating more value in my work and making conscious decisions to increase my income.

☐    I have set specific goals to make shifts in the <u>type of work</u> I engage in and the <u>value I create</u> in order to move towards Profit, Excellence, and Greatness.

☐    I have taken the time to clearly define and write down my deepest values. I have identified the reasons why I work and the causes I care most about. If my values and career are not in harmony, I am committed to bringing them into alignment.

☐    I will strive for excellence in my work at every level.

☐    I understand that business ownership, career advancement, and all other forms of investment involve risk and uncertainty. I am prepared to mitigate this risk by implementing the first six pillars.

## CHAPTER 20

# INVESTING IN YOU

## PART I: INCREASING YOUR VALUE QUOTIENT

Progressing through the *Five Levels of Financial Merit*™ requires constant investments in your greatest asset: <u>YOU</u>. Your capacity to create value for others grows as you increase your knowledge, experience, and credibility. The more resources you have to offer, the more value you can create. I call your ability to create value your *Value Quotient*. Whereas IQ (Intelligence Quotient) describes your ability to reason and think, VQ describes your potential for adding value to the work you do. Managing your VQ is a pivotal aspect of managing your income.

What specific actions can you take to develop a high *Value Quotient*? From my experiences helping clients, I have identified four areas of personal growth that you should be continually investing in:

# 1. CAREER DEVELOPMENT

Whether you work for an employer or for yourself, your career makes a huge difference in your lifetime income and financial success. One of the best pieces of advice I can offer is this: *choose a field of work that you enjoy AND have a natural aptitude for*. People who enjoy their work have little trouble staying motivated, and when you are also good at something that you enjoy, the combination breeds excellence. If you excel at what you do for a living, your income will likely excel in direct proportion. Developing the right career is very important to reaching Financial Greatness.

Hard work, good ideas, and demonstrated leadership abilities seldom go unnoticed in the marketplace. Business success depends on constant reinvention to meet the needs of customers, while maintaining core company values and managing profits and resources. An innovative business owner can distance him or herself from the competition and become an industry leader. Successful businesses never stop developing and improving, or they cease to be relevant to the market.

The same principle applies to people who work for employers. Employees who consistently excel at what they do will find doors opening repeatedly in their career. Further, employees who become leaders in their organizations will have the greatest opportunities to make an impact for good, as well as a profit for themselves. In order to achieve excellence and leadership as an employee, you need to continually develop yourself both personally and professionally.

**How to Invest in your Career**

The vast majority of working Americans work for organizations, so it makes sense to address employees first. The key to career development as an employee is to *think like a business owner*. As you interview, ask for a raise, seek promotions, and move up the corporate ladder, it is important to put yourself in the employer's shoes. Hiring an employee is a significant investment—it involves costs for training, pay, benefits, and so forth.

Your organization is taking many risks to hire you. They have no guarantees that you will work hard, perform well, take care of their customers, or stay long enough to cover the costs of training. You, as the investment, need to provide ROI to your employer in order to boost the value of your career. So ask yourself these two questions:

1. "If I owned a company, what type of employee would I want to hire?"

2. "What attributes would I want in an employee?"

The answers to these questions provide you with a pattern for developing your career with any company. Employers look for the following qualities in the people they hire, promote, and invest in:

I   **Positive**: Customers and co-workers like to work with people who are optimistic about life and the company they work for.  Happy employees foster a healthy workplace culture that ultimately improves their company's bottom line. If you have a reputation for complaining, gossiping, being cynical, or being unfriendly, you need to change your negative behavior into positive attributes. Being positive is one of the first and most crucial qualities employers are looking for in an employee.

I   **Hard Working**: Employers want to hire self-starters who are motivated to get the job done right. Usually when a business owner complains that "it's so hard to find good help these days," they mean that the people taking their job positions tend to be lazy. Working hard does not always have to mean putting in long hours, although that can get you noticed. Most employers just want to see work done correctly and on time with a high level of attention. They want quality work, not just quantity. Doing things right the first time and staying on top of your work require good organization and time management skills. If you have a reputation for doing sub-par work or constantly missing deadlines, over time, you will find yourself with fewer and fewer career opportunities.

I   **Honest**: Fraud, unethical conduct, theft, fudged reports, and other dishonest behaviors cost employers untold amounts of time and money every year. Having employees who can be trusted increases an organization's effectiveness drastically.  In today's marketplace, trust pays high dividends to those who have earned it. If you have a reputation for cheating, bending the truth, or taking advantage of people, you need to reevaluate your priorities immediately. Not only will dishonest behavior eventually catch up with you financially, it erodes your character <u>now</u> and prevents you from reaching Financial Greatness.

I   **Intelligent:** No employer wants to invest their resources into an employee who can't understand his or her job. High IQ and advanced education are not prerequisites for most employers, but they do look for employees who demonstrate the ability to learn quickly, process details, and think on their feet. Smart employers know that your track record from schooling and previous work is the best indicator of how you will perform in the future. If you don't have a good recent track record of intelligent decisions (also known as a *resume* and *references*), you need to start building one. Do something every week to demonstrate your creativity and analytical abilities at work and build a reputation for being a problem solver.

I   **Leadership:** Employers in every field and every industry consistently reward leadership qualities. Leaders excel at creating and seizing opportunities for their organization, inspiring those they work with to strive for greatness. Every person, no matter what his or her vocation or temperament, has the potential to become a leader in the workplace. Employers know that leadership characteristics impact and spill over into every aspect of an employee's work. If you do not have a reputation for showing leadership on the job, commit yourself to helping your co-workers step up to a higher level and lead by example first.

Based on the qualities that employers look for, are you the type of person you would hire? Would you give more responsibility to someone like you if you were the boss? If another employee had your attitude, work ethic, character, brains, and leadership skills, would you promote them? You need to develop these qualities every day if you want to better develop your career. Invest the time and energy necessary to acquire these traits, and career opportunities will abound. Your *Value Quotient* depends in large measure on how well you develop these qualities.

It is important to note that possessing these attributes will not automatically earn you better job offers or promotions. You need to get good at <u>communicating</u> the fact that you have these essential attributes. Notice that in each of the descriptions above, I mentioned your *reputation.* How you are perceived matters almost as much to your career as who you really are. Even if you possess every quality an employer wants, you may still miss out if these attributes don't come across in the interview or performance review. Communication skills play a crucial part in almost every modern day job. If you can communicate effectively in an interview or evaluation, doors will open and opportunities will present themselves.


## Give Yourself a Raise

In a sense, everyone who works has to be in sales. Even if you never sell a product or service, you have to be able to sell yourself every time you apply for a position or seek a promotion. Business owners have to sell their ideas to investors or lenders before they can even open their doors, and then successfully sell to customers in order to stay in business. A simple way to increase your earned income is to get the raises you deserve by up-selling your value to your customers or employer.

If you work for an employer, you probably feel like you deserve more pay than you get (if you think you are more than fairly compensated, by all means skip this section). What keeps you from making the money you feel you are worth? Often, you simply haven't asked for it well enough—or enough times. Of course, if you don't have the qualities and track record to back up your claims, you will need to work on yourself first. But if you really do deserve to earn more money for what you do, you need to communicate that to your company in a convincing way. That means learning how to sell yourself—how to demonstrate the value you bring to your employer.

The beautiful thing about *The Value Creation Matrix*™ is that it gives you the tools you need to sell your boss on a raise or promotion. *Labor* represents your official job description—what you are paid to do. *Ideas* include all of the improvements you have brought to the company above and beyond your normal duties. *Leadership* represents the ways you have acted like an owner—building up your team, setting the bar, wowing customers, and any other additional value you have created for your company. You can prepare yourself to communicate your value in three simple steps:

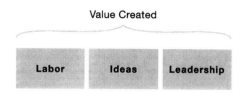

I   **First**, focus on your _Labor_ by writing down in your own words
    what your job description really includes, point by point. Then
    jot down a sentence next to each point describing how you excel
    at it.

I   **Second**, list every good _Idea_ you have ever had on the job that
    improved your company in some way. Write a sentence next to
    each idea describing exactly how it benefited the company—
    tangibly or not.

I   **Third**, make a list of situations at work in which you
    demonstrated _Leadership_. Difficult challenges, special
    assignments, and outstanding performances are all excellent
    scenarios to start with. Briefly describe the situation, what
    you did to demonstrate leadership, and how it improved your
    company.

Now you have a page of proof to draw from when you ask for that raise or
promotion. Review it regularly and memorize it if you can—this benefit
sheet is your leverage for selling your company on the value you provide.
Keep looking for opportunities to add to your list—just having it in writing
will help you focus on the right kinds of behaviors at work and help your
benefit sheet to grow.

Another way to build your confidence as an employee is to study
books on sales or even practice actual selling part-time. Learning _how_
to communicate the benefits you bring and the value you create for
your employer will greatly increase your chances of being heard. I
recommend joining a local Toastmasters club to work on your speaking
and communication skills. Anything you can do to become a better
communicator will enhance your ability to get a raise.

No matter how amazing you are or how finely honed your communication skills, you will miss out on 100% of the raises you <u>never ask</u> for. Even if you don't feel completely ready, ask for that raise and apply for that promotion right now. If you are turned down, you can then ask what you need to do in order to get a "yes" next time, and build on the experience. Employers value tenacity and resilience, and seeing you turn rejection into growth opportunities immediately begins to increase your standing with them. The key is to ask early and often for the pay and positions you deserve, rather than just hoping someone in authority will notice the good job you do.

What if you are self-employed—do the same qualities merit higher pay when you own your own business? Can you still give yourself a raise when you don't have a boss to hear and assess your case? The answer to both questions is a resounding YES. When you are in business, your customers view you and everyone who represents your company the same way employers view their employees. Customers expect to have the same positive experience with your products or services again and again.

View every facet of your business through the eyes of your customers. Take the time to experience your company as a customer would. To help facilitate a wonderful customer experience, you should hire the kind of people you would want to interact with if YOU were the customer. Evaluate yourself and everyone involved in your customers' experiences using the same criteria that a hiring manager would use on a potential employee. The better your business reflects the qualities of positivity, hard work, honesty, intelligence, and leadership, the more customer loyalty you will earn.

Customers want to be respected by the companies with whom they do business. When your customer service comes across as positive, honest, highly competent, committed to excellence, and ready to do whatever it takes to resolve any issues, your customers will respond with appreciation and more business. The same goes for marketing, selling, delivering goods and services, and handling problems. You might want to create a benefits sheet listing the reasons your customers do business with you, the innovations you have made for them, and the ways you lead your competitors. It can be eye-opening to do this exercise from a customer perspective.

How can business owners give themselves a raise? The answer may surprise you: increase prices over time. Inflation causes the price of wages, materials, office space, retail space, utilities, fuel, and every other business operating cost to go up eventually. Businesses that engage in price wars and rely on gimmicky pricing tactics usually don't last during tough economic times. If you are self-employed you need to gradually and prudently increase what you charge for your goods and services. Now, if the quality of your products and services does not merit a higher price, don't bother asking customers to pay more for them. But if you deserve to earn more for what you provide, your customers are likely to stay with you through reasonable price increases.

## 2. NETWORKING AND MENTORSHIPS

Another important component of your *Value Quotient* is your <u>network</u> of past and present friends, associates, and co-workers. The personal connections you make in various companies, industries, and geographic areas can exponentially multiply your *Value Quotient*. It takes very little effort to stay in touch with people in the Information Age, and maintaining an active network of relationships will prove well worth the time and energy for your long-term career.

Often the best opportunities in life come through the people who know us. Your network encompasses a vast array of ideas, skills, experience, and support that you can both contribute to and draw from. The larger you build your network, the greater resources you will have. Some of the best sources for growing your personal network are the causes you care most about. When you can meet and work with people who share your deepest values, you will rapidly expand the size and quality of your network.

The possible benefits of having a large, strong personal network are too numerous to list. At a minimum, you will have more career opportunities than you could find on your own, not to mention a better pool of references to draw on when you do pursue an opportunity. You may even find your dream job or calling in life through your network. You never know when you might need to go to your network for support, so keep building and maintaining your invaluable connections with people.

In my experience, we learn best of all not by seeing or hearing or even doing, but by *teaching others*. You can hone your *Value Quotient* by mentoring others in your network. This accomplishes two things at once: you will be surprised by how much better you master your own knowledge, and you will fill a great need for those you mentor. You can also seek out mentors from within your network who can help you grow your own career. I have seen too many people burn out trying to forge their way to success alone when they could have succeeded with a little expert coaching and assistance.

There are no limits to the number of mentors a person can have. The best way to find a mentor is to simply ask someone you want to model if he or she would mentor you in his or her field of expertise. The best way to become a mentor is to offer to share your expertise with someone else. A mentorship can be a simple and informal arrangement or a specific and well-defined relationship. The format is less important than the fact that you are mentoring others and being mentored.

## 3. CONTINUING EDUCATION

By now you may be tired of hearing how much I unequivocally support education—both formal education and self-education. Education grows your *Value Quotient* across the board, making you a better investment for any employer. All successful business owners go through a tremendous learning curve as they build their companies, and the more educated they are going into it, the better. Study after study finds that, in general, higher education results in higher incomes. But even without formal degrees, lifelong learning will do more to increase your wealth than almost anything else.

More books have been written on how to find your best career, increase your income, and manage your money than any person could read in a lifetime. The principles I am sharing with you in this chapter only scratch the surface of what you can do to earn more money. I recommend you continue to expand your financial education throughout your life and take advantage of the many educational resources available to you. *8 Pillars University*™ includes a comprehensive curriculum of interactive web learning modules, recommended reading lists, and an online community of learning resources (to learn more about *8 Pillars University*™ please visit www.8pillars.com).

Whether you pursue additional formal education, enroll in a financial education program such as *8 Pillars University*™, take continuing education courses in your field, or follow your own informal course of study, the rewards will be significant for your career. Your mind is a formidable asset, but unless you continue to exercise it and use it constantly, you risk letting it deteriorate and atrophy. Continuing to gain education keeps you sharp, interesting, and valuable.

Understanding basic economic realities should be an important part of your education if you are going to achieve Financial Greatness. The better you understand the language and perspective of economists, the better you can sort out the financial graffiti in the media from the important economic indicators reported on every week. When you maintain a balanced, fact-based perspective on markets and the economy, you can make better career and financial decisions throughout your life.

Your financial education extends to areas such as avoiding scams, evaluating opportunities, preparing for potential setbacks, and helping others to do the same. You need to learn some of the "psychology of money" to understand why people so frequently make poor financial decisions. Never stop seeking education; the more you learn about Financial Greatness, the more people you will be able to point in that direction.

## 4. LEADERSHIP TRAINING

Leadership skills carry a very high *Value Quotient* and affect your income potential considerably. You can increase your leadership ability through experience (seeking positions of influence and learning by doing), through study (reading books on leadership, studying the lives and traits of great leaders, and so on), and through formal leadership training programs. I encourage you to utilize all three methods of leadership training, since we learn best when we combine studying, teaching, and doing.

I have said enough about leadership in the context of Pillar Seven already. Firmly grasp the concepts in Chapter Nineteen and remember that leadership is one of the most powerful ways in which you can create value for others. No matter what you might think, you have the potential to be a leader in your sphere of influence. If you need additional help developing your leadership potential, seek out formal training from well-known and respected sources. In addition, *The 8 Pillars Workbook* provides many resources to help you become an effective leader.

# PART II: DIVERSIFYING YOUR INCOME SOURCES

Managing your income sources takes careful and systematic planning and effort. No matter how much income your work merits, you need to earn financial rewards from multiple sources. Relying on a single source of income (such as an employer) for the length of your career is like purchasing only one investment for all of your financial goals and objectives. It is important to spread out your sources of income just as carefully as you would diversify your investment portfolio. Throughout your life you need to effectively manage the <u>number</u> and <u>variety</u> of income sources that supply your values.

The income you earn at any of the five levels in the matrix (wage, opportunity, profit, excellence, and greatness) always depends in part on your doing something to earn it. While financial rewards at the higher levels (such as excellence and greatness) may continue without much day-to-day effort on your part, eventually you will retire from vocational endeavors. When that time comes you will rely 100% on your *money to work for you*. As I said in Chapter Nineteen, usually before you have anything to invest you have to *work for money*. Between those two extremes and during your working life you need to be slowly but surely shifting your income sources from *active* to *passive*. Over the course of your career, <u>earned</u> income gives way to <u>investment</u> or <u>passive</u> income. The earlier you can make this transition in life, the earlier you can retire.

I am not fond of the word "retirement." The sooner you can formally "retire" from working to earn a living, the sooner you can engage in *working full time for the causes you care most about*. My definition of retirement hardly means slowing down. Whether that means traveling the world, rendering humanitarian service, spending time with your family, or any number of worthwhile pursuits, retirement to me stands for <u>financial freedom</u> to do more. In this sense, the sooner you are financially free, the better. This will allow you to be even more diligent in your pursuit of personal greatness and of helping the world become a better place. If you still want to work for money after you no longer need to, you will enjoy your work that much more doing it by choice and not necessity.

Now let's take a brief look at the three major income sources that will help you diversify your earnings and work towards financial freedom.

## INCOME SOURCE NUMBER ONE:
### BUSINESS INVESTMENTS

Up to now, I have focused on running a business as an active owner, a self-employed entrepreneur who earns profits and finds income opportunities by creating value for others. But business ownership has another potential benefit: the capacity to generate residual income. Residual income does not require you to continue working in order to receive payments. In this way, businesses become investments that represent your money working for you instead of the other way around.

Business investing takes many forms. The most common form of business investing involves owning common stock in public companies. But you can also invest in private companies, start-up companies, and other business ventures as well. The best business investment often comes from building your own profitable business and then selling most of your stake to someone else. The return on your time and effort can be astonishing, and if you maintain some ownership in the company, you can continue to profit from it long after you give up the management of the business.

Business investing has another important benefit for your potential income: legal tax breaks. I won't go into detail in this book about the specific tax strategies that business owners utilize to reduce their tax liability. However, you can get the gist of these tax advantages by comparing the way an employee pays taxes to the way a business owner pays them. When an <u>employee</u> earns money, his employer deducts income taxes BEFORE paying the net amount to him. Then the employee pays for the things he needs and saves the rest. On the other hand, a <u>business owner</u> earns money, buys what the business needs, and THEN pays taxes on the rest, meaning less income gets taxed and more is left to save and invest. Every business owner needs a good tax specialist who can help him or her take advantage of potential tax savings.

Business Investing should play a part in your financial plans. This does not mean you have to quit your job and devote your life to building a global enterprise. In addition to making passive investments in existing businesses, you could start a home-based business, Internet business, affiliate marketing program, or networking marketing business. While these business models are fraught with examples of scams and illegitimate schemes, if you sort the good from the bad, you can find some great opportunities to get your feet wet in business. Judge any business opportunity in terms of the value it will create for customers, the income it will actually generate, and its effect on your values and the causes you believe in.

If you are serious about starting your own business but are not sure where to begin, please take the opportunity to review the affiliate program for *8 Pillars University*™ by visiting www.8pillars.com and clicking on the "Become an Affiliate" link.

## INCOME SOURCE NUMBER TWO:
### REAL ESTATE INVESTMENTS

You have learned from Pillar Six what a powerful investment your own home can be. Investing in additional real estate multiplies that effect for you financially. Owning real estate offers a great combination of advantages to investors: tax-deferred gains, tax deductions from interest paid and depreciation, relative stability and security, leverage options from financing, the possibility to produce current income, the potential for long-term appreciation in value, and various ways to increase return on investment through your own efforts (fixer-uppers, bargain buys, foreclosures and bank sales, and a whole variety of creative strategies).

Remember to evaluate real estate investments as thoroughly and carefully as you do any other investments you make. Although we sometimes ignore the fact, investing in real estate does involve serious risks to your cash flow, principal, liquidity, and credit. The purpose of this book is not to make you a great real estate investor, but rather to teach you the principles of Financial Greatness. However, I wholeheartedly encourage you to learn more about real estate investing and tap into this income source as soon as you can wisely do so. Again, you need to have a good CPA or tax advisor who can help you maximize the tax-savings potential from your real estate investments.

## INCOME SOURCE NUMBER THREE:
### INTEREST INVESTMENTS

Business and equity investments generate profits and pay dividends from their earnings, and real estate investments generate income from rents. Both of these types of investments have the potential to appreciate substantially in value over time. Virtually every other kind of investment generates returns as some form of interest. Interest investments are not very exciting and don't usually offer big returns on investment, but they are predictable, steady, and allow you to take advantage of compounding.

While you shouldn't concentrate all of your assets in interest-earning investments, neither should you neglect them altogether. These simple investments, such as bonds, CDs, fixed annuities, and similar vehicles can benefit your liquidity, reduce your portfolio volatility, and may provide current income that can be spent or used to fund additional investments. Review Pillar Five to better understand how to evaluate investments and put them to work for you.

## PILLAR SEVEN IN A NUTSHELL

Time for a recap: Usually before you have anything to invest, you have to spend some time *working for money*. Your money-making potential over the course of your career represents one of the single largest assets you may ever have. Ultimately, the value of your economic engine depends on how effective you are at *creating value for others*. This means putting as much forethought, time, effort, and care into managing your career and income sources as you do to managing the rest of your financial health. Your capacity to create value for others grows as you increase your knowledge, experience, and credibility. The more resources you have to offer, the more value you can create. Let's review the key concepts you have learned in Pillar Seven:

I   You increase your income sources by creating value for others.
I   Understanding *The Value Creation Matrix™* helps you maximize Labor, Ideas, Leadership, and the three ways to work.
I   Progressing through *The Five Levels of Financial Merit™* (Wage, Opportunity, Profit, Excellence, and Greatness) can substantially grow your income potential.
I   You can increase your *Value Quotient (VQ)* through Career Development, Networking and Mentorships, Continuing Education, and Leadership Training.
I   Diversifying your income sources through business, real estate,

and interest investments enables you to eventually stop working for money and allows your money to work for you.

It is vital to *choose a field of work that you enjoy AND have a natural aptitude for*. As your income grows, slowly but surely shift your income sources from *active* to *passive*. When your money makes more money, your economic engine gains horsepower and you become freer to work for the causes you believe in regardless of pay. Don't expect these results to come about by themselves. Having a *Financial Greatness Mindset* means taking the initiative to manage your income as carefully as you manage the rest of your financial life.

On one hand, some of the concepts discussed in Pillar Seven are simple and can be applied immediately. On the other hand, many of the principles (such as leadership) are not as simple and may require more thought and planning if they are to become a mainstay in your life. Because some of the principles are more complex, you may want to re-read Pillar Seven and review *The Value Creation Matrix*™ more than once. This will allow you to create specific goals and personalize the material. As these principles and concepts sink in more deeply, they will help you to *Maximize Your Money-Making Machine*™.

Remember that your earning potential has no limits. From the standpoint of possible ROI, the principles in Pillar Seven can have more financial impact than all of the other pillars combined. Managing your career should be an important aspect of your overall financial plan. Increasing your income magnifies your ability to live each of the other pillars. Funding a *Financial Confidence Account*™, saving for specific goals, breaking the bonds of debt, paying for insurance, funding investments, and owning a home all require income sources. The higher your income goes, the faster you can implement *The 8 Pillars*™.

**Thoughts, Feelings, and Ideas** – What are some of the thoughts or feelings you had while reading Chapter Twenty? What insights occurred to you while reading? Did any particular action ideas pop into your mind as you read?

_____

_____

_____

_____

_____

_____

_____

_____

Can you see how increasing your *Value Quotient* will affect your income over time?

In addition, can you see how diversifying your income sources will help you achieve Financial Greatness?

How will increasing your *Value Quotient* and diversifying your income sources affect your ability to reach Financial Greatness?

_____

_____

_____

_____

_____

_____

_____

# DOER CHECKLIST – CHAPTER 20

☐    I am committed to increasing my VQ through continual career development.

☐    I have a plan in place to ask for a raise or promotion at work. I have completed the steps to create a proof-of-value list that will help prepare me to ask for and get a raise or promotion.

☐    I have a mentor at work or in my career as a business owner.

☐    I mentor other people at work or in other facets of my life.

☐    I am committed to investing in continuing education and leadership training throughout my career. I have a plan mapped out for the next 12-24 months of exactly what training, coursework, and other education I will obtain.

☐    I understand the three main sources of income (business, real estate, and interest income) and how they can help me reach Financial Greatness. I have a plan to systematically go after and access these three income sources.

# PILLAR EIGHT

*Get Perspective by Giving Back*

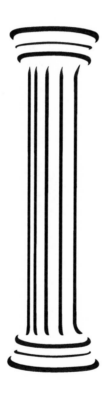

## CHAPTER 21

# GREATNESS

*"Remember, what you possess in the world will be found at the day of your death to belong to someone else, but what you are will be yours forever."*

- Henry Van Dyke

Of all the sections in *The 8 Pillars of Financial Greatness*, this chapter on gaining perspective and giving back is the most difficult for me to write. I find it challenging to put into words a subject that is so near to my heart. You will notice that I quote several other people in this chapter who have already said so eloquently what I feel. I hope their words will help you, as they have helped me, to connect deeply with the message of giving back.

I wish that you and I could have a one-on-one conversation about this subject instead of you merely reading a chapter in a book. If we engaged in personal dialogue, I believe you would be able to feel and sense my genuine concern and desire for your happiness. I think you would recognize the sincerity in my facial expressions and tone of voice and would come to understand how important Pillar Eight is to me. If you looked into my heart and examined my intentions, you would discover that I have great confidence in your ability to become a person of greatness. My primary intent for this book (and especially this final chapter) is to promote your well-being and success.

## STEP BACK TO STEP FORWARD

While you have been reading *The 8 Pillars*™, I have asked you to focus intensely on improving one aspect of your life: your financial health. I have presented, in great detail, many strategies that will help you save, organize, protect, and grow your money. I truly believe that this book blueprints the way to a fantastic financial future.

In this chapter, I would like you to take a step back and look at the big picture of your life. Throughout the final pages of this book, try to view your life from an objective distance so you can gain the necessary perspective to move forward. Leonardo Da Vinci, the great Italian sculptor, inventor, engineer, musician, scientist, and painter understood the need to step back in order gain perspective. In speaking about creating a *work of art*, Leonardo once said, "Go some distance away because the work appears smaller and more of it can be taken in at a glance, and a lack of harmony or proportion is more readily seen." I would like you to view your life as *a work of art*.

This holistic perspective will allow you to accomplish two major objectives: First, you will gain insights about managing your money with greater wisdom. Second, you will understand the deeper role money plays in your life and your priorities. As you step back and view your life as a whole, you will gain clarity. You may even notice evidence of the "lack of harmony" that Leonardo mentions. The word *harmony* means agreement or accord, as when one thing combines pleasantly and consistently with something else. What *something else* in your life do you need to find harmony with? I believe your most important *something else* is your unique set of values—the ideals, relationships, and principles that you hold most dear.

Your happiness depends, to a large degree, on making your everyday life congruent with your values. When your thoughts and actions are in harmony with your values, you will find peace, joy, and happiness. You will have true integrity, a treasure that no amount of money can ever purchase. Though I am not perfect at it, I live my values to the best of my ability. I share this pillar with a personal conviction born of experience. Some of the things I value most are family, health, spirituality, deep happiness, security, safety, freedom, and balance. As I give my time and energy to living and protecting these values, I gain peace.

## GIVING BACK

One of the best ways to get perspective is by giving back. Giving back means sharing the time, talents, energy, and abundance you enjoy with other people around you. Sharing your blessings allows you to focus on something or someone other than you. As you shift your attention away from your own needs and desires, you become aware that you are a part of something much larger than any one person. You realize that you are a member of a vast human family. As the Buddha once stated, "If you knew what I know about the power of giving, you would not let a single meal pass without sharing it in some way." I submit that giving has just as powerful an effect on the giver as it does on the receiver.

When I was in high school, I thought that my best opportunity to make the world a better place would come with great wealth. I wanted the wonderful feeling I believed that the "rich" experienced when they donated large sums to charity. Shortly after high school, I had the opportunity to volunteer for a couple of years in England helping individuals and families improve their lives. While away from home, I learned to serve and love others without thinking about how it would make me feel. As I worked for others rather than for money or my own satisfaction, I learned a valuable lesson. I realized that the greatest joy comes not from the *amount* you give, but from how generously you give it.

Albert Camus observed somewhat wryly that "too many have dispensed with generosity in order to practice charity." One of the best ways to feel truly wealthy, regardless of your net worth, is to share what you do have with others. Remember the New Testament parable of the Widow's Mite? Watching the rich men make large donations in the temple, Jesus observed a poor widow giving two mites (the least valuable coin of the times). Then he told his listeners, "This poor widow hath cast more in, than all they which have cast into the treasury: For all they did cast in of their abundance; but she of her want did cast in all that she had, even all her living" (Mark 12:43-44 KJV). It means very little for a billionaire to donate a small percentage of his riches to charity. The habit of giving needs to become part of you long before you gain material wealth.

As I discovered in England, the essence of giving is self-sacrifice. I have learned and relearned that lesson many times over since then. When my wife and I were newlyweds and struggling to pay for college by each working two jobs, we always found joy in giving back. We donated at least 10% of our income to charity during these lean years and discovered for ourselves the truth of Simone de Beauvoir's statement about generosity: "You give your all, and yet you always feel as if it costs you nothing." Giving back helped us remember what was most important to us. Any time we went out of our way to donate time or resources to worthy causes, we felt richer afterwards than we did before.

I remember sitting in my algebra class when I was just a freshman in college and having the distinct impression that a certain single mother in the room needed help financially. The next day, I asked if I could speak with my professor in private. During the conversation, I handed my teacher some money and asked if she would anonymously give it to this particular woman. Some days later, my teacher related to me how much this meant to that struggling mother. I did not have much to give, but I gave what I had. Maya Angelou expressed exactly how it affected me: "I have found that among its other benefits, giving liberates the soul of the giver." I felt richer and freer after *giving* that money away than if I had *received* any amount of money from someone else.

I mention these very personal stories not to glorify my good deeds, but to attempt to share one of the sources of my greatest happiness. I freely admit that I forget to give back more often than I can excuse. At times I lose sight of my intent to make the world a better place and get caught up in promoting selfish ends. After college, as my income increased, for a time I cared more about impressing others with the nice things I could buy than about sharing my good fortune. I now recognize that my selfishness and ego need to be continually checked. That is why I have to regularly step back, gain some perspective, and reconnect with my values. Giving helps me to continually find harmony in my life.

I have observed some telling philanthropic patterns as I have studied the traits of many financially wealthy people. The vast majority of those I observed gave tremendous amounts of their time and money to causes greater than themselves *long before* they were well-off. Financial Greatness does not need to take a lifetime to achieve—these givers were headed there before their net worth had even begun to grow. Now they continue to give substantial portions of their wealth to others. Perhaps they took Voltaire's words to heart and realized what really matters in life: "The man who leaves money to charity in his will is only giving away what no longer belongs to him." Don't wait to give.

# LOVE TO GIVE BACK

At the heart of giving back are the principles of love and kindness. When I was very young, my father and I set a goal to travel around the world. When I say *around the world*, I literally mean we wanted to fly completely around the entire globe, not just go to a distant country and fly home the same way we left.

After years of planning and saving for this trip, we finally achieved our goal and set off around the world. We visited eleven major world cities spanning five continents and heard several different languages spoken. We also had the wonderful experience of seeing every major world religion up close. Even in circumstances where language prohibited me from verbally communicating with the locals, I think my smile and warm demeanor communicated my friendly intentions. By genuinely showing kindness, I connected with people on a level deeper than words. Love is the great universal language, the ultimate equalizer. No matter what race, age, nationality, religion, or economic status, all people understand the languages of love and kindness. As Mark Twain so eloquently said, "Kindness is a language which the deaf can hear and the blind can see."

Mother Teresa beautifully summed up my feelings about giving: "It's not how much we give, but how much love we put into giving." When I have found myself discouraged in life, the love and kindness of others was like a warm blanket on a cold night. I wholeheartedly agree with the statement made by Albert Einstein when he said, "The ideals which have lighted my way, and time after time have given me new courage to face life cheerfully, have been kindness, beauty and truth."

I am convinced that for you and me to find happiness and become people of greatness, we need to give back generously. Our lives should be more about <u>giving and becoming</u> and less about <u>wanting and accumulating</u>. I encourage all of my clients to give back at least 10% of their time and income. The actual amount is less important than giving enough to constitute a real sacrifice. By giving consistently and generously, you will *feel* wealthier, no matter what your current income is. As I have reiterated from the Introduction of this book to now, becoming rich does not always equate to Financial Greatness. *The 8 Pillars*™ demonstrate how to build real riches by applying enduring principles to your entire life.

> **In order for you to reach true Financial Greatness, you need to give back at least 10% of your time and money to worthy causes that will make the world a better place.**

Not only is sharing your means the right thing to do, it will also yield tremendous benefits in your financial life. When you give back, you gain more control of your money and learn to manage your remaining assets better. You learn to appreciate what you have and make it count. You remind yourself of the true value of money and tend to waste less. I know this is true from personal experience. I am far less likely to waste money when I am consistently giving back 10% of my income. The purpose of this book is to help you reach *greatness*—not just *financial* greatness—but make no mistake about it: giving back will help you achieve <u>both</u>.

For many great individuals, giving back was never an optional component to financial success. Og Mandino, author of *The Greatest Salesman in the World*, believed that wealthy people should give back *half* of their fortune! This is just another way of reiterating that money is not your end goal. The happiness of your family, the contributions you make in life, and the dreams you pursue are your end goals. When you connect your values and emotions with your financial life, you make a direct investment in your future Financial Greatness. Over time, such investments will yield the *true riches* of more time for your family, for serving others, and for pursuing your dreams.

> *Remember that there is no happiness in having or in getting, but only in giving. Reach out. Share. Smile. Hug. Happiness is a perfume you cannot pour on others without getting a few drops on yourself.*

- Og Mandino

## THE END OF THE BEGINNING

As you implement *The 8 Pillars*™ and especially Pillar Eight, you will enjoy the freedom to live in control of your money. When you keep money matters in their proper perspective, they cease to be significant driving forces in your life. With money no longer controlling any part of you, something deep inside you will be freed to make a profound difference in this world. I would like to re-quote the words of Marianne Williamson from her book, *A Return to Love*:

> Our deepest fear is not that we are inadequate. Our
> deepest fear is that we are powerful beyond measure.
> It is our light, not our darkness that most frightens
> us. We ask ourselves, '*who am I to be brilliant,*
> *gorgeous, talented, fabulous?*' Actually, who are
> you not to be? You are a child of God. Your playing
> small does not serve the world. There is nothing
> enlightened about shrinking so that other people
> won't feel insecure around you. We are all meant
> to shine, as children do. We were born to make
> manifest the glory of God that is within us. It is not
> just in some of us; it is in everyone.

I believe that you *are* unique and amazing. I know that you have wonderful gifts that are meant to be developed and shared. Your gifts may be reserved for the people who live within the walls of your own home, or they may one day bless the whole world. You may use your gifts to serve those who reside in your neighborhood or those who support the same causes that you do. No matter where or how much you give, *giving back* will help put your financial life in harmony with your values. Giving sets you free to fully live for what matters most and realize your greatest dreams.

I feel so certain about the human need to get perspective that I created a full-color coffee table book to better reflect my feelings on the subject. The book is called "**Financial Wisdom** – *Timeless as Nature*" and contains a number of inspirational quotations from some of the greatest thinkers, artists, and spiritual leaders of the past. Each quotation is coupled with wonderful, full-color landscape photography.

**FINANCIAL WISDOM**
TIMELESS AS NATURE

I frequently find myself reading and pondering the thought-provoking words to help reconnect me with the principle of giving back. I have appreciated it so much myself that I include this book with every enrollment into *8 Pillars University™*. The following excerpts give you a small sample of the book, and apply especially well to Pillar Eight:

**"Happiness is found in doing, not merely in possessing."**
> - Napoleon Hill

**"If you want to feel rich, just count all of the things you have that money can't buy."**
> - Unknown

**". . . For a man's life consisteth not in the abundance of the things which he possesseth."**
> - Holy Bible – KJV (Luke 12:15)

**"Money is not required to buy one necessity of the soul."**
> - Henry David Thoreau

As I mentioned in the Introduction, I value your time. I am honored that you have invested your time into reading *The 8 Pillars of Financial Greatness*. I truly believe that this book blueprints the way to a fantastic financial future for you. As a result of building your financial house with *The 8 Pillars™*, many unexpected but wonderful things will come into your life. It is important to remember that *to know how to do something* and *to do it* are two very different things. A wise man once said that we need to be doers and not hearers only. If you have been casually reading,

I urge you to take action today. The biggest risk to your financial health is *doing nothing about it.*

If you want help taking action, I encourage you to enroll in *8 Pillars University™.* I developed *8 Pillars University™* to further solidify these principles for my readers and to provide assistance putting them into practice. I want you to reap the rewards of <u>living</u> *The 8 Pillars™.* Please visit my website at www.8pillars.com and consider taking the next step to becoming a person of greatness. This program can become your bridge to a lifetime of financial discovery and freedom.

# 8 PILLARS
## UNIVERSITY™

I truly am excited about your future. You have an amazing life before you. No matter what your particular dreams are, living *The 8 Pillars of Financial Greatness* will help you reach them more quickly, while ensuring that your success is sustainable. This book and the financial principles it teaches are sure and true. Thank you for investing your time and money in my book—may it help you find your path to Financial Greatness!

I would enjoy hearing from you. If you have a comment about *The 8 Pillars™* or would like to share a success story, please e-mail me: brian@8pillars.com

I wish you success and happiness as you continue your quest to become A PERSON OF GREATNESS!

**Brian Nelson Ford**
brian@8pillars.com
www.8pillars.com

**Thoughts, Feelings, and Ideas** – What are some of the thoughts or feelings you had while reading Chapter Twenty-One? What insights occurred to you while reading? Did any particular action ideas pop into your mind as you read?

_____

_____

_____

_____

_____

How will your life specifically improve through getting perspective and giving back?

_____

_____

_____

_____

_____

## DOER CHECKLIST – CHAPTER 21

☐    I will gain perspective by regularly taking a step back to review my life and personal finances in relation to my values.

☐    I commit to giving back at least 10% of my income and time to worthy causes!

☐    I commit to becoming a person of greatness by continually furthering my financial education. I have visited www.8pillars. com to learn more about _8 Pillars University_™.

# THE COMPLETE
# FINANCIAL GREATNESS CHECKLIST

### DOER CHECKLIST – CHAPTER 2

☐ I understand my values (what is most important to me), and I have committed them to paper.

My Values:

1._____

2._____

3._____

4._____

5._____

6._____

7._____

8._____

### DOER CHECKLIST – CHAPTER 3

☐ I am committed to reaching Financial Greatness by completing each of *The 8 Pillars*™!

# DOER CHECKLIST – CHAPTER 5

Part I:

☐   I have at least $850 saved in a separate, no-touch online or regular savings account.

☐   I have $150 cash in a fire/water-proof safe that I can access immediately.

It is important to remember that you do not need to have these items checked off before moving on to Pillar Two. However, you do need to take immediate action before moving on: start saving a fixed amount of money every month in your *Financial Confidence Account*™ and put this savings process on autopilot. Once you have begun to save, you can keep your momentum going by moving on to Pillar Two: *Organize and Systematize for Success*™.

Part II:

☐   I have 85% of 3 months of my living expenses saved in a separate, no-touch online or regular savings account.

☐   I have 15% of 3 months of my living expenses saved as cash in a fire/water-proof safe that I can access immediately in my home.

After checking off these two items, you should be very proud of yourself—you have successfully completed Pillar One! If you have been following the program closely, this means that Pillars Two through Four are likely also complete or under way. You are now ready to Invest for Happiness by understanding Pillar Five.

# DOER CHECKLIST – CHAPTER 6

☐   I have clarified my core values / dreams and committed them to paper.

- ☐ I have calculated my net worth, and I am committed to growing it in a balanced way.

- ☐ I have tracked my expenses and taken inventory of my fixed and variable costs.

- ☐ I have analyzed my income and determined my net cash flow.

- ☐ I have a working budget that the entire household is committed to supporting.

## DOER CHECKLIST – CHAPTER 7

- ☐ I have written down specific long-term financial goals that connect with my values.

- ☐ I have developed a plan to achieve my long-term financial goals by identifying and writing out short-term milestone goals.

## DOER CHECKLIST – CHAPTER 8

- ☐ I have eliminated as much financial clutter from my life as possible and will continue to keep my finances as simple as I can.

- ☐ I have my savings plans and financial goals on autopilot.

- ☐ I have a fire/water-proof home safe with my vital documents and cash portion of my *Financial Confidence Account*™ in it.

- ☐ I have an organized financial filing system.

- ☐ I have scheduled systematic and regular reviews of my *Financial Greatness Blueprint* and my automatic plans.

## DOER CHECKLIST – CHAPTER 9

☐ I understand the principle of interest and the idea of depreciating assets. I am committed to eliminating and completely avoiding consumer debt.

☐ If I have consumer debt, I have created a plan to eliminate it.

☐ I understand what "acceptable" forms of debt are. I will be very careful to only use "acceptable" forms of debt to help me reach Financial Greatness.

## DOER CHECKLIST – CHAPTER 10

☐ I know my credit score.

☐ I am committed to playing by the rules and achieving/ maintaining a credit score of 720 or higher.

## DOER CHECKLIST – CHAPTER 11

☐ I understand that knowledge is the keystone to Financial Greatness.

☐ I commit to becoming a person of greatness by continually furthering my financial education. I have visited www.8pillars. com to learn more about *8 Pillars University*™.

## DOER CHECKLIST – CHAPTER 12

☐ I have all of the *Fundamental Insurance Types* in place that apply to my situation.

☐ If I do not have all of the insurance I should, I have a plan to follow the 3-step process to obtain the needed insurance policies to protect my financial plan from *fatal* falls.

- [ ] I am committed to being very careful about the types of *Insurance to Scrutinize*. I will never purchase insurance too quickly or out of fear or from a pushy insurance salesperson.

- [ ] Once I have a fully funded *Financial Confidence Account*™, I will raise my deductibles to save premium costs where appropriate.

## DOER CHECKLIST – CHAPTER 13

- [ ] I have a properly constructed written WILL, along with the necessary corresponding estate planning documents.

- [ ] I have updated and checked the accuracy of my named beneficiaries on all of my financial accounts and insurance policies.

- [ ] If I am near or above $500,000 in net worth, I have discussed the need for a trust with my estate planning attorney.

- [ ] I can rest assured that I have done all that I can do to financially prepare for "what if."

## DOER CHECKLIST – CHAPTER 14

- [ ] I have clearly defined values and long-term investment goals centered on those values.

- [ ] I understand the difference between speculation and investing.

- [ ] I will not invest in something that I do not understand.

- [ ] I have completed the Doer Checklists from Pillars One through Four including fully funding a *Financial Confidence Account*™.

## DOER CHECKLIST – CHAPTER 15

☐     I have established the habit of saving 10-15% of my income for long-term goals.

☐     I know my own risk tolerance and what investment tradeoffs I can live with.

☐     If this is my first time investing, I have begun implementing the appropriate advice from the "First Time Investors" section relative to my situation.

## DOER CHECKLIST – CHAPTER 16

☐     I am committed to setting *The Five Mousetraps of Investing*™.

       I will:

-   Take a long-term view of my investments
-   Diversify
-   Implement systematic strategies
-   Utilize tax-advantaged investment vehicles
-   Keep expenses low

☐     I have a trusted financial advisor or have interviewed at least two potential advisors.

## DOER CHECKLIST – CHAPTER 17

☐     I view my home as an investment. I understand that my home is first and foremost an investment in my values and my everyday quality of life. Second, my home is a true financial investment with the potential to appreciate over time.

☐     If I am currently renting, I have set specific goals to save and prepare for buying my own home.

## DOER CHECKLIST – CHAPTER 18

☐   I am committed to growing and guarding my home's equity.

☐   When purchasing or refinancing a home, I will use a simple
     fixed-rate loan that I completely understand unless I have
     a very good, sound reason to do otherwise.

☐   Because I have applied my knowledge from Pillars One, Two,
     and Three by having adequate cash, low levels of debt, and
     a credit score of 720 or higher, I am committed to getting the
     most competitive interest rate available.

☐   I will purchase a home that does not cost me more than 30% of
     my gross income to pay for and maintain.

☐   I will increase my home's chances for appreciation by always
     applying what I have learned about finding, buying, maintaining,
     and selling homes.

☐   I will be very careful about tapping into my *magic number* for
     any reason.

## DOER CHECKLIST – CHAPTER 19

☐   I understand that the principles in Pillar Seven can have more
     financial impact than all of the other pillars combined. I know
     that managing my career and income should be an important
     aspect of my overall financial plan.

☐   I have located where my current occupation and income sources
     fit into *The Value Creation Matrix*™.

☐   Circle where your current occupation falls within the *Five Levels
     of Financial Merit*™ :

1. Wage
2. Opportunity
3. Profit
4. Excellence
5. Greatness

☐ I am committed to creating more value in my work and making conscious decisions to increase my income.

☐ I have set specific goals to make shifts in the <u>type of work</u> I engage in and the <u>value I create</u> in order to move towards Profit, Excellence, and Greatness.

☐ I have taken the time to clearly define and write down my deepest values. I have identified the reasons why I work and the causes I care most about. If my values and career are not in harmony, I am committed to bringing them into alignment.

☐ I will strive for excellence in my work at every level.

☐ I understand that business ownership, career advancement, and all other forms of investment involve risk and uncertainty. I am prepared to mitigate this risk by implementing the first six pillars.

## DOER CHECKLIST – CHAPTER 20

☐ I am committed to increasing my VQ through continual career development.

☐ I have a plan in place to ask for a raise or promotion at work. I have completed the steps to create a proof-of-value list that will help prepare me to ask for and get a raise or promotion.

☐ I have a mentor at work or in my career as a business owner.

☐ I mentor other people at work or in other facets of my life.

☐ I am committed to investing in continuing education and leadership training throughout my career. I have a plan mapped out for the next 12-24 months of exactly what training, coursework, and other education I will obtain.

☐ I understand the three main sources of income (business, real estate, and interest income) and how they can help me reach Financial Greatness. I have a plan to systematically go after and access these three income sources.

## DOER CHECKLIST – CHAPTER 21

☐ I will gain perspective by regularly taking a step back to review my life and personal finances in relation to my values.

☐ I commit to giving back at least 10% of my income and time to worthy causes!

☐ I commit to becoming a person of greatness by continually furthering my financial education. I have visited www.8pillars. com to learn more about *8 Pillars University*™.

# ABOUT THE AUTHOR

Brian Nelson Ford is the Founder and President of *8 Pillars*™ Financial Education Company. He has a passion for teaching personal finance. Because of the current flood of financial advice, Brian has set a goal to bring simplicity and sound principles to financial education.

Brian received Bachelors Degrees in Business Management as well as Marriage, Family & Human Development from Brigham Young University. Further, he holds a Masters Degree in Personal Finance from the College for Financial Planning.

Brian's experience as a financial coach combined with his background in business and education uniquely qualify him to impact people's lives for good. He takes great pride in helping families reach their financial goals and achieve their dreams.

Brian currently lives in Highland, Utah with his wife and three children. In addition to *The 8 Pillars of Financial Greatness*, Brian has authored an award-winning children's book titled *Marshmallows and Bikes – Teaching Children (and Adults) Personal Finance*. His latest title is a stunning, full-color book of inspirational quotations called *Financial Wisdom – Timeless as Nature*.

You can learn more about Brian's books and his education company at www.8pillars.com.